LA

Everyday Memory
Actions and Absent

396

Everyday Memory
Actions and Absent-Mindedness

edited by

J.E. Harris

SCICON Limited
London

P.E. Morris

Department of Psychology
University of Lancaster

1984

Academic Press

Harcourt Brace Jovanovich, Publishers

London · Orlando · San Diego · New York · Austin
Montreal · Sydney · Tokyo · Toronto

ACADEMIC PRESS INC. (LONDON) LTD.
24/28 Oval Road
London NW1

United States Edition published by
ACADEMIC PRESS INC.
Orlando, Florida 32887

British Library Cataloguing in Publication Data

Everyday memory, actions and absent-mindedness.
1. Memory
I. Harris, J.E. II. Morris, Peter, E.
153.1′2 BF371

ISBN 0-12-327640-3
ISBN 0-12-327641-1 (Pbk)

LCCCN 83-73146

Phototypeset by Deltatype Limited, Ellesmere Port
Printed in Great Britain by St. Edmundsbury Press, Bury St Edmunds

CONTRIBUTORS

A. D. BADDELEY MRC Applied Psychology Unit, 15 Chaucer Road, Cambridge CB2 2EF, UK

H. P. BAHRICK Department of Psychology, Ohio Wesleyan University, Delaware, Ohio 43015, USA

D. BARTRAM Department of Psychology, University of Hull, Hull HU6 7RX, UK

J. E. HARRIS MRC Applied Psychology Unit, 15 Chaucer Road, Cambridge CB2 2EF, UK; present address: Scicon Limited, 49 Berners Street, London W1P 4AQ, UK

D. J. HERRMANN Department of Psychology, Hamilton College, Clinton, New York 13323, USA

G. V. JONES Department of Psychology, University of Bristol, 8–10 Berkeley Square, Bristol BS8 1HH, UK

R. L. LEVY School of Social Work, University of Washington, 1417 N.E. 42nd Street, Seattle, Washington 98105, USA

G. R. LOFTUS Department of Psychology, University of Washington, Seattle, Washington 98195, USA

D. LUCAS Department of Psychology, University of Manchester, Manchester M13 9PL, UK

M. MARTIN Department of Experimental Psychology, South Parks Road, Oxford OX1 3UD, UK

N. MOFFAT District Psychology Service, Branksome Clinic, Layton Road, Parkstone, Poole BH12 2BJ, UK

P. E. MORRIS Department of Psychology, Fylde College, University of Lancaster, Bailrigg, Lancaster LA1 4YF, UK

J. T. REASON Department of Psychology, University of Manchester, Manchester M13 9PL, UK

P. SMITH Department of Psychology, University of Hull, Hull HU6 7RX, UK

A. SUNDERLAND MRC Applied Psychology Unit, 15 Chaucer Road, Cambridge CB2 2EF, UK

A. J. WILKINS MRC Applied Psychology Unit, 15 Chaucer Road, Cambridge CB2 2EF, UK

B. WILSON Rivermead Rehabilitation Centre, Abingdon Road, Oxford OX1 4XD, UK

Preface

The first International Conference on Practical Aspects of Memory was held in September 1978 and marked a new willingness of academic psychologists to become involved in studies of practical memory issues. Since then a number of books have dealt with various practical and applied aspects of memory. Most have covered special topics, such as eye-witness testimony (Loftus, 1979), or person recognition (Clifford and Bull, 1978), and Neisser's (1982) book emphasized observational methods in the study of memory. Other books have covered a wider range of topics (e.g. Gruneberg and Morris, 1979), but some related and important ones have not been adequately covered. In this book we try to bring together a number of these topics into one volume.

The book has several overlapping focuses. One concerns the relationship between memory as studied in laboratory experiments and the use of memory in everyday life. While in such a book most chapters relate to this theme, Chapters 1, 2, 3 and 12 are particularly relevant. A second focus concerns "remembering to do things" or prospective remembering (mainly Chapters 1, 5, 6 and 7), and is clearly related to a third focus — absent-mindedness, and slips of action and of memory (Chapters 4, 7 and 10). A fourth focus concerns self-report methods of collecting data in the forms of questionnaires, diaries and daily checklists (Chapters 8, 9, 10 and 11). The last focus concerns the practical, clinical aspects of everyday memory research in assessment (Chapters 10 and 11), rehabilitation (Chapter 12), and compliance (Chapter 6). So the book is likely to be of interest to those involved in the management of clinical memory problems, as well as to academics and students of memory generally.

In the first chapter, Baddeley and Wilkins consider some of the issues involved in taking memory research out of the laboratory, such as what is to be gained, problems involved and how some of the issues and hypothetical constructs that have arisen relate to each other and to those studied in the laboratory.

In the next chapter Bahrick reports two experiments on memory for people. This is, of course, a very rich concept including our memories of people's personalities, voices, hobbies, occupations, relationships, times we have spent with them, their names and appearances. Names and particularly photographs have been used as material in a good many laboratory studies of memory. However, Bahrick's first experiment shows that, at least for photographs, there is a low correlation between performance on the typical, espisodic laboratory task and an equivalent test of "natural" memory for people derived from extended exposure to them. Bahrick discusses some of the possible implications of the low correlation, though supporters of Munsat's (1966) and Tulving's (1972) distinction between episodic and semantic memory may regard it as being in line with their expectations.

With Bartram and Smith's chapter we move from people to places. They discuss how people's memories for routes and the general layout of the area in which they live often fail to match the actual physical angles and distances. Distortions in the representation that we have of the world around us seem to follow from the ways in which we learn about our environment.

The good use Reason has made of diaries for "netting" and studying people's absent-mindedness is already well established, and in Chapter 4 he joins with Deborah Lucas in describing the use of diaries in studying natural occurrences of the tip-of-the-tongue (TOT) phenomenon, a type of everyday memory failure that has, unusually, also found its way into the laboratory. In particular, their studies compare "blocked" TOTs (when an incorrect word repeatedly intrudes) with unblocked TOTs. The results are discussed in terms of the activation of schemata, according to the theoretical position put forward by Reason in Chapter 7.

The following two chapters (5 and 6) both review work on remembering to do things or "prospective" memory as it is increasingly becoming known. The first, by Harris, covers psychological studies, while the second by Levy and Loftus describes studies of medical compliance: i.e. doing what the doctor, psychologist, etc. tells you. In both types of study the subject or patient is asked to do, at a later time, something that the researcher can detect. However, there is very little overlap between the two chapters in the studies covered, and the different content is also reflected in the different issues that are covered and approaches that are taken.

To understand failures in remembering to do things we need to know how our cognitive system normally copes with planning and controlling actions. Reason, in Chapter 7, presents a challenging attempt to capture with a general model many widely agreed principles about the control of actions. Reason hopes that this model will encourage discussion of the system controlling our actions so that more fully specified models may be developed. One potentially controversial aspect of the model is the absence of a separate intention system with executive control over the planning of actions.

The next group of chapters deals with various aspects of memory or cognitive failures questionnaires and subjective data. In the first, Herrmann follows up his 1982 comprehensive review of memory-related questionnaires with some additional thoughts on differentiating questionnaires that *test* memory from those that ask respondents for their own estimates of their own memory abilities. He also examines the content of these latter "metamemory" questionnaires.

In the following chapter, Morris considers why memory failure questionnaires have relatively poor correlations with objective measures of memory ability. He argues that the samples of memory failures that are normally recalled when a memory questionnaire is being completed are not representative of our actual memory failures. He discusses the general issues of individual differences in memory ability, and the advantages and disadvantages of subjective reports of memory performance.

Martin and Jones's chapter is about cognitive failures in everyday life and focusses primarily on one particular questionnaire, the Cognitive Failures Questionnaire (CFQ) of Broadbent and his colleagues. The chapter covers how the CFQ relates to other questionnaires on memory, action-slips and attention, to various measures of performance and to personality. In many instances divided attention is implicated as a factor in the cognitive failures.

The chapter by Sunderland, Harris and Baddeley concerns the use of questionnaires and daily checklists for assessing everyday memory after head injury. Their subjects have included groups of severely and mildly head-injured patients as well as groups of normal young and old subjects. There is, therefore, likely to be some generality to their findings, well supported in the sequence of studies reported, that there are factors acting to bias subjective assessments of memory, but that at least assessment by relatives appears to have a useful degree of validity.

Wilson and Moffat take a clinical view of everyday memory, dealing in particular with rehabilitation of those with memory problems. They cover a wide range of techniques and issues, such as the use of faculties that remain intact in order to support or substitute for those that are impaired. The section on Planning and Administration deals with very practical issues, covering group treatment, evaluation, strategies and when to begin memory training. This section should be of particular interest to those involved in helping people with impaired memories to return to normal everyday life.

July 1983

John Harris, London
Peter Morris, Lancaster

Contents

1

Taking Memory out of the Laboratory

A. D. Baddeley and A. Wilkins

I. WHY STUDY MEMORY OUTSIDE THE LABORATORY?

In 1978, the Welsh branch of the British Psychological Society organized a conference on practical aspects of memory. In the opening address, Ulrich Neisser eloquently presented the view that psychologists had in the past been far too unwilling to emerge from their laboratories and tackle the wealth of interesting problems posed by everyday aspects of human memory (Neisser, 1978). In the days that followed, it became obvious that Neisser had articulated a concern that had been preoccupying many of the participants. The conference contained numerous papers that were concerned with taking memory out of the laboratory; Neisser's plea for ecological validity was a powerful one, but one that had in many cases been heeded before it was uttered at least by those who attended the conference. The curious feature of the conference, however, was that almost all the participants, like Neisser himself, believed that they were working largely in isolation against what was perceived as the dominant experimental paradigm. In the years immediately following, the trend towards the study of everyday memory has become more firmly established, and the signs are that it will continue to play an important part in the study of human memory.

Why this shift in emphasis? Looked at historically, the present situation should perhaps be regarded as a return to normal concerns rather than a completely new departure. There has always been within the psychology of memory, a tension between the Ebbinghaus approach with its concern for ruthless simplification in order to make the problem of human memory tractable, and the need for ecological validity. The attempt to capture the richness of human memory rather than simplify has been an important thread in psychology, extending back through Bartlett to Galton in Britain and to William James in the US. While the Ebbinghaus approach dominated associationist interference theory which in turn dominated the study of memory up to the 1960s, the development of cognitive psychology allowed an escape from the rigidity of earlier laboratory-bound approaches. The escape came partly through the development of new concepts, and indeed the rediscovery of old ones. Take for example the reawakening of interest in the role of organization in learning that occurred in the 1960s, notably in the work of Mandler and Tulving. This led to a return to the concept of an active learner which had been out of favour since the decline of Gestalt psychology in the 1930s. It has been followed by a wide range of interesting developments from the analysis of mnemonic systems (Bower, 1970) to the role of expertise in memory for material as diverse as chess positions (de Groot, 1966), bridge hands (Charness, 1979) and football results (Morris *et al.*, 1981).

One reason why cognitive psychology has been more broadly applicable than S-R associationism is probably its eclecticism. Cognitive psychology does not represent a single integrated theory so much as a collection of attitudes to theorizing. Such attitudes allow, and indeed encourage the confrontation of complex aspects of human memory that simply did not lend themselves to discussion in terms of associationist interference theory. As a result it has become respectable to ask broad questions, and to carry out studies of intrinsically interesting phenomena even though they might not be of immediate theoretical significance and might not necessarily suggest clearly defined explanatory models. The work of Roger Brown and others on flashbulb memories (see Neisser, 1982) and of Nickerson and Adams (1979) on remembering the detailed appearance of a penny are good examples of this.

Another reason for the growing interest in memory in everyday life stems from the desire to check the ecological validity of laboratory memory results. A good example of the influence of this concern comes from the area of mathematical psychology, where the initial enthusiasm for quantitative models led to a preoccupation with producing experimental data that could be modelled within the range of available techniques. This in turn led to a series of studies in which subjects were required to associate a very limited set of single-item responses with an equally limited range of stimuli (see Kintsch, 1970, for a good overview of this approach). The models concerned were able to fit a subject's behaviour on certain very limited tasks, but could say little or nothing about more complex and ecologically relevant memory situations. One could not avoid the suspicion that the psychologist was merely devising games which his subjects were clever enough to play according to his rules. Given the choice between elegant models of trivial data, or untidy approaches to phenomena of greater practical or theoretical importance, psychology could have followed the route that appears to have been taken by certain approaches to economics. These seem to prefer to cling to elegant models of ever increasing complexity rather than be concerned with the mundane question of validating such models against the inelegant and intractable problems of the real world. Fortunately, a substantial number of psychologists have chosen not to take this route and one of the results of this has been the development of interest in everyday memory.

At the same time as attempts to apply detailed quantitative mathematical models to human memory were becoming bogged down, attempts to develop broad principles were proving sufficiently successful to encourage their broader application. For example, a concept such as Levels of Processing (Craik and Lockhart, 1972) can be criticized in many ways (Baddeley, 1978), but it does offer a simple rule of thumb that can fruitfully be applied in tackling a broad range of practical problems (Baddeley, 1982). In short, success in the laboratory provided both conceptual tools and the confidence to apply them to everyday problems.

One final reason why psychologists are increasingly showing a willingness to move out of the laboratory is economic. In the last few years, research funds have become tighter, and demands for accountability have become stronger. In such a climate, it is much harder to justify research on human memory that appears to say nothing about memory as it impinges on everyday life. This has led to a greater interest in carrying out research that might potentially be applied, and in the area of human learning and memory this has often involved a willingness to tackle problems in more realistic settings (Baddeley, 1982).

II. ADVANTAGES OF MOVING OUT OF THE LABORATORY

We have so far been concerned largely with speculation as to the historical antecedents of the current growth in interest in everyday memory. In the section that follows, we shall briefly describe some of the possible advantages to extending memory research beyond the confines of the psychology department.

A. Establishing generality

As mentioned earlier, it is clearly desirable for theories to be generalizable. We carry out experiments in the laboratory typically in order to discover the general characteristics of the mind. For reasons of convenience and control, we test these theories most commonly within the laboratory, but implicitly or explicitly we intend them to apply to a much wider range of situations. The only way in which we can check whether this is indeed the case is to widen the scope of our enquiry, if necessary sacrificing some of our control over the situation in order to extend the generality of our findings.

Consider for instance the role of distribution of practice in the learning and retention of motor skill. Much of the laboratory work was based on studying pursuit rotor performance, a task of questionable generality typically studied over a very short time period (Bilodeau and Bilodeau, 1961). Fortunately the advantage of distributing practice proved to be robust when studied over a period of months, using the more ecologically valid task of learning to type (Baddeley and Longman, 1978).

B. The need to check before applying theories

When an issue of practical importance is at stake, it is always wise to check the predictions of even a well-established theory under realistic conditions. Such a need is quite general in science and is not by any means limited to the application of cognitive psychology. Take for example an extensively researched and well understood area of physics, such as the study of laminar flow. This body of theory and expertise can and is used in attempting to design more effectively streamlined car bodies. However, no sensible manufacturer would rely on theory to design the shape of his next car without very extensive empirical work using models and wind tunnels. Given the much less developed state of cognitive psychology, it is clearly unwise to base practical decisions on theory, without first checking them under conditions that are as realistic as possible.

C. Everyday memory as a source of new phenomena

Laboratory research has an unfortunate tendency to produce what Tulving and Madigan (1970) have referred to as "the functional autonomy of methods". This occurs when a method that was originally devised in order to tackle some substantive and important question, itself becomes the primary object of study, generating experiments that are primarily about other experiments rather than about the underlying processes. It is important to counteract this tendency, first of all by continuing to check the generality of results, and secondly by seeking new phenomena that are not as yet captured by existing laboratory paradigms. The recent development of interest in plans of action (Reason, 1979; 1984—chapter 7 of this volume) and remembering to do things (Wilkins and Baddeley, 1978; 1983—chapter 5) are examples of this; in both cases, the questions involved are of considerable practical importance, but had virtually never been studied in the laboratory, and hence tended to have been ignored by memory theorists. One hopes that such problems can be reformulated in a way that allows them to be studied within the more tractable environment of the laboratory, enabling the development of theories that can then be tested in the world outside.

D. The limits of simulation

A laboratory task typically attempts to simulate the essence of the situation that one wishes to study. For the most part, this can be done with a good deal of success. Hence for example, the simple transfer of training designs explored in the laboratory do have implications for interference effects outside (Fitts and Seeger, 1953), and studies of distributed practice mentioned above in which college students perform artificial tasks such as learning a pursuit rotor did seem to produce results that generalize to the more practical problem of postmen learning to type (Baddeley and Longman, 1978).

However, where emotional and motivational variables are important, it is rarely either practicable or ethically acceptable to perform adequate laboratory simulations.

Possibly for this reason, we still know very little about memory for pain, for example; there are only two studies known to us on this topic. One looking at the pain experienced during childbirth suggests marked forgetting (Robinson *et al.*, 1980), while the other, based on painful exploratory procedures such as lumbar puncture suggests, if anything, the opposite (Hunter *et al.*, 1978). Since ratings of pain used in a medical context are often retrospective, relying on memory, such a question is of some practical importance. It is clearly a question that can be answered much more easily in the hospital than in the laboratory.

The role of the emotion in cognition is another area in which laboratory research appears to have substantial limitations. Despite the ingenious use of hypnotic suggestion by Bower and his colleagues (Bower, 1981), the most promising line of development for the future would seem to lie in applying the methods and techniques of the psychological laboratory within the clinic.

III. PRACTICAL PROBLEMS IN STUDYING EVERYDAY MEMORY

There are essentially two broad approaches to studying memory outside the laboratory. The first of these is to concentrate on collecting memory information from as wide a range of realistic situations as possible. Such an approach characterizes the intriguing collection of papers presented by Neisser in his recent book "Memory Observed" (Neisser, 1982). We are still very much at the natural history phase of everyday memory, a phase during which observation is more prominent than theory, although ideally the two should go hand in hand. Since we know so little about everyday memory, almost any information is likely to be useful, provided it is based on reliable evidence. The very range and diversity of work carried out in this tradition makes it extremely difficult to summarize. It is however worth pointing out some of the characteristics of this approach that differentiate it from the more traditional approach to the study of memory due to Ebbinghaus.

The traditional laboratory study of human memory involves presenting carefully designed material to the subject under controlled conditions, and then requiring recall or recognition after a specified interval, given clearly defined cues. The essence of this is that the experimenter should control as much of the situation as possible. When studying memory in everyday life, it is hardly ever possible to exercise this degree of control, and technical developments have primarily been concerned with exploring ways in which reliable data can be obtained under less controlled conditions.

A. Conventional paradigms in naturalistic settings

Perhaps the simplest way of extending the ecological validity of current techniques has been simply to use these techniques outside the laboratory. For example, a study by Baddeley (1981) was concerned with the question of whether the results of experiments on the effect of alcohol on performance carried out under laboratory conditions would generalize to the performance of subjects who had imbibed their alcohol under normal pub conditions, and who were tested in a group. Results on the whole did support laboratory studies. Another good example of extending the generality of laboratory findings comes from experiments by Wagner (1978) on the memory capacities of students of a village Koranic school in Morocco, whose training involved principally rote memorization of the Koran. Their memory performance was if anything rather worse than one would expect from an equivalent North American student sample, but the group showed the standard recency effect for free recall performance, implying that this is a phenomenon of some robustness. A second study concerned memory for the patterns on oriental rugs, comparing Koranic students, Moroccan rug sellers and American college students. Somewhat surprisingly, the college students were about as good as the rug sellers, who in turn were better than the Koranic scholars. One would have predicted poorer performance by the non-rug-selling college students; this illustrates the general point that although there is considerable evidence for expertise enhancing memory across tasks ranging from re-membering bridge hands (Charness, 1979) to recalling football scores (Morris et al., 1981), in any given situation, this may be over-ridden by other factors: in this case, possibly, the more extensive and flexible learning strategies employed by the college students.

While testing under such real-life conditions can present unexpected problems (Baddeley, 1981), conceptually the experimental procedure is identical with that in the laboratory. Frequently it is the case that potentially interesting phenomena simply cannot be studied under such carefully controlled conditions. The question then arises as to what can be concluded, given lack of control.

B. Studies where learning can not be controlled

We shall begin by considering the case in which the process of learning is not under the control of the experimenter. A good example of this is raised by the question of studying retrograde amnesia, and we shall consider it in some detail to illustrate the problems that arise.

A severe blow on the head can lead to problems in the memory for prior events, sometimes extending back for a period of many years. This retrograde amnesia typically "shrinks" until the patient can eventually recall almost everything except the few seconds prior to the injury. The retrograde component of other types of amnesia such as that associated with the

Korsakoff syndrome, may however be less benign, and tend not to show shrinkage. How can one study this? It is possible to ask each individual about his earlier life, but it is often difficult to obtain accurate information against which to check his answers. Warrington and Sanders (1971) decided to use prominent news events, culled from the newspaper headlines of each year as a test of a subject's long-term memory. While this is broadly satisfactory, there are a number of problems (cf. Squire and Cohen, 1982). First, subjects clearly differ in the interest they take in current events, and this interest itself may vary over time. A second problem is raised by the question of making items equally easy. Should one select items of equivalent prominence? If not, the nature of the test will change as a function of the delay interval. Performance after a long delay will primarily depend on retention of a few prominent items, while after a short interval of time, performance is likely to be limited by the ability of subjects to remember relatively obscure events, since virtually all subjects will remember the recent major incidents. Bearing this in mind, it might be argued that early items rely on memory for events that are salient or frequently referred to, as compared with later items that are less significant or noteworthy.

A practical problem in this area is set by the fact that the questionnaire itself will continually be ageing, and hence needs to be updated, and presumably re-standardized every year. This is a particularly acute problem when one selects items in the first instance so as to be equally easy to answer rather than equally prominent. While it is easy to point out the shortcomings of this kind of test, it is far from easy to suggest a single solution, and it seems likely that any theoretical conclusions will need to be based on a range of techniques rather than a single procedure.

There are of course situations in which clear conclusions can be drawn without requiring a precise estimate of the degree of learning preceding a particular memory test. A good example is offered by a study by Morton (1967), of incidental memory for the combinations of letters and digits that at that time were located on British telephone dials. He found that despite frequent use, none of his 50 subjects correctly located all the letters and numbers. Nickerson and Adams (1979) made a similar demonstration, this time asking their American subjects to recall the detailed characteristics of the US penny piece, and again finding remarkably poor performance. Both these cases illustrate the point made in laboratory studies by Tulving (1966) and Craik and Watkins (1973) that even a very frequent acquaintance with the material in question, does not guarantee learning.

Other occasions occur when one may be able to estimate the frequency of exposure. In a recent study, Bekerian and Baddeley (1980) examined the effectiveness of a saturation advertising campaign to acquaint radio listeners with proposed changes in the assignment of programmes to particular wavelengths. It was possible by asking the subjects how much time they spent listening to the radio each day, and obtaining the frequency with which advertisements were presented, to arrive at a rough estimate of the number of presentations. Here again the mismatch between the enormous number of exposures, and the almost complete lack of precise learning allowed the point that repeated exposure does not guarantee learning to be made, without requiring a very precise specification of learning conditions.

It is the case however that these last three were largely demonstrations of a striking and counterintuitive effect, rather than systematic investigations. It remains true that the absence of accurate information about the time and degree of learning is probably the most significant limitation on studies of everyday memory.

C. Studies where retention interval can not be controlled

A much less severe limitation occurs in the case where it is possible to control learning and recall but not the retention interval. Under some circumstances, it may prove possible to record though not control delay, in which case forgetting curves can be plotted simply by categorizing subjects into groups on the basis of *post hoc* computation of retention interval. Baddeley *et al.* (1978) used this technique in studying the capacity for experimental subjects to remember features of a prior visit to the experimental laboratory; this has the drawback of yielding uneven numbers in different groups, but provided a sufficiently large sample is tested this need not be a major problem. A more severe limitation occurs when the retention interval is simply not known. This clearly prevents any estimate of rate of forgetting, but still allows one to investigate more general characteristics of long-term memory for the material in question. It is indeed almost always the case with semantic memory that the time and conditions of learning are unknown.

D. Studies where retrieval is not controlled

A third class of problems occurs when instead of controlling the time and manner of retrieval the experimenter is interested in the subjects' ability to do this. Perhaps the best example here stems from experiments on remembering to do things (see Harris, 1984, Chapter 5 of this volume). An example of this is the study by Wilkins and Baddeley (1978) in which subjects were asked to perform a task analogous to remembering to take pills four times a day. It proved possible to estimate the overall accuracy with which subjects performed this test and to relate it to their performance on a more standard laboratory task of free recall, producing the rather counterintuitive result that subjects who were better at free recall were worse at remembering to do things.

IV. THE NEED FOR THEORY

There is no doubt that simply collecting reliable data on everyday memory presents some interesting technical challenges. For that reason, and because of the lack of good everyday memory data, we foresee the next few years producing a large number of studies that are essentially empirical investigations as to the role of memory in a wide range of everyday tasks. The danger here is that we become so preoccupied with the technical problems of collecting interpretable data of any kind, that we shirk the need to develop theories that can cope with these data. In many areas, existing theories developed with conventional laboratory paradigms will probably provide the necessary background and will themselves be enriched in the process (Baddeley, 1982). Where comparatively unexplored problems are concerned such as that of remembering to do things for example, there is danger that in the absence of theory, we are likely to find ourselves gradually being engulfed in a mass of unrelated empirical observation. One answer is obviously to try to derive theories from these data. Unfortunately that is often far from easy. A good case in point is offered by the recent work on face recognition.

Several dramatic legal cases in recent years have reawakened psychologists to the importance and unreliability of the eyewitness. While work in this area was active in the early years of the century, it was largely neglected during the days of laboratory-based associationism, and has seen a welcome recovery over the last decade. During that time considerable evidence has accumulated showing just how unreliable is an eyewitness's ability to recognize the face of a person seen briefly in connection with a simulated crime, and a great deal of useful information has been accumulated about the various factors that might make such poor recognition memory even worse (Clifford and Bull, 1978; Loftus, 1979).

Attempts to understand the process of face recognition and if possible improve the eyewitness's performance have, however, met with depressingly little success. We know that instructing the subject to analyse a face into its component features is unhelpful (Woodhead *et al.*, 1979), and that an instruction to estimate the honesty, intelligence, or indeed the weight of the person being studied will marginally enhance subsequent recognition performance over that of a naïve subject (Winograd, 1976), but the magnitude of such effects is too small to be of practical significance. In short, attempts to capitalize on the phenomena of verbal learning via concepts such as levels of processing and semantic elaboration have proved relatively unproductive (Baddeley and Woodhead, 1982).

We suspect that the lack of progress in this area has stemmed from an excessive preoccupation with a specific practical problem: that of recognizing a briefly seen unfamiliar face. To limit study to unfamiliar faces is in our view equivalent to attempting to limit verbal memory to the study of nonsense syllables. We therefore welcome the advent of research on the recognition of familiar faces (Bruce, 1979; see Bahrick, 1984, Chapter 2 of this volume), which we hope may have a comparable effect on theoretical development in this field to that observed in the study of verbal memory with the 1960s switch from nonsense syllables to words.

(1) The generalization of existing theoretical concepts
In general however, it is important to try to use what theoretical concepts we have in order to come to grips with the phenomena of everyday memory (Baddeley, 1982). One way of doing this is to start with existing concepts and attempt to generalize them. A very good example of the application of laboratory memory research to a practical problem is presented by the work of Ley and his collaborators (Ley, 1979). This work began with an attempt to explore the complaint of many patients that they had not been adequately informed by their doctor regarding their condition. This was denied by the doctors, and further investigation suggested that much of the discrepancy between the doctors' and the patient's views stemmed from the fact that patients forgot most of what the doctor said.

Ley and his colleagues set out to attempt to remedy this, using the standard findings of the memory laboratory to guide them, but continually checking these out under hospital conditions. They found a surprisingly clear relationship between memory for medical information and the findings of the memory laboratory. For example they observed a clear primacy effect, together with a correlation between probability of recall and rated importance (Ley, 1972), both effects that had previously been observed in the laboratory. Another powerful laboratory variable was that of categorization, and Ley *et al.* (1973) showed that dividing medical information into labelled categories significantly increased the amount recalled both under laboratory conditions and with patients in general practice. Rubenstein and Aborn (1958) have shown that the probability of remembering prose is related to its readability, and this also proved to be an important factor in patients' ability to remember the content of medical leaflets (Ley *et al.*, 1973). This study also indicated that mere repetition was a not very powerful variable, a result that is consistent with a number of findings from the memory laboratory (e.g. Tulving, 1966). In learning lists of unrelated words, Murdock (1962) has shown that percentage recall declines with increasing list length; Ley (1979) showed a similar function for recalling medical information. This study also showed a correlation between amount recalled and a subject's medical knowledge, a result consistent with a range of studies relating memory to expertise. In contrast, the age of the patient was not a good predictor of amount remembered. Finally, Bradshaw *et al.* (1975) showed that advice presented in concrete specific statements was substantially more likely to be recalled than the same advice couched in more abstract general statements. On the basis of these results, Ley and his colleagues produced a manual containing suggestions for improving communication and enhancing the likelihood that the patient will remember what he is told. The recall of information presented was studied in the case of four general practitioners before and after receiving the booklet. Mean amount recalled increased from 55% to 70%, an improvement that was characteristic of all four doctors included in the study.

(2) The generation of new concepts

Ley has shown that laboratory phenomena can be very robust and can be demonstrated in the real world. His work justifies both laboratory studies and the studies that seek to apply their findings. But work on everyday memory does not simply justify laboratory studies or provide useful applications of their findings. We would claim that exposure to the complexities of the real world can aid in the development of theory as well as testing the generality of existing theory. As an example, consider the study of absent-mindedness by Reason. Reason's research began when he was reading through the reports of aircraft accidents and was struck by the frequency with which an accident could be traced to a failure of memory which is referred to in common parlance as "absentmindedness". The experimental study of the phenomena of absentmindedness which then ensued has led Reason to a theory of action and slips of action which has broadened the study of memory and raised important questions which are unlikely ever to have been raised within the tradition of laboratory-based research (see Chapter 7).

Consider the following example of absentmindedness. Suppose you are making a cup of instant coffee and omit to put the coffee in the cup before pouring in the water. One action in a sequence of actions has been forgotten because the necessary information was not retrieved in response to the appropriate cue in the action–event sequence. This may be because the sequence of actions was overlearned and only intermittently under conscious control, indeed it is perhaps for this reason that failures of retrieval of this kind are attributed to absentmindedness. A similar sequence of actions and events provides the cue for recall in many everyday situations: after all, there is no experimenter there to say "Now I want you to recall the information that you learned earlier". The sequence of actions and events that provides the prompts can be seen as resulting from a hierarchy of plans for action, some of which are a response to the immediate environment, but many of which look forward to events that are expected to occur at some future time. Suppose you forget one of the things you went to the shops to buy. Several subcomponents of your plan may have been at fault. You may have failed to predict the necessity of constructing an *aide-mémoire* such as a shopping list, or else you may have failed to take the list with you, or failed to consult it when it was appropriate to do so. The latter two failures are clearly failures of memory, but memory that is "prospective" rather than "retrospective" in nature. "Prospective memory", as the name suggests, refers to memory for future actions or events and "retrospective memory" to events or actions that have occurred in the past (see Meacham and Singer, 1977 and Harris, 1984, Chapter 5).

Most laboratory studies have been concerned with retrospective memory. In the example above, laboratory studies have much to say about the best way of memorizing a sequence of items on a shopping list, but should you choose not to rely on retrospective memory of this kind but choose instead to write out the shopping list, laboratory studies have very little indeed to say about the reasons why you forget to take the list with you when you leave for the shops! The prospective memory involved in remembering to do something at the appropriate time is such an obvious feature of everyday life that it is surprising that it has received so little study.

(3) A new area for research and its overlap with conventional theory
The theoretical basis of the distinction between retrospective and prospective memory is something of a minefield. We suspect that of all the dichotomies that have been used to divide up memory, the dichotomy between retrospective and prospective memory is one of the weakest. It is immediately obvious that much prospective remembering involves retrospective memory. We would suggest, however, that the distinction is a useful one, if only because it provides a label for a large area of memory that has been ignored.

To what extent do the theoretical constructs that have been developed in the course of the last 30 years or so apply to this newly-identified aspect of memory? Over the years memory has been successively fragmented into short- versus long-term, and within long-term into episodic versus semantic memory. The dimensions that these dichotomies are an attempt to define are of sufficient importance to have found expression in natural language as components of the concepts of attention, memory and knowledge. Although these distinctions have been exclusively applied to retrospective memory they appear to have considerable relevance for prospective memory as well.

Already in the embryonic literature on prospective memory there are examples of both semantic and episodic types. The study by Reason (1979) on slips of action might be classified as falling within a category of prospective semantic memory. It can be contrasted with the prospective episodic memory exemplified in the studies of Wilkins and Baddeley (1978) and Harris and Wilkins (1982), the first of which involved a button-pressing task analogous to remembering to take pills four times a day, and the second a task analogous to watching a television film while intermittently monitoring the cooking of a meal (see Chapter 5). Both studies required subjects to remember an arbitrary novel action at some prearranged time.

Tulving (1972) identified several criteria for distinguishing between episodic and semantic memory, the first of which concerned the nature of stored information. The nature of the stored information differs in the two types of study outlined above. In Reason's studies the action sequences are overlearned components of habitual behaviour in which absentminded errors are made, and in the other studies novel arbitrary actions are recalled. This distinction can be likened to that between semantic knowledge of linguistic rules and episodic memory for isolated events.

The second of Tulving's criteria concerned the nature of the reference. In Reason's studies the reference is cognitive: there is, for example, a pre-existing cognitive structure for the action sequence involved in making coffee, and the occasions on which this information was learned can no longer be recalled. By way of contrast, in the studies that involved the remembering of relatively novel action sequences, the specific episode in which the action-plan was acquired can easily be recalled and related to previous auto-biographical events.

In the case of the action sequence of making coffee it is only rarely that an action will fail to cue the next in an appropriate and orderly sequence. In the case of remembering an arbitrary and novel action the components are higher-order plans consisting of many subcomponents, and although these subcomponents may be sequentially constrained, the higher-order plans may not necessarily be so. This point raises the issue discussed originally by Tulving, namely the interdependence of semantic and episodic systems. It is evident that in some sense semantic memories must evolve from a succession of overlaid episodic memories; conversely episodic memories can be thought of as composed of a novel rearrangement of semantic units. Episodic memory of a list of words, for example, depends on semantic memory for the words themselves, a semantic memory that is presumably acquired from a succession of episodes. This interdependence of the two systems forces one to be explicit about the level of analysis involved. This is perhaps less of a problem as regards memory for plans where hierarchic level is implicit and would be the central feature of any theory of action.

Consider the high-level plan to entertain someone for dinner. This plan will comprise a plan to go shopping before a plan for cooking and the plan for cooking might have as one component a plan to make coffee. It is this concatenation of plans at different levels that might explain why "absent-minded" errors generally involve habitual behaviour. The habitual behaviour presumably derives from a low-level plan that can be run off without conscious control when the mind is "absent" elsewhere. It may be only on these occasions that errors in low-level plans can occur. Failures of high-level plans on the other hand, may have a more complex origin and can less often be explained as absentmindedness. At this level the actor is assumed to be in conscious control of his actions and is held responsible for any failures in his plan!

The distinction between episodic and semantic memory is not the only well-established theoretical construct that appears to apply to prospective as well as retrospective memory. Another example is the distinction between the short- and long-term. There is very little work indeed on short-term prospective memory. Harris and Wilkins (1982) have shown that when people are required to respond at prearranged times they may forget to do so although they show all the signs of remembering to make the required response up to a few seconds before it is due. It would appear that episodic plans of the kind they studied may show very rapid forgetting. This is perhaps particularly the case when, as in Harris and Wilkins' experiment, the sequence of actions in which the subject is engaged provides no cue for the to-be-remembered response. Under these circumstances it is perhaps only by maintaining a plan in conscious awareness that one can be sure of carrying it out.

As an example consider the plan to telephone someone. If the number is engaged and one is forced to wait before trying again, a subsequent distraction may mean that the plan is forgotten altogether. This rapid forgetting may be analogous to the rapid forgetting of information in short-term retrospective memory, which can be circumvented by conscious rehearsal of the items, a process that sets up retrieval strategies based on the semantic property of the items. It is conceivable that the same applies within prospective memory. Perhaps it is only when plans can be integrated into a cohesive sequence of behaviour that the several components are not subject to short-term forgetting.

We have attempted to show how the classifications that have been used to describe retrospective memory might also apply to prospective memory. The classification system underlying the discussion is illustrated in table I. We offer it not as a theoretical treatise but only as a crude classificatory system that highlights the gaps in current research on memory. The underlying similarities between prospective and retrospective memory show that the theories developed for one type of memory may well apply to the other, and that there is no intrinsic reason why exploration of this underworked area should not prove both tractable and exciting.

Table I. A broad categorization of memory tasks.

	Short term	Long term	
		Episodic	Semantic
Retrospective	STM Tasks	Event recall	Knowledge access
Prospective	Short-term action plans	Remembering to do things	Plans for action

V. CONCLUSION

In this chapter we have discussed the practical and theoretical advantages of studying memory in a naturalistic setting. We have identified some of the problems that arise and ways in which they can be overcome. We have argued that the growth of theories of naturalistic memory will be slow and dependent on a considerable increase in empirical studies, many of which may have little theoretical motivation. Already these studies have identified the new underworked area of prospective memory. We suspect that the theoretical development of this area will depend on the integration of theories of memory with theories of action. This theoretical development will need to encompass the problem of motivation within a framework of plans for action.

The framework of action plans is at least partly hierarchical, and a prospective memory task, whether short- or long-term, may involve memory for several plans at different levels in the hierarchy. The content of memory is clearly a very complex concatenation of plans at different levels. This degree of complexity has never been acknowledged in theories of retrospective episodic memory which prefer to cling to the simplistic notion of a to-be-remembered "item", a notion that belies the hierarchical content of memory.

The study of human memory appears to be undergoing a subtle metamorphosis as the late result of a fashion for ecological validity. When fashions change direction again it will be interesting to see whether this metamorphosis has produced sufficient progress to establish a durable bridge between memory in the laboratory and memory in everyday life.

ACKNOWLEDGMENT

We are grateful to Douglas Hintzman for his helpful comments on an earlier draft.

VI. REFERENCES

Baddeley, A. D. (1978). The trouble with levels: A re-examination of Craik and Lockhart's framework for memory research. *Psychological Review*, 85, 139–152.

Baddeley, A. D. (1981). The cognitive psychology of everyday life. *British Journal of Psychology*, 72, 257–269.

Baddeley, A. D. (1982). Domains of recollection. *Psychological Review*, 89, 708–729.

Baddeley, A. D., Lewis, V. and Nimmo-Smith, M. I. (1978). When did you last . . . ? *In* "Practical Aspects of Memory" (M. M. Gruneberg, R. N. Sykes and P. E. Morris, eds), Academic Press, London, Orlando and New York.

Baddeley, A. D. and Longman, D. J. A. (1978). The influence of length and frequency on training sessions on the rate of learning to type. *Ergonomics*, 21, 627–635.

Baddeley, A. D. and Woodhead, M. M. (1982). Depth of processing, context of face recognition. *Canadian Journal of Psychology*, 36, 148–164.

Bekerian, D. A. and Baddeley, A. D. (1980). Saturation advertising and the repetition effect. *Journal of Verbal Learning and Verbal Behavior*, 19, 17–25.

Bilodeau, E. A. and Bilodeau, I. McD. (1961). Motor skills learning. *Annual Review of Psychology*, 12, 243–280.

Bower, G. H. (1970). Analysis of a mnemonic device. *American Scientist*, 58, 496–510.

Bower, G. H. (1981). Mood and memory. *American Psychologist*, 36, 129–148.

Bradshaw, P. W., Ley, P., Kincey, J. A., and Bradshaw, J. (1975). Recall of medical advice: comprehensibility and specificity. *British Journal of Social and Clinical Psychology*, 14, 55.

Bahrick, H. P. (1983). Memory for people. *In* "Everyday Memory, Actions and

Absent-Mindedness" (J. E. Harris and P. E. Morris, eds), Academic Press, London, Orlando and New York.

Bruce, V. (1979). Searching for politicians: an information-processing approach to face recognition. *Quarterly Journal of Experimental Psychology*, 31, 373–396.

Charness, N. (1979). Components of skill in bridge. *Canadian Journal of Psychology*, 33, 1–16.

Clifford, B. R. and Bull, R. (1978). *The Psychology of Person Identification*. Routledge and Kegan Paul, London.

Craik, F. I. M and Lockhart, R. S. (1972). Levels of processing: A framework for memory research. *Journal of Verbal Learning and Verbal Behavior*, 11, 671–689.

Craik, F. I. M. and Watkins, M. J. (1973). The role of rehearsal in short-term memory. *Journal of Verbal Learning and Verbal Behavior*, 12, 599–607.

Fitts, P. M. and Seeger, C. M. (1953). S-R compatibility: spatial characteristics of stimulus and response codes. *Journal of Experimental Psychology*, 46, 199–210.

de Groot, A. (1966). Perception and memory versus thought: some old ideas and recent findings. *In* "Problem Solving" (B. Kleinmuntz, ed.), Wiley, New York.

Harris, J. E. (1984). Remembering to do things: a forgotten topic. *In* "Everyday Memory, Actions and Absent-Mindedness" (J. E. Harris and P. E. Morris, eds), Academic Press, London, Orlando and New York.

Harris, J. E. and Wilkins, A. J. (1982). Remembering to do things: a theoretical framework and an illustrative experiment. *Human Learning*, 1, 123–136.

Hunter, M., Philips, C. and Rachman, S. (1978). Memory for pain. *Pain*, 6, 35–46. Elsevier/North Holland Biomedical Press, Amsterdam.

Kintsch, W. (1970). "Learning, Memory and Conceptual Processes", Wiley, New York.

Ley, P. (1972). Primacy, rated importance, and the recall of medical statements. *Journal of Health and Social Behavior*, 13, 311–317.

Ley, P. (1979). Memory for medical information. *British Journal of Social and Clinical Psychology*, 18, 245–255.

Ley, P., Bradshaw, P. W., Eaves, D. and Walker, C. M. (1973). A method for increasing patients' recall of information presented by doctors. *Psychological Medicine*, 3, 217–220.

Ley, P., Goldman, M., Bradshaw, P. W., Kincey, J. A. and Walker, C. M. (1973). The comprehensibility of some X-ray leaflets. *Journal of the Institute of Health Education*, 10, 47–55.

Loftus, E. F. (1979). "Eyewitness Testimony", Harvard University Press, Cambridge, Mass.

Meacham, J. A. and Singer, J. (1977). Incentive in prospective remembering. *Journal of Psychology*, 97, 191–197.

Morris, P. E., Gruneberg, M. M., Sykes, R. N. and Merrick, A. (1981). Football knowledge and the acquisition of new results. *British Journal of Psychology*, 72, 479–484.

Morton, J. (1967). A singular lack of incidental learning. *Nature*, 215, 203–204.

Murdock, B. B. Jr. (1962). The serial position effect of free recall. *Journal of Experimental Psychology*, 64, 482–488.

Neisser, U. (1978). Memory: What are the important questions? *In* "Practical Aspects of Memory" (M. M. Gruneberg, P. E. Morris and R. N. Sykes, eds), Academic Press, London, Orlando and New York.

Neisser, U. (1982). "Memory Observed: Remembering in Natural Contexts", W. H. Freeman, San Francisco.

Nickerson, R. S. and Adams, M. J. (1979). Long-term memory for a common object. *Cognitive Psychology*, **11**, 287–307.

Reason, J. T. (1979). Actions not as planned: the price of automation. *In* "Aspects of Consciousness Vol. 1" (G. Underwood and R. Stevens, eds), Academic Press, London, Orlando and New York.

Reason, J. T. (1983). Absent-mindedness and cognitive control. *In* "Everyday Memory, Actions and Absent-Mindedness" (J. E. Harris and P. E. Morris, eds), Academic Press, London, Orlando and New York.

Robinson, J. O., Rosen, M., Revill, S. I., David, H. and Rees, G. A. D. (1980). Self-administered intravenous and intramuscular pethodine. *Anaesthesia*, **35**, 763–770.

Rubenstein, H. and Aborn, M. (1958). Learning, prediction and readability. *Journal of Applied Psychology*, **42**, 28–32.

Squire, L. R. and Cohen, N. J. (1982). Remote memory, retrograde amnesia, and the neuropsychology of memory. *In* "Memory and Amnesia" (L. S. Cermak, ed.), Lawrence Erlbaum Associates, Hillsdale, N. J.

Tulving, E. (1966). Subjective organization and effects of repetition in multi-trial free-recall learning. *Journal of Verbal Learning and Verbal Behavior*, **5**, 193–197.

Tulving, E. (1972) Episodic and semantic memory. *In* "Organization of Memory" (E. Tulving and W. Donaldson, eds), Academic Press, Orlando, New York and London.

Tulving, E. and Madigan, S. A. (1970). Memory and verbal learning. *Annual Review of Psychology*, **21**, 437–484.

Wagner, D. (1978). Memories of Morocco: The influence of age, schooling and environment on memory. *Cognitive Psychology*, **10**, 1–28.

Warrington, E. K. and Sanders, H. I. (1971). The fate of old memories. *Quarterly Journal of Experimental Psychology*, **23**, 432–442.

Wilkins, A. J. and Baddeley, A. D. (1978). Remembering to recall in everyday life: an approach to absentmindedness. *In* "Practical Aspects of Memory" (M. M. Gruneberg, P. E. Morris and R. N. Sykes, eds), Academic Press, London, Orlando and New York.

Winograd, E. (1976). Recognition memory for faces following nine different judgments. *Bulletin of the Psychonomic Society*, **8**, 419–421.

Woodhead, M. M., Baddeley, A. D. and Simmonds, D. C. V. (1979). On training people to recognise faces. *Ergonomics*, **22**, 333–343.

2

Memory for People

H. P. Bahrick

This chapter deals with memory for names and faces, although the title suggests a much broader coverage. Memory for people includes the physical and behavioural characteristics of individuals as well as a rich context of past interactions, feelings and experiences associated with them. The gap between the title and our coverage underlines the narrow focus of past memory research and the challenge of broadening this emphasis to cover other areas. Even within the limited domain of facial memory, investigators have concentrated on short term, episodic tasks. The research reported in this chapter illustrates some of the methodological problems encountered by extending research to cover memory based upon prolonged interactions. In traditional facial memory research, portraits are presented under conditions that permit manipulation of encoding processes, and tests are administered later to determine accuracy of recognition. Such research has both theoretical and practical significance, but it does not answer questions about facial memory based on real-life interactions over extended periods. Ecologically realistic research concerned with long-term memory for people is method-ologically difficult, and this contributes to its paucity. If portraits of public figures are used (Warrington and Sanders, 1971; Read and Bruce, 1982) the type and amount of exposure of subjects are usually unspecifiable and uncontrolled; and these factors are likely to vary considerably for subjects of different ages or cultural backgrounds. If the portraits are selected on the basis of biographical information obtained from individual subjects, test con-struction becomes cumbersome. This chapter reports two investigations. Both deal with semantic rather than episodic memory, that is, they are based upon extended real-life interaction. The duration of interaction is reasonably well controlled at about 10 weeks, and is thus substantially shorter than the interaction explored in an earlier investigation (Bahrick *et al.*, 1975) of memory for the names and faces of high school classmates. The studies reported here deal respectively with memory of college students for the faces of their classmates, and with the memory of college teachers for the names and faces of former students. The first study relates performance on a laboratory-based episodic facial memory task to performance in the naturalistic task based upon extended interaction in the classroom. The second study permits a separation of the effect of age of the subject from the effects of age of the memory trace *per se*. This is done by comparing performance over the same retention intervals for teachers belonging to different age groups.

I. MEMORY OF COLLEGE STUDENTS FOR THE FACES
OF THEIR CLASSMATES

One purpose of this study was to determine the relation between scores on a facial recognition test for portraits shown in the laboratory and scores on a test for recognition of people's faces known through extended real-life interaction. Forty-nine students at Ohio Wesleyan University were tested for facial memory of their classmates and also for recognition of portraits previously presented in the laboratory. The correlation between scores on these two tasks was assessed.

A. Procedure

The subjects were 21 male and 28 female students in various sections of an introductory psychology course. They were tested during the tenth week of the term after each section had met from 40 to 45 times in lecture-discussion sessions of 50-minute duration. The number of students in each section varied from 32 to 45.

In the laboratory, the students were first shown the material for the episodic facial memory test. This material consisted of 20 portraits of 10 male and 10 female faces. The portraits used throughout this study were black and white high school graduation pictures, 4×5 cm. For this task the portraits were of individuals not known to the subjects. The subjects were instructed to commit the faces to memory so as to be able to recognize them on a later test, and portraits were exposed individually for 5 seconds each, in a random sequence.

The facial memory test for classmates was administered next. The subjects were shown 10 sets of 10 portraits each. Each set contained 2 portraits of classmates, and 8 foil portraits. All 10 portraits in a set were of individuals of the same sex, and the foil portraits were also of students at Ohio Wesleyan University, but not of members of the introductory psychology course. Portraits of individuals likely to be familiar to the subjects were used as foils in order to minimize identification of classmate portraits based only upon familiarity of the face. Five of the 10 sets of portraits were of male students, and 5 were of female students. The 10 sets were presented in random sequence, and each set was exposed for 30 seconds. The subjects were asked to identify the 2 portraits of their classmates, and they were required to guess if they had not made 2 identifications at the end of 30 seconds.

Immediately after completing the classmate identification, task subjects took a recognition test for the portraits presented to them at the beginning of the session. For this test the same procedure was used as in the classmate identification test, except that the 8 foil portraits were of individuals unfamiliar to the subjects.

B. Results and discussion

Performance on both tasks was scored by awarding 1 point for each correct identification, so that a maximum score of 20 could be obtained for each task. Table I shows the result, with separate means reported for male and female subjects, and for male and female target portraits. Overall means for a task are therefore the sums of the means obtained for male and female targets.

Table I. Mean recognition of male and female portraits by male and female subjects.

	Laboratory exposure		Ecological exposure	
	Male subjects	Female subjects	Male subjects	Female subjects
Male portraits	5.5	6.2	8.0	7.5
Female portraits	5.6	6.7	7.7	7.9

Analysis of variance indicates that scores on the classmate identification task are higher than the scores on the laboratory task $F(1,47) = 27.4$, $p<.01$ but neither the main effect of sex of subject, nor the effect of sex of target are significant $(p>.05)$. The mean performance of female subjects is only slightly higher than the mean for male subjects, and this agrees with most previous findings regarding overall sex-differences on laboratory facial memory tasks (Shepherd, 1981). Slight superiority in the performance of females based mainly upon their superior recognition of female faces has been reported by Ellis *et al.* (1973), Goldstein and Chance (1971) and others. The most significant interaction effect revealed in the analysis of variance is that of sex of subject with type of task $F(1,47) = 17.0$, $p<.01$, with females scoring relatively higher on the laboratory memory task, and males on the classmate identification task. Total scores on the two tasks were correlated for the 49 subjects, and the resulting correlation is $-.15$.

The implications of this low correlation between scores on the two facial recognition tasks require comment.[1] During recent years investigators have responded to demands that memory research address problems encountered in real life, rather than be restricted to problems which lend themselves readily to laboratory analysis (Neisser, 1976; Bahrick and Karis, 1982). The present volume is a contribution to these efforts. A priority task for ecologically relevant memory research is to find out how well the generalizations established in the laboratory apply to a variety of real-life situations. When results cannot be generalized it is important to establish the conditions that differentially affect performance in the laboratory and in real life. Such differences may be systematic, i.e. they may reflect the effect of specific variables that affect the tasks differently, or they may be random, i.e. they reflect low reliability of data, a condition that attenuates correlations between tasks. The present results reflect both types of effects.

Laboratory memory tasks typically offer a high degree of control over conditions of motivation and attention. Subjects receive uniform instructions and incentives, and this greatly reduces the range of individual differences in motivation and attention during the encoding phase of learning and memory tasks, in comparison with most real-life learning situations. In this laboratory task, subjects were instructed to commit to memory the portraits presented to them. Variation in the amount of information retained is likely to reflect primarily individual differences in the capacity to learn and in the effectiveness of encoding strategies, and only to a much lesser degree variation in sustained attention to the target portraits. The circumstances governing encoding of information about the faces of classmates during real-life interactions are markedly different. The learning is incidental, and subjects are unlikely to engage in deliberate rehearsal for the purpose of committing the information to memory. Therefore individual differences in the effectiveness of encoding strategies can only play a minor role. To be sure, several investigations (Bower and Karlin, 1974; Chance and Goldstein, 1976; Strnad and Mueller, 1977) have failed to show significant differences in facial recognition when the encoding occurred under intentional vs incidental learning conditions, but in all of these investigations the incidental orienting task assured consistent attention to the faces. This is not the case in the present investigation. Variation of interest and motivation, habits of gregariousness and of social interaction, and their consequences in regard to attention to the

---

[1] Editors' Footnote: We suggested to Professor Bahrick that some readers may regard the low correlation as no more than a reflection of Munsat's (1966) and Tulving's (1972) distinction between episodic (the single laboratory exposure) and semantic (the extended real-life exposure) memories. His reply was:

I did not bring this classification into my discussion because I do not believe that the distinction *per se* accounts for the low correlation. In other words I can conceive of episodic and semantic facial recognition tasks which would correlate highly. It happens that my episodic task is one in which attention is directed to the portraits, but my semantic task is one in which the subject's habits and motives determine attention, and I attribute the low correlation to this factor, rather than to intrinsic characteristics of semantic *vs* episodic tasks.

individual faces of classmates are certain to influence how much is learned about each face. Thus individuals are likely to excel in the laboratory task on the basis of their superior encoding strategies, but in the real-life task on the basis of social motives and habits which yield sustained attention to the faces of their classmates. Memory for people in real-life situations is thus strongly affected by variables that are usually controlled in the laboratory and therefore have little influence on individual differences in laboratory memory tasks. Even when the duration and type of interaction among individuals is reasonably well controlled as in the present investigation, social and motivational variables determine what is learned about others. The significant interaction effect of type of task by sex of subject obtained in the present investigation may well reflect this difference. The overall performance of female subjects is slightly superior to the performance of males, but this is due entirely to the results obtained with the laboratory task. On the classmate identification task there is a reversal of the overall sex difference.

Lack of control over motivational and attentional variables also affects the reliability of individual scores on the classmate identification task. The present investigation permits an estimate of this effect. Subscores based upon two arbitrarily selected sets of 10 of the 20 target faces were calculated for all subjects in both tasks. The correlation between the subscores of the same task provides an estimate of split-half reliability of the scores. The correlations corrected by the Spearman-Brown formula are .81 for the laboratory task and .52 for the classmate identification task. It is clear that these reliability estimates limit the extent to which individual differences can be established dependably, and that particularly the low reliability of the classmate identification task attenuates the correlation of this task with any other task. Shepherd (1981) in reviewing the very scant evidence regarding intra-individual consistency in face recognition tasks concluded that high correlations are obtained only when the tasks are very similar, but not when different paradigms are involved. The present results indicate that this conclusion is particularly applicable when one task is an episodic laboratory task in which attention is controlled, and the other a semantic, naturalistic task in which attention is uncontrolled. The present results also underline the importance of establishing the reliability of scores when intra-individual consistency is to be interpreted. Applied psychologists routinely determine the reliability of indicants, but reliability is rarely specified in laboratory investigations.

We can conclude that memory for people's faces based on ecologically realistic interaction reflects attentional and motivational variables which are difficult to control or specify and which have little influence upon performance in the usual facial memory tasks presented in the laboratory. As a result, the reliability of facial memory is likely to be lower in real life than in the laboratory, and individual differences in the two types of situations are not highly correlated.

II. MEMORY OF COLLEGE TEACHERS FOR THE NAMES
AND FACES OF THEIR STUDENTS

A previous study (Bahrick *et al.*, 1975) showed that recognition of portraits of high school classmates remains remarkably high for a period of at least 35 years, and that this is followed by a decline in recognition during the last 13 years of the 48-year retention interval. Earlier and more pronounced declines occur for name recognition, picture-name matching, and picture-cued recall.

The previous study cannot answer the question of whether the decline of memory reflects the ageing of the individual, or the ageing of the memory trace *per se*, because age of the individual and age of the memory trace are confounded in a design in which all subjects are of the same age at the time of learning. The design of the present study differs in several important ways from the design of the first study. In the present study three groups of subjects were of different age at the time of learning. Age of the subject is therefore not confounded with age of the memory trace, and it is possible to determine the extent to which the decline of retention is associated with each factor. The present study also achieves higher control over other important variables. By testing the same subjects for memories of different ages, comparisons of retention are longitudinal, within-group, rather than cross-sectional and between group. This achieves control over individual differences. Control over the conditions of learning the names and faces of approximately 40 students during a 10-week term is also higher than control over the conditions of learning the names and faces of classmates over a period of 4 years, with class size and the nature of interactions varying greatly. Finally, control over rehearsals during the retention interval is superior in the present study, because yearbooks which give access to the material are rarely available to college teachers. This improved control makes it possible to use fewer subjects, and to dispense with the use of multiple regression analysis and cross-sectional adjustments essential to the earlier design.

Twenty-two faculty members of Ohio Wesleyan University participated as subjects. They ranged in age from 36 to 75 years and all had taught at the college for at least 8 years. They were assigned according to their age to a young group (N = 7, $\bar{X}$ = 39, s.d. = 2.4) a middle-aged group (N = 7, $\bar{X}$ = 54, s.d. = 4.0) and an older group (N = 8, $\bar{X}$ = 68, s.d. = 3.6). Three individuals in the older group were retired.

A. Selection of test material

Tests were constructed from class lists obtained from the registrar for introductory level courses taught by each instructor during terms dating back 8 years, 4 years, 1 year and 2 weeks. The more recent material had to be omitted for the retired teachers. The classes had met 3–5 times per week for a term of 10 weeks. Names and portraits of students who took subsequent courses from the same instructor were eliminated from the test material in order to achieve better control over the duration of interaction. Class size was kept as closely as possible to 40 students ($\bar{X}$ = 39.7, s.d. = 5.8). Portraits were photocopies of those submitted by students at the time of their application to the university.

B. Subtests and test sequence

Five subtests were administered in three sessions. The subtests measured picture-cued name recall, picture recognition, name recognition, picture name matching, and picture name relearning. During the first session the first four subtests were administered in the order listed and the test material was selected from classes taught 1, 4, and 8 years ago. Within each subtest the material taken from the three retention intervals was randomly sequenced into a series of items. The second session was administered 1–3 weeks after the first session and consisted only of the relearning subtest. During the interval between the two sessions individual relearning tests were constructed for each subject based upon items failed on the picture cued recall test in Session 1. The third session tested memory for students taught recently, and was administered within two weeks of the end of an academic term. The session involved the same subtests administered in the same order as in the first session, with the test material selected only from a class taught during the preceding term.

(1) *Picture cued name recall*
Ten portraits approximately 4 × 5 cm, were selected randomly from each of the classes chosen for the subject. The portraits were presented individually and in random order. The instructor was asked to recall the first and last name of the individual portrayed. Guessing was encouraged, and a time limit of 15 seconds was imposed in all tests except the picture-name relearning test.

(2) *Picture-recognition*
Ten portraits not selected for the picture-cued recall test were randomly selected from the remaining members of each class, to be tested. Each portrait was presented together with four foils. The foils were photo copies of portraits of applicants to Ohio Wesleyan University who had not enrolled at the school. Subjects were instructed to select the portrait that they recognized as one of a former student.

(3) *Name recognition test*
The names of ten individuals not previously selected for either the picture recognition or the picture-cued recall subtests were randomly selected from among the remaining members of each class, and each name was shown together with four foil names in a multiple choice format. Both first and last names were used. The subjects were asked to identify the names of former students.

(4) *Name-picture matching test*
The ten portraits previously selected for the picture-recognition test were
shown individually, together with 5 first and last names, one of them, the
correct name. The 4 foil names were selected at random from among members
of the same class who were of the same sex as the student shown in the
portrait. Names from the same class were used as foils in order to assure that
correct responses were based upon name-face association rather than
familiarity with the name. The subjects were asked to identify the correct
names.

(5) *Picture-name relearning test*
Seven portraits for which each subject had failed to recall the name on the
picture-cued name recall tests, were selected from each of the classes taught 1,
4, and 8 years ago. In a few instances, the total number of pairs selected was
smaller than 21 because no one-year test had been administered (3 retired Ss)
or because the individual had fewer than 7 response failures on a picture-cued
name recall test. To provide a base line control, 9 additional portrait-name
pairs were selected randomly from the available portraits of applicants to the
university who had not enrolled. Thus the test material usually consisted of 30
portrait-name pairs. Twenty-one of these were of former students which the
subject had taught 1, 4, or 8 years ago, but whose names were not recalled,
and 9 were unfamiliar to the subject. The portrait-name pairs were presented
individually for 5 seconds in random sequence, with the name printed below
each portrait. This presentation series was followed by a test in which each
portrait alone was shown and the subject was required to give the first and last
name presented with it. A time limit of 10 seconds was imposed for each
answer, and the portraits were then presented together with the name in a new
random series. A drop-out procedure was used for the next presentation
series so that only those portraits were shown for which the subject had failed
to give a correct name on the previous test. The alternating sequence of test
and presentation series was continued until the subject gave correct names to
all remaining portraits on a given test.

(6) *Scoring*
Recognition responses were scored correct or incorrect. A recall score of
one-half point was awarded in cases where only the first or last name was
given correctly. Separate scores were obtained for each subject, for each
subtest, for each of the four time intervals. The relearning data from Session 2
were scored by determining the number of test trials needed to produce a
correct response. Separate means were calculated for each subject for
picture-name pairs which were new (controls) and for picture-name pairs of
former students taught 1, 4, and 8 years ago, respectively.

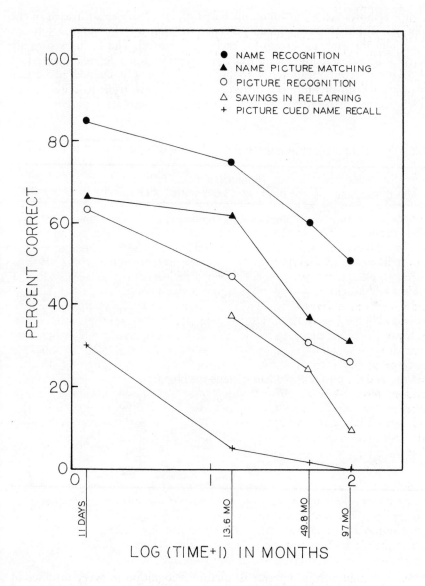

Fig. 1. Memory of college teachers for the names and faces of former students.

C. Results and discussion

Figure 1 shows retention functions based on all 22 subjects for each of the subtests. Table II shows mean percent retention for the various subtests separately for each age group for each time interval. The saving scores are derived by subtracting mean trials to criterion for relearned name-face associations from mean trials to criterion for newly learned name-face association, and dividing the difference by the mean trials to criterion for newly learned associations. Several general conclusions are apparent.

Table II. Mean percentage retention of three age groups on each of five tasks.

Age of subjects	Retention interval			
	11 days	13.6 months	49.8 months	97 months
	Picture cued name recall			
39	37.5	7.1	3.8	0
54	34.1	5.0	1.4	0
68	—	—	2.3	0
	Picture recognition			
39	70	46	31	24
54	68	49	33	33
68	—	—	29	22
	Name recognition			
39	88	80	69	57
54	87	71	56	50
68	—	—	53	48
	Picture name matching			
39	67	56	33	41
54	79	68	43	33
68	—	—	33	20
	% Savings			
39	—	34	13	15
54	—	38	40	12
68	—	—	22	9

Name recognition is superior to picture recognition in every instance in which a comparison is possible. Picture recognition declines to near chance level (20%) over the eight-year retention interval, while name recognition remains substantially higher. Performance on picture recognition is approximately equal to performance on picture-name matching. The relearning data indicate substantial savings for items failed on the picture-cued recall test, at least for retention intervals up to four years. Age differences in retention are minor.

These results differ in some important respects from those obtained in the earlier study of memory for high-school classmates (Bahrick *et al.*, 1975). Figure 2 shows data from the earlier investigation for comparison. The earlier results show much better retention on all comparable subtests and this difference reflects primarily the lower degree of original learning for the items

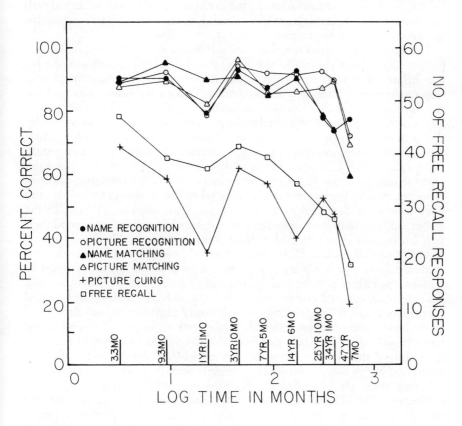

Fig. 2. Memory for high-school classmates. (From Bahrick, H. P., Bahrick, P. O. and Wittlinger, R. P. (1975). Fifty Years of Memory for Names and Faces: A Cross-Sectional Approach. *Journal of Experimental Psychology: General*, **104**, 54–75. Copyright 1975 by the American Psychological Association. Reprinted by permission.)

in the present study. The names and faces of high-school classmates are learned over a period of several years, in contrast with the 10-week exposure used in the present study. Equally important, the nature of interactions among high-school classmates leads to greater depth of processing in a greater variety of encoding contexts than the interaction typical for an instructor with most students in a large college class. These differences affect initial performance and later retention. Only for name recognition is initial performance comparable in the two investigations. The present data show substantial losses of information during the first year of the retention interval. In contrast, the earlier data show no decline of recognition performance for the first 15 years of the retention interval.

The earlier study does not show the advantage of name recognition over picture recognition evident in the present study. Several factors account for this difference. Instructors may be exposed to student names more frequently than to their faces (especially for students with poor attendance records) and this is not true for the interactions among high-school classmates. More important, the portraits presented in the present study had never been seen by the instructors prior to the memory tests, so that correct recognition depended entirely upon an association generalized from person to portrait. Egan *et al.* (1977) estimated that such generalizations lower recognition performance by about 12%, and this estimate may be conservative, since the portraits used in the present study were taken about two years earlier, and were somewhat degraded as a result of the photo-copying process. In the earlier study, it may be assumed that all subjects had originally perused their year-book, and therefore had at least some exposure to *both person and portrait* prior to the test. Differential rehearsal of names and faces in the two studies may also play a role. In spite of a regression correction designed to remove the effects of rehearsals in the earlier study, some effects persisted because of attenuated corrections (Bahrick and Karis, 1982). High-school yearbooks afford the opportunity for additional exposure to both names and faces during the retention interval, while class registers only provide the opportunity for re-exposure to names. Although some exposure to student faces during the retention interval was possible in the present study, the likelihood of this was diminished for the early part of the retention interval by selecting only those students who took no further courses from the instructor. This likelihood was quite small after the students left the university. Both the present and the earlier investigation provide a biased estimate in favour of name recognition over face recognition. This is so because tests of name recognition reinstate the original stimulus with fidelity, while photocopies of portraits taken at an earlier time represent a comparatively degraded visual stimulus which adversely affects performance (Goldstein and Chance, 1981). It is clear from the rationale provided why this bias is likely to be more significant in the present study than in the earlier one.

The only indications of a significant decline of performance with age are observed for the picture-name matching and the relearning subtests. The oldest teachers learn new picture-name pairs more slowly than younger teachers, but this difference is obscured in Table II because learning and relearning are approximately equally affected by age, so that all groups achieve approximately comparable saving scores in relearning the names of former students. The overall correlation between the age of the instructor and the mean number of trials needed to learn new portrait-name pairs if .45 (p<.05). This suggests an ageing effect on the speed of learning, but not on degree of retention *per se*. This important distinction has been neglected in most previous discussions of the effects of ageing on memory. If original exposure to material is held constant for all age groups, and older subjects learn less from this exposure than younger subjects, then poorer performance of older subjects on later tests of retention may reflect the lower degree of original learning, rather than accelerated forgetting. Thus Warrington and Sanders (1971) concluded that older subjects show poorer retention than younger subjects for the names and faces of famous individuals, when original exposure is presumed to have been comparable for all age groups. It is difficult to determine to what extent these age differences reflect unequal degrees of original learning and to what extent they reflect differential rates of forgetting. This issue affects all investigations of age and memory in which the subjects were of different ages at the time of original exposure, and original learning did not continue to a fixed criterion.

Burke and Light (1981) in their important review of the literature on memory and ageing, reached this same conclusion. They pointed out that there have been no adequate checks on whether orienting tasks produce similar initial encoding in young and old subjects, and that the problem is particularly troublesome in naturalistic studies because it is impossible to equate people of different ages on initial learning or exposure to the materials. Eysenck (1974) and Craik and Simon (1980) attributed differences in initial encoding to a processing deficiency of older subjects.

Picture-name matching has declined to chance levels after eight years for the oldest subjects, and performance of the young instructors is significantly (p<.01) higher. This age difference may also be subject to the above interpretation, but the data are less definitive since no significant age difference is observed for classes taught 4 years earlier.

Previous findings by Ferris *et al.* (1980) and by Smith and Winograd (1978) also indicated age deficits in recognizing photographs of faces, but these investigations dealt with episodic memory for photographs unfamiliar to the subjects prior to the experiment.

No significant age differences are observed for the name recognition subtest, and picture recognition and picture cued recall have declined to chance levels for all groups at the end of eight years, so that the data are no longer sensitive to age differences.

In the earlier study (Bahrick *et al.*, 1975), all subjects were of approximately the same age at the time of original exposure, and the lower retention of those tested after very long intervals cannot therefore be explained in terms of lower degrees of original learning. However, that study confounded age of subjects with age of the memory traces, and therefore does not permit unequivocal attribution of the decline to ageing effects. The results of the present study suggest that at least some of the decline observed in the earlier study is due to ageing of the memory trace, rather than ageing of the individual. For memory traces of the same age, the older individuals in this study show no pronounced deficits in name recognition. Performance for name-face matching does show a significant difference which has been discussed, and no conclusions can be reached for the other subtests.

The performance of various age groups in this study may also be affected differentially by cumulative interference. Younger instructors had fewer classes preceding the ones on which they were tested, while those older instructors who had retired were less subject to retroactive inhibition from learning subsequent class lists. These factors tend to offset each other, and since the task of associating names and faces also continues outside the classroom for all subjects, the net effect of these differences is probably minor.

It is concluded that college teachers are better at recognizing names than portraits of former students; that eight years after the teaching contacts, portrait recognition is very poor if students were taught in only a single class, but relearning of name-face associations still shows substantial savings. Age differences are minor for instructors between the ages of 36 and 75, and the data suggest that at least some of the differences reflect lower degrees of original learning, rather than accelerated forgetting.

The research discussed in this chapter reveals methodological problems associated with the study of naturalistic memory for names and faces. The study of memory for the faces of college classmates shows that problems of reliability arise from the failure to control variables that are typically well controlled in the laboratory. Motivational and attentional variables appear to have a great influence upon what is learned during prolonged real-life interaction, and this affects retention in a naturalistic task. As a result, individual differences in an episodic laboratory task do not correlate with individual differences in a semantic, naturalistic task. To understand naturalistic memory we must develop better means of assessing the influence of motivational variables.

The study of memory for the names and faces of former students reveals the difficulties of sorting out the effects of cognitive and maturational variables on retention over long time-periods. It is useful to compare retention of subjects who acquired the same information at different ages, but limitations of the life-span preclude extending this design over very long intervals. When individuals learn at different ages retention losses are often confounded with differences in the degree of original learning and with the type and duration of interference during the retention interval. More effective techniques for sorting out these effects are needed in the study of long-term naturalistic memory.

NOTE

This research was supported by U.S. Public Health Service Research Grant HD00926-16 from the National Institute of Child Health and Human Development. The author is indebted to Phyllis Bahrick, Melva Hunter and Mark Richards for their help in the collection and analysis of data.

REFERENCES

Bahrick, H. P. and Karis, D. (1982). Long-term ecological memory. *In* "Handbook of Research Methods in Human Memory and Cognition" (R. Puff, ed.), Academic Press, New York and London.

Bahrick, H. P., Bahrick, P. O. and Wittlinger, R. P. (1975). Fifty years of memory for names and faces: A cross-sectional approach. *Journal of Experimental Psychology: General*, **104**, 54–75.

Bower, G. H. and Karlin, M. B. (1974). Depth of processing pictures of faces and recognition memory. *Journal of Experimental Psychology*, **103**, 751–757.

Burke, D. B. and Light, L. L. (1981). Memory and Aging: The Role of Retrieval Processes. *Psychological Bulletin*, **90**, 513–546.

Chance, J. E. and Goldstein, A. G. (1976). Recognition of faces and verbal labels. *Bulletin of the Psychonomic Society*, **7**, 384–386.

Craik, F. I. M. and Simon, E. (1980). Age differences in memory: The roles of attention and depth of processing. *In* "New directions in memory and aging; Proceedings of the George Talland memorial conference" (L. W. Poon, J. L. Fozard, L. S. Cermak, D. Arenberg, and L. W. Thompson, eds), Erlbaum, Hillsdale, N.J.

Egan, D., Pittner, M. and Goldstein, A. G. (1977). Eyewitness identification — Photographs vs live models. *Law and Human Behavior*, **1**, 199–206.

Ellis, D. H., Shepherd, J. W. and Bruce, A. (1973). The effects of age and sex upon adolescents' recognition of faces. *Journal of Genetic Psychology*, **123**, 173–174.

Eysenck, M. W. (1974). Age difference in incidental learning. *Developmental Psychology*, **10**, 936–941.

Ferris, S. J., Crook, T., Clark, E., McCarthy, M., and Rae, D. (1980). Facial recognition memory deficits in normal aging and senile dementia. *Journal of Gerontology*, **35**, 707–714.

Goldstein, A. G. and Chance, J. E. (1971). Visual recognition memory for complex configurations. *Perception and Psychophysics*, **9**, 237–241.

Goldstein, A. G. and Chance, J. E. (1981). Laboratory studies of face recognition. *In* "Perceiving and Remembering Faces" (G. Davies, H. Ellis, and J. Shepherd, eds), Academic Press, New York and London.

Neisser, U. (1976). "Cognition and Reality: Principles and implications of cognitive psychology". Freeman, San Francisco.

Read, J. D. and Bruce, D. (1982). Longitudinal tracking of difficult memory retrievals. *Cognitive Psychology*, **14** (in press).

Shepherd, John (1981). Social factors in face recognition. *In* "Perceiving and Remembering Faces" (G. Davies, H. Ellis and J. Shepherd, eds), Academic Press, New York and London.

Smith, A. D. and Winograd, E. (1978). Adult age differences in remembering faces. *Developmental Psychology*, **14**, 443–444.

Strnad, B. N. and Mueller, J. H. (1977). Levels of processing in facial recognition memory. *Bulletin of the Psychonomic Society*, **9**, 17–18.

Warrington, E. K. and Sanders, H. I. (1971). The fate of old memories. *Quarterly Journal of Experimental Psychology*, **23**, 432–442.

3

Everyday Memory for Everyday Places

D. Bartram and P. Smith

I. INTRODUCTION

Paradoxically, we become most acutely aware of our "sense of place" and "sense of direction" when we are lost. The feeling of being lost involves far more than just finding ourselves in a strange and unfamiliar setting. Indeed we can feel "lost" and yet be in a place that is quite familiar to us. For example, when emerging from a familiar cinema or theatre, it is relatively common to feel temporarily disoriented. We may have to stop for a moment to decide which way to go, or may even walk off in the completely wrong direction. We "know" where we are, but have temporarily misplaced or lost track of the relationship between our current location and the locations of other nearby familiar places.

The essence of being lost is an inability to relate the place we are in (be it strange or familiar) to other known places, a failure to fit our current location into our internal representation of the spatial environment. In other words, it is a failure of our internal navigation system. Such failures may have various causes and manifest themselves in many different ways. For example, we can set off to visit a new location along a familiar route and find ourselves inadvertently travelling to our customary destination. We may also get lost if we try to navigate using distorted knowledge of the layout of the environment. Such distortions are clearly revealed in a study by Milgram and Jodelet (1976). They found that most Parisians (91.6% of their sample) drew the River Seine as a fairly shallow smooth curve rather than as it really is (i.e. sharply curved in places). As they located places in Paris by reference to the river, the relative positions of such places and the distances between them were grossly distorted.

We tend to rely most on our sense of direction when we are in unfamiliar places. For example, emerging from the station in a strange town, we see our destination some distance away. However, there is no direct route to it and as soon as we walk away from the station our destination disappears from view. In such a situation we may try to use our sense of direction to keep track of the twists and turns in our route. However, as we shall see later, a number of features of the environment can make this difficult: when our guidance system tells us we should have reached our destination, we may in fact find that we are nowhere near it.

In this chapter we shall attempt to explain the reasons for such navigational problems. In order to do so, we shall need to outline the nature of this internal navigation system. This can best be done by considering two questions:

(1) From what sources do we acquire our spatial knowledge of the world?
(2) How is that knowledge internally represented and used?

In trying to answer these questions, it is hoped that we shall gain a clearer understanding of three interrelated "everyday" questions:

(1) How do we know where we are?
(2) How do we find our way from one place to another?
(3) Why do we sometimes get lost?

To appreciate the relevance of actual research findings relating to these questions it will be necessary first to examine the (often implicit) theoretical frameworks underlying the studies. In particular, it will be necessary to consider the relative importance of different sources of information (Section II) and the distinctions made between the internal representation of specific information about particular routes and general information about the relationships between places (Section III). Having done this, we shall be in a position to evaluate the research dealing with factors that produce distortions in our spatial knowledge (Section IV). Finally, we shall consider the question of individual differences in navigational ability (Section V).

II. SOURCES OF SPATIAL KNOWLEDGE

Our sources of spatial information may be either direct or indirect. Through direct experience (e.g. walking around a town, or driving from one place to another) we gain knowledge about the perceptual characteristics of places and landmarks. Furthermore, we gain information about the spatial relationships between such places when we move from one to another. The information gained by this direct interaction with the environment is extremely rich but is also very limited. If this were all we had, we should only be able to navigate with confidence along previously trodden paths between places already known to us. We can supplement this direct input with less rich sources of information about places and routes from other people, written media, films and photographs and, of course, printed maps. Even maps come in a variety of forms designed to represent different aspects of information about the environment. They differ in terms of scale, detail, and the type of information they contain. Some are designed to show accurately the objective distances between places (e.g. Ordnance Survey Maps), while others only convey information about relative locations (e.g. the London Underground Map). Maps designed for motorists are very different from those designed for the pilots of low-flying fast-jets (the latter containing detailed information on power lines, and other important obstructions and landmarks).

While these second-hand sources of information may lack the impact and richness of direct experience, they are likely to contribute a considerable proportion of our world-knowledge. Indeed, much of our knowledge is only attainable by indirect means. Apart from a few astronauts, most of us only know the shape of the British Isles indirectly from maps or photographs.

A distinction has been drawn between the scale at which the environment is, or can be, experienced directly, and that at which such experience is not possible. Sommer (1969) called the former the proximate environment and the latter the macro environment. Others have referred to the latter as the "invisible" (Stea, 1967) or "extra" (Goodey, 1968) environment. One's home address, for example, refers to a nested sequence of environmental scales; while the house and street may be the subject of direct experience, the town, county and country as wholes are not. From the various parts that we perceive directly, and from indirect sources (such as maps), we are able to abstract a unitary concept of the town, county or country. Thus, when someone says, "go down the M1 to London", they are using London as a conceptual label to refer to a large area.

III. THE INTERNAL REPRESENTATION OF SPATIAL KNOWLEDGE

Once information has been acquired in the ways described above, it is reasonable to assume that it is used to build up a representation of the environment. Any system designed to move within a complex environment requires some internalized representation of the layout of that environment. This representation might be descriptive (e.g. in the form of a network of nodes that represent places, and links that represent the relationships between places) or procedural (e.g. in the form of a store of "production rules" that specify how to get from place A to place B). This distinction between descriptive and procedural knowledge (cf. Anderson, 1976) is one that has been made repeatedly during the short history of research on spatial cognition.

Tolman, who first introduced the notion of "cognitive maps" (Tolman, 1948) as internal descriptions of routes ("strip maps") or interrelated collections of routes ("comprehensive maps"), also developed the notion of "means-ends-readiness" (Tolman, 1959). This readiness was defined as being a belief that a certain sort of stimulus situation, if reacted to by a certain sort of response, could be expected to lead to a different but predictable sort of stimulus situation. As Clayton and Woodyard (1981) have argued, if one replaces stimulus-response-stimulus with situation-action-outcome, we have a general description of a production system (Newell, 1973).

Siegel and White (1975) clearly echoed Tolman when they drew the distinction between route representation (i.e. action sequences) and configural representations (i.e. network-like representations of the relationships between places). They also added a third category, implicit in Tolman's approach: memory for landmarks. However, landmarks are a special instance of a general category of place-identifiers. Just as we are able to describe how to get from one landmark to another (e.g. from the Houses of Parliament to the Tate Gallery), so we can describe how to get from one city to another. In the latter case, city names stand as identifiers for macro-scale places. The nodes of the network which are linked together to produce a route or configural representation may represent relatively abstract descriptions of places.

These different levels of description are clearly seen in Lynch's (1960) work on city images. He described the content of the city maps produced by his subjects in terms of landmarks, nodes, paths, districts and edges. Nodes, districts and landmarks can all be considered to be place-identifiers. Both nodes and landmarks are identifiers on the proximate-scale environment while districts are macro-scale identifiers. Paths and edges, on the other hand describe the relationships between places. Paths link non-adjacent places: landmarks at the proximate scale (e.g. the Mall between Admiralty Arch and Buckingham Palace), and districts at the macro-scale (e.g. the M1 between Leeds and London). Edges define the conjunctions between adjacent districts (e.g. the Berlin Wall).

Thorndyke (1981) described representations of landmarks as perceptual icons or images of places whose elicitation is strongly tied to perceptual cues. These perceptual primitives form the building blocks from which more abstract levels of description can be produced. Such higher level descriptions may be classed as semantic rather than episodic (cf. Tulving, 1972): for example, the label "Houses of Parliament" is a symbolic label that can elicit specific perceptual icons. While perceptual icons are necessarily tied to the proximate-scale environment (e.g. images of your house), the more abstract descriptions can refer to nodes at any level of place-identifier scale (e.g. your house, England, the Solar System etc.).

Thus one can conceptualize the internal representation of the environment in terms of a network of interrelated nodes. Each node represents a place-identifier, referring to a specific place (a "landmark") or a generalized place (a macro-scale description such as the district of a city, or at a higher level, the city itself). The links between nodes describe relationships of "distance", "adjacency" and "direction". Within such an hierarchical network, a route-representation can be regarded as a specific pathway from one node (the starting place) through others to a final node (the destination).

A. The nature of route representations

Thorndyke (1981) distinguished between two types of route knowledge: ordered and unordered productions. As described above, a production rule specifies a current situation, and an action that is required to achieve a goal (the outcome). In terms of routes, the current situation will relate to one's present location, and the outcome to the location one is trying to reach. When links between one segment of a route and the next rely on contextual cues picked up from the environment, the set of production rules describing the route are deemed unordered. Selection of the next rule in the sequence requires one to have satisfied the goal of the previous rule in order to pick up the contextual cues that define the "situation" of the next production rule. Thus there is no explicit representation within the system of the ordering of the segments of the route. Clayton and Woodyard (1981) referred to this as "memory for actions in context".

Ordered productions differ from unordered ones in that the former involve explicit internal representations of the sequence of route segments. According to Thorndyke (1981), routes can be successfully travelled using either ordered or unordered productions. The main distinction appears to be in terms of the ease with which the route can be described. For unordered productions, the outcome of each rule can only be recognized when reached, whereas for ordered productions the outcomes and hence the sequence can be recalled. It seems likely that rather than being a difference of kind, this is a difference of degree.

While production rules provide a convenient way of describing how we actually travel from one place to another, it does not follow that our knowledge of the environment is stored in this form. We would argue that routes are represented as linked sequences of nodes in the spatial memory network described at the beginning of Section II. Such information may be derived from experiences of actual journeys or from indirect inputs such as maps or descriptions, or may be generated from the network by processes of inference (e.g. If A is one mile north of B, and C is two miles west of B, then C is just over two miles, approximately west-south-west of A).

Just as a portion of the network at one level of environmental scale can be labelled as a single district at a macro-scale level, so one might expect that a well-learnt route could be given a single macro-label ("going to work"). Such representations of well-learnt routes may have the stereotypical properties of "scripts" (cf. Schank and Abelson, 1975).

Routes that are explicitly derived from information in the network database using means-ends-analysis (i.e. plans) correspond to ordered productions. For any new route that one actively travels along (i.e. not as a passenger), the initial ordering has to be planned. As the route becomes more familiar, so increasingly large sections of it will become abstracted into single labellable nodes: each such section being executable as an automatic script. For example the route: "Hull to Doncaster" might subsume descriptions of how to get from one's house in Hull to the M62 motorway, to transfer to the M18, to exit the M18 at the appropriate point and finally to enter Doncaster. In turn, the first (Home to M62) and last (M62 exit into Doncaster) segments are each higher-order descriptions subsuming sequences of productions. Necessarily, unordered productions must derive from routes that have been directly experienced; (perhaps one has been driven along the route by someone else, or one discovered it by chance).

Procedural representations of knowledge, as embodied in production rule systems, may well play an important role in the translation of route plans into action. Their main role is likely to be in the actual control of movement in the environment. However, the underlying database from which such plans are derived or recalled need not itself be procedural. It is far more economical to generate procedures from a network, than to try to store the amount of information contained in such a network in procedural form.

B. The internal representation of spatial configurations

The integration of information about place-identity and the spatial relationships between places into a network representation is sufficient for the production of an internal topological representation of large-scale space. Such a representation is not something over and above the route information it is based on: routes, as argued above, may be considered to be pathways in the network.

A number of researchers (e.g. Byrne, 1979; Moar, 1978; Thorndyke, 1981), have argued that it is important to distinguish between on the one hand network or schematic maps and on the other hand veridical Euclidean or "vector-maps". The former are generally regarded as simplified representations of spatial layout which are likely to contain distortions of true distance and direction information (a good analogue in the real world being the London Underground map), while the latter accurately represent the distances between each pair of nodes (a real world analogue being Ordnance Survey maps).

Moar (1978) made a further distinction between egocentric and topological representations of space (both being non-Euclidean). Egocentric representations are those that are route-dependent: that is, they are a memory of the event-sequence that the person experienced when travelling the route. The topological information contained within the memory of this event-sequence must, presumably, be abstracted and incorporated into the topological spatial network. This distinction between egocentric representations and topological ones can be likened to the distinction drawn between episodic and semantic memory (e.g. Tulving, 1972). An egocentric representation of how one got from A to B could not be used to travel from B to A, whereas a topological representation abstracted from it could.

Thus there appear to be three stages in the representation of directly experienced spatial information. Egocentric, or episodic, route-representations provide information from which topological networks can be derived. These, in turn, may approximate to Euclidean vector-representations as increasing amounts of information are incorporated into them. However, learning about the environment does not necessarily involve an ordered sequence of transitions from egocentric, through topological to Euclidean representation. Detailed Euclidean information is available directly from certain types of printed maps, and topological information is available from topological sketch maps and verbal descriptions. Two studies have shown very clearly the relationships between these forms of representation and the learning of new spatial environments.

Moar (1978) gave one group of subjects a three-minute tour of an unfamiliar building, while a second group were given a ground plan of the same building. to study for the same time. Subjects were then asked to recall directions and distances between places on the ground floor of the building. Those who had studied the plan produced "maps" that were holistic and approximately Euclidean, while the "tour" subjects' maps were highly fragmented and route-dependent. However, a third group of subjects who were familiar with the building produced maps that correlated highly with the properties of Euclidean space. Moar concluded that with increasing experience of a spatial environment, the properties of the internal representations of that environment tend towards the properties of Euclidean space.

A similar study was carried out by Thorndyke and Hayes-Roth (1978) using the Rand Corporation building. They used a number of groups having different levels of experience of the building (from one to 24 months) and a group who learnt the layout from a map. In terms of the ability to point to locations that were not visible, the map-group were the worst, with level of performance increasing with experience. However, when subjects were asked to indicate the location of a place on a piece of paper containing the locations of two reference places, the map-group performed best, with performance decreasing from the most to least experienced groups. Finally, in a distance estimation task, the map-group were good at estimating both actual and Euclidean (i.e. "as the crow flies") distances. The inexperienced group were good at estimating actual distances, but poor at estimating Euclidean ones. However, those with one or more years of experience were good at both tasks and superior to the map-group. These results show that detailed Euclidean representations can be produced either directly (from Euclidean media) or indirectly through extensive experience. Furthermore, the superiority of the experienced groups on the distance estimation tasks suggests that their "network", while having the same Euclidean properties as that of the map-group, is far richer in terms of the detail it contains.

IV. DISTORTIONS IN THE REPRESENTATION OF DISTANCE AND DIRECTION

There is now an extensive literature concerning distance and direction judgements in the large-scale environment. These studies fall into two main categories: those concerned with judgements of the macro-scale environment (such as Stevens and Coupe, 1978; and Milgram and Jodelet, 1976) and those concerned with judgements based on direct or indirect knowledge of the proximate scale environment (e.g. Byrne, 1979; Golledge and Zannaras,

1973; Lee 1970; Canter and Tagg, 1975; Chase and Chi, 1981; Sadalla and Staplin, 1980a, 1980b; Sadalla and Magel, 1980).

It is important to clarify a number of points before trying to summarize the results of such studies. Consider three places, A, B and C, which in Euclidean space lie at the apices of an equilateral triangle. Suppose that we have travelled the route A→B→C, and internally represent A→B as longer than B→C. If we correctly represent the angle ABC as 60°, we may infer that the other two angles must be unequal. This is a correct inference based on inaccurate distance information which would lead to inaccurate direction estimates. If, on the other hand, we represent A→B as equal in distance to B→C, but incorrectly judge the angle ABC to be 90°, then we may reasonably but incorrectly infer that A→C is greater than both A→B and B—→C, and that the angles BCA and CAB are both 45°. Hence it is important to try independently to assess (a) the representation of directional information, (b) the representation of distance information and (c) the inferential processes used to "bridge" untraversed links in the network.

The assessment of direction information is relatively simple: people can be asked to point to places that are known but not visible, or can be asked to draw specific junctions of paths. The assessment of information about distance is far more complex. Consider again the three equidistant places A, B and C. If A and B were joined by a straight motorway while B and C were joined by a twisting footpath, then it does not seem unreasonable to judge B→C as being a greater distance than A→B (cf. Ewing, 1981). Indeed, to show that the two Euclidean distances were the same, we would either need to use a ruler and a map or else know that A→B and A→C were of equal Euclidean distance and that CAB was 60°. Not only are the actual route-distances different, but also the travel times per unit distance will be very different. Thus, there is a problem of deciding upon an appropriate baseline for assessing the accuracy of any distance judgement.

A. Estimation of direction

There is a relatively small literature directly concerned with this question. What there is suggests that we tend to store information about direction in "normalized" form. Byrne (1979) asked subjects to draw ten different familiar road junctions, stressing that they should pay particular attention to the angle at which the roads met. The roads were chosen so that five pairs met as acute angles of between 64° and 70°, and five at obtuse angles of between 110° and 116°. He found a very strong tendency for subjects to represent all of these as being 90° angles: the means for the ten pairs varied from 83.5° to 103.7°. The mean for the acute angle junctions was 89.7°, while that for the obtuse angles was 94.5°.

Other evidence for this "normalization" can be found in a study reported by Chase and Chi (1981). They asked 16 subjects to draw maps of the Carnegie-Mellon campus. One street intersection, which was not rectilinear with respect to the rest of the campus, produced very large errors and distortions. Most subjects drew these streets meeting at 90°, instead of the correct 45°. Lynch (1960) also reported that subjects had problems in correctly representing Boston Common in their maps: the Common was represented as having four sides when in fact it is five-sided.

Similar direction normalization errors can be found in studies that involve subjects pointing to buildings that were not visible. Kozlowski and Bryant (1977) found a systematic tendency for their subjects to point to the left of the target buildings on a trapezoid campus. This error can be accounted for if one assumes that subjects represented the campus as rectangular. The second author (Smith, 1978) has found a similar constant error with blind subjects on the Hull University Campus: with the size of the error in pointing relating to the angle by which the campus deviates from a true rectangle.

A description of a route, or a plan of how to travel a route, need only contain information about major changes in direction. In addition, information about the sequence of places to be visited and some indications of the relative distances between those places. However, for everyday navigation it is not important to know the precise angle at which paths meet: frequently all one needs to know is whether to go on, turn left or turn right. Complex junctions may require more detailed coding (e.g. "turn sharp left" or "veer left"). As far as we know, the representation of complex junctions has not been investigated. It seems likely though that some form of normalization would be used, as precise Euclidean angles are difficult to assess and, for the most part, unnecessary.

Distortion of direction and relative location also occur in macro-scale representations (though often for rather different reasons). As described earlier, Milgram and Jodelet (1976) found that their subjects distorted the locations of places due to their misperception of the shape of River Seine. Stevens and Coupe (1978) asked people to indicate the direction from one American city to another. They showed how substantial errors can occur when inferences are based on over-simplified (or normalized) spatial networks. For example, nearly all their subjects asserted that Reno, Nevada, lay northeast of San Diego, when in fact it is north-northwest. Stevens and Coupe argued that such errors arise through the processes of inference used to produce the response. From their spatial network, subjects can derive the premises:

(a) Nevada is east of California;
(b) San Diego is in Southern part of California on the West coast; and
(c) Reno is in the central part of Nevada on the Californian border.

From these premises, it would follow that Reno must be northeast of San Diego. The error seems to arise from treating the States as single elements and then, by implication, asserting that *All* of one State lies to the west of the other.

This sort of simplification, which is strongly supported by Stevens and Coupe's data, supports the idea of a hierarchically arranged network. Each

State is represented as a node at a macro-scale level and has normalized directional links to other States. In turn, each State node has links to subordinate levels of the hierarchy which specify the relative locations of towns within the State. In making judgements about relative directions of towns that are in different States, the relative directions of the superordinate (State-to-State) links may introduce distortions. Similar distortions do not arise for intra-State judgements as these do not involve combining information from different levels of scale. This effect of superordinate level distortion can be readily elicited in British people by asking them whether Bristol lies to the east or west of Edinburgh. Unsuspecting subjects will readily reply "west", on the assumption that the UK is north-south oriented; Edinburgh is on the east coast and Bristol on the west.

B. Distance estimation

The literature on distance estimation is complex and at times confused. Lee (1962, 1970) found that while estimates of distance towards the centre of a town tended to be underestimated, those for distances away from the centre were overestimated. Golledge et al. (1969) and Briggs (1973) found the opposite. Lee (1970) found no effect of objective distance on over- or underestimation, while Cadwallader (1973) found a tendency to overestimate short routes relative to longer ones. Other studies (e.g. Canter and Tagg, 1975) have found complex relationships between the Lynchian "legibility" of a city (i.e. the ease with which information about the parts of a city can be organized into a coherent pattern) and distance estimation within that city.

Much of the confusion has arisen from the fact that many studies have looked at distance estimation in the real world without adequate control over relevant variables (e.g. the skill and experience of the subjects, the nature of the buildings and structure of the city). In addition, confusions often arise for methodological reasons.

An example of this type of confusion can be seen in the apparent inconsistencies between one study by Canter (1977) and another by MacEachren (1980). Both studies examined the prediction of estimated, or cognitive distance from (a) actual, or objective distance and (b) journey time. Canter found a strong positive correlation between actual and estimated distance and a weak negative one between travel time and estimated distance. MacEachren, on the other hand, found that travel time correlated more highly with estimated distance than did actual distance (though both correlations were strongly positive). Ewing (1981) attempted to explain the apparent conflict between these results by looking at their differences in methodology and experimental setting. Canter asked people to estimate distances between pairs of stations on a London Underground route, while MacEachren asked people to estimate distances between their homes and four supermarkets familiar to them. Normal modes of transport differed, in that MacEachren's subjects primarily travelled by car. However, Ewing concluded that the main reason for the conflicting results was the difference in procedures for data aggregation and analysis. Canter correlated objective distances with their mean estimated distances (across subjects), while MacEachren used the more appropriate procedure of using regression analysis on non-aggregated data to determine which of objective distance and travel time was the better predictor of estimated distance.

More adequate levels of experimental control are found in a number of recent studies (Byrne, 1979; Sadalla and Staplin, 1980a, 1980b and Sadalla and Magel, 1980). Byrne (1979), using ratio-scaling techniques, obtained distance estimates for twelve routes well known to his subjects. Half the routes were in the centre of a town (St. Andrews), and half were in residential outskirts. In each case, there were three straight routes and three containing between two and four bends. Within each subgroup the objective distance was 300, 540 or 750 metres. The results of the study were quite clear:

(1) The short routes were overestimated and the long ones underestimated (cf. Cadwallader, 1973).

(2) Short routes with bends were overestimated to a greater degree than short straight routes.

(3) The effects of both objective length and bends were more pronounced for routes in the town centre than for routes in the outskirts.

In a laboratory study, Sadalla and Magel (1980) obtained distance estimates for paths that were of equal objective length but differed in having either two or seven right-angle bends. Using ratio-scaling, subjects estimated the 7-turn paths to be longer than the 2-turn paths. They also drew the former paths longer than the latter. This effect could not be accounted for simply in terms of "travel-time", as there were no significant differences in either the actual times or their estimates of the times taken to walk each type of path. Furthermore, the straight-line distance between the start and end-point of each path was controlled.

Sadalla and Magel considered three hypotheses:

(1) *The Scaling Hypothesis.* Dainoff *et al.* (1974) found that psychological distance varied as a power function of actual distance (cf. Stevens, 1957). The relationship between actual and psychological distance when using double logarithmic coordinates was a straight line having a slope less than one (indicating that short-objective distances are over-estimated relative to longer ones). Assuming that turns in a route segment it into a number of shorter paths, then if the estimated route length is an additive function of the estimated lengths of each segment, paths with many turns will be estimated as being longer than those with fewer turns.

(2) *The Storage Hypothesis.* This is based on Milgram's (1973) argument that the judged length of a path is a function of the amount of information stored about it. Hence paths with large numbers of turns will have more information stored and therefore be judged longer than those with few turns.

(3) *The Effort Hypothesis.* This attributes overestimation to the effort involved making turns when travelling a route.

Sadalla and Staplin (1980a) manipulated information load by labelling 15 intersections on an L-shaped path with either high or low-frequency names. High frequency names have been shown to be easier to recall than low frequency ones (e.g. Hall, 1954; Deese, 1960). Routes that had high frequency junction-names were estimated as longer than those with low frequency ones (furthermore, the expected superior recall for high frequency names was found). There was also evidence of a von Restorff effect for the intersection that came immediately after the turn. These results are counter to the Effort Hypothesis, which would predict that low-frequency names, being harder to remember, should produce overestimation. However, both the Scaling and Storage Hypotheses are supported. Labelling nodes (whether they are intersections of turns) may act to segment the route: the more it is segmented, the more its length will be overestimated according to the Scaling Hypothesis.

A further study (Sadalla and Staplin, 1980b) suggested that the crucial variable is the number of segments and not the amount of information encoded about each node. In this study, a complex network of paths and intersections was used. Having made their distance estimates, subjects had to estimate the number of intersections on each path and the number of paths converging at each intersection. They found that varying the number of paths at each junction had no effect on distance estimation.

C. The role of functional utility in the representation of spatial information

Environments (such as some University campuses and the insides of buildings) that contain places linked by relatively straight paths which can be travelled at uniform rates can be internally represented by detailed networks that have strict Euclidean properties. The same is not true for more complex variable environments. For such environments, a Euclidean representation would be accurate, but it would also be both difficult to obtain, and less useful than a representation that embodied information about journey time, difficulty and actual (as opposed to straight-line) distance. Indeed, as previously discussed, in cases where the main source of information about distance is travel-time and the utility of distance information is low (car-driving in inner-city areas), estimates of distance are better predicted by travel-time than by objective distance (MacEachren, 1980).

As argued by Foulke (1971), it seems that the system's criteria for selecting information about places and relationships between places are primarily the functional utility of that information and its availability. In MacEachren's study (1980), travel-time had high functional utility and was immediately available while information about distance was not. In regular environments Euclidean information is useful and available, in complex irregular ones it is neither. Thus, it is inappropriate to regard Euclidean representations as the ultimate goal of the system (cf. Downs and Siegel, 1981). As Griffin (1948) said:

The better oriented a person is, the more closely his schema is likely to resemble a map. For many people, however, geographical accuracy is not necessary or even important.

The major problem with non-Euclidean topographies is that the introduction of extra information into one link in the network will distort vital information about the relative directions of other places in the network. The system has to accept some form of trade-off between the utility of normalization procedures and non-veridical information about distance on the one hand, with the disadvantages of the non-Euclidean distortions they introduce into other parts of the network on the other.

V. INDIVIDUAL DIFFERENCES IN NAVIGATIONAL ABILITY

While it is a truism to assert that people differ in their navigational ability, we are only just beginning to understand the mechanisms underlying these differences. Kozlowski and Bryant (1977) have provided support for the lay concept of having a sense of direction. They found a strong relationship between self-reported sense of direction and accuracy at pointing to unseen locations (though all subjects tended to produce the same normalization errors; see above). In a second study, two groups of subjects (self-assessed by questionnaire as having either a good or a poor sense-of-direction) walked round an irregular maze. On the first trial the need for orientation was not emphasized, and no difference was found between the accuracy of maps produced by the two groups. However, with repeated exposure to the maze and the realization that orientation was being assessed, the good sense-of-direction group showed significant improvements while the other group showed none. Possible confounding variables (such as level of attention, motivation, interest in the task and so on) were also assessed. No differences were found between the two groups for these variables.

A number of other differences were found between good and poor sense-of-direction subjects. The former were better at giving and following directions, at remembering routes while a passenger in a car and at remembering written route instructions. In addition, they liked reading maps, enjoyed giving directions, exploring new places and finding new routes to known places. They also reported being less prone to anxiety when lost. In general they found successful navigation an intrinsically satisfying experience. A similar pattern of spatial aptitude profile has been noted by Beck and Wood (1976).

Thorndyke and Stasz (1980) examined individual differences in spatial learning strategies by analysing subject protocols in a map-learning task. They identified three main classes of procedure:

(1) Attentional procedures concerned the selection of subsets of information upon which to focus (i.e. the subjects' scheduling strategy). Fast

learners showed a more systematic control of focus of attention, breaking the map down into manageable parts.

(2) Encoding procedures related to techniques for storing and elaborating upon spatial information. The fast learners showed a greater use of visual-image mnemonics, relational statements (such as "place A is west of place B"), and configural images (such as "this road system looks like a stick-man running to the west").

(3) Evaluation procedures involved the subjects' estimates of how well they were doing. The fast learners had more realistic estimates of their performances and were better at identifying and concentrating upon areas with which they were having difficulty.

Having identified good strategies, they trained subjects in the use of these. They found that only those with good spatial memory improved with training.

Such results suggest that experience provides the opportunity for the development of spatial knowledge. However, such opportunities are a necessary but not sufficient condition for the development of that knowledge. People seem to differ not only in terms of what they derive from their spatial experience, but also in terms of the extent to which they actively seek such experiences.

VI. CONCLUSIONS

It is important to distinguish between our "semantic" knowledge of the spatial environment, "episodic" memories of places and journeys and procedures for generating and executing journey-plans. We have suggested that our semantic knowledge is represented as an hierarchical network of place-identifier nodes. Different levels of this network correspond to different environmental scales, with the lowest being the proximate-scale where nodes are ostensively defined (see Russell, 1948) by links to episodic memories. Such ostensive links provide an interface between semantic and episodic memory.

However, such interfaces must exist at all levels of the system. Studies such as those by Thorndyke and Hayes-Roth (1978) and Moar (1978) show that information from different forms of input medium (both direct and indirect) are mapped onto the network at different levels. The same conclusion was drawn by one of us (Bartram, 1980) in a study comparing the comprehension of map and time-table information about bus-routes. In general, most indirect sources of spatial knowledge (books, maps, verbal descriptions and so on) involve some degree of symbolic abstraction and tend to relate to macro-scale environmental features. Rather than seeing episodic and semantic memory as two separate systems, linked at a single interface, it seems more appropriate to view them as aspects of one system in which a semantic network structure provides the cohesion and organization for episodic content. A similar account was given by Anderson and Bower (1973) of the relationship between perceptual and linguistic information in HAM.

How is such a system used in the process of navigation? It has been argued that well-known routes may be explicitly represented and labelled by a single route-node. Such routes are analogous to scripts, and will be linked to the production-rule systems required to travel the route. In other situations, the production of a route-plan will involve a mean-ends-analysis of the network, to find a suitable sequence of links between the origin and destination. In producing such route-plans, inferential processes may be used to bridge gaps in the network or find short-cuts (cf. Kuipers, 1978).

The difference between travelling routes through known as opposed to unknown places is an important one. In the former case, information about landmarks and decision points are explicitly represented in memory. In the latter case, we have to rely on our ability to recognize certain types of place. For example, suppose you are in a strange town and are told to "walk past the Town Hall, through the park to the station, and you will see the memorial on your right". It is necessary to be able to recognize certain environmental features as instances of town halls, stations, memorials and parks. Each of these are conceptual abstractions which presumably relate to prototypical representations or "frames" (cf. Minsky, 1975). Successfully travelling such a route would involve checking information about the actual places we pass with this sequence of prototypes: the crucial feature of landmarks is not that they are known, but that they are recognizable.

In order to keep track of one's progress during a journey, it is necessary to relate external environmental features to locations in the network or route-description. Such navigational checking may be non-continuous (route-segment related) or continuous (cf. Griffin, 1948). Each segment of a journey can be defined in terms of environmental cues which, once picked up, signal the end of one segment and the start of the next.

There are a number of reasons why people may get lost using such a system. First, their prototype descriptions, or schema, for types of landmarks may be inadequate for recognizing certain actual instances of those landmarks. As a result they will lose track of their location in the network. Secondly, generation of the route-description may have involved inferences about relative distances and directions that were inaccurate. Third, major changes in the environment (e.g. new roads and buildings) may conflict with a previously adequate representation.

In this chapter we have argued that spatial knowledge is represented within a single complex database: a semantic network providing the necessary cohesion and organization for our knowledge of the world. Furthermore, we have stressed the point that the criterion for selecting information for inclusion in the database is primarily one of functional utility. Just as the maps produced for use by fell-walkers differ in both their form and content from maps of the same areas produced for fast-jet pilots, so our internal spatial representations reflect our navigational requirements. As Foulke (1971) has said:

The selection of information for inclusion in the schema is governed by the individual's needs, and these needs are determined by the nature of his interactions with his environment. The functional significance of this schema is that it greatly reduces the amount of information about a terrain that must be obtained to interact with it successfully. Once the schema has been organized, the individual can base his behavior on it, and he need only sample his environment for the feedback information required to keep the schema in proper registration with the terrain it represents. (pp. 2–3)

REFERENCES

Anderson, J. R. (1976). "Language, Memory and Thought", Lawrence Erlbaum Associates, New Jersy.

Anderson, J. R. and Bower, G. H. (1973). "Human Associative Memory", Winston, Washington D.C.

Bartram D. (1980). Comprehending spatial information: the relative efficiency of different methods of presenting information about bus routes. *Journal of Applied Psychology*, **65**, 103–110.

Beck, R. J. and Wood, D. (1976). Cognitive transformation of information from urban geographic fields to mental maps. *Environment and Behavior*, **8**, 199–238.

Briggs, R. (1973). Urban cognitive distance. *In* "Image and Environment" (R. M. Downs and D. Stea, eds), Arnold, London.

Byrne, R. (1979). Memory for urban geography. *Quarterly Journal of Experimental Psychology*, **31**, 147–154.

Cadwallader, M. T. (1973). A methodological analysis of cognitive distance. *In* Environmental Design Research. (W. F. E. Prieser, ed.), Dowden, Hutchison and Ross, Stroudsbury.

Canter, D. V. (1977). "The psychology of place", The Architectural Press, London.

Canter, D. V. and Tagg, S. (1975). Distance estimation in cities. *Environment and Behavior*, **7**, 59–80.

Chase, W. G. and Chi, M. T. H. (1981). Cognitive skill: implications for spatial skill in large-scale environments. *In* "Cognition, Social Behavior and the Environment" (J. H. Harvey, ed.), Lawrence Erlbaum Associates, New Jersey.

Clayton, K. and Woodyard, M. (1981). The acquisition and utilisation of spatial knowledge. *In* "Cognition, Social Behavior and the Environment" (J. H. Harvey, ed.), Lawrence Erlbaum Associates, New Jersey.

Dainoff, M., Miskie, D., Wilson, C. and Crane, P. (1974). Psychophysical measurements of environmental distance. *In* "Man-Environment Interactions: Evaluations and Associations EDRA 5 Proceedings" (D. H. Carlson, ed.), Milwaukee.

Deese, J. (1960). Frequency of usage and number of words in free recall: the role of association. *Psychological Reports*, **7**, 337–344.

Downs R. M. and Siegel A. W. (1981). On mapping researchers mapping children mapping space. *In* "Spatial Representation and Behavior across the Life Span" (L. S. Liben, A. H. Patterson and N. Newcombe, eds), Academic Press, New York.

Ewing, G. O. (1981). On the sensitivity of conclusions about the bases of cognitive distance. *Professional Geographer*, **33**, 311–314.

Foulke, E. (1971). The perceptual basis for mobility. *American Foundation for the Blind Research Bulletin*, **23**, 1–8.

Golledge, R., Briggs, R. and Demko, D. (1969). The configuration of distances in intra-urban space. *Proceedings of the Association of American Geographers*, **1**, 60–65.

Golledge, R. and Zannaras, G. (1973). Cognitive approaches to the analysis of human spatial behavior. *In* "Environment and Cognition", (W. H. Ittelson, ed.), Seminar Press, New York.

Goodey, B. (1968). Environmental, extra-environmental and preferential perception in geography. *Proceedings of the North Dakota Academy of Science*, **22**, 73–78.

Griffin, D. R. (1948). Topographical orientation. *In* "Foundations of Psychology" (G. G. Boring, H. S. Longfield and H. P. Weld, eds), Wiley, New York.

Hall, J. (1954). Learning as a function of word frequency. *American Journal of Psychology*, **67**, 138–140.

Kozlowski, L. T. and Bryant, K. J. (1977). Sense of direction, spatial orientation and cognitive maps. *Journal of Experimental Psychology: Human Perception and Performance*, **3**, 590–598.

Kuipers, B. (1978). Modelling spatial knowledge. *Cognitive Science*, **2**, 129–153.

Lee, T. R. (1962). "Brennan's Law" of shopping behavior. *Psychological Reports*, **11**, 662.

Lee, T. R. (1970). Perceived distance as a function of direction in the city. *Environment and Behavior*, **2**, 40–51.

Lynch, K. (1960). "The Image of the City", Cambridge, MIT Press, Massachusetts.

MacEachren, A. M. Travel time as the basis of cognitive distance. *The Professional Geographer*, **32**, 30–36.

Milgram, S. (1973). Chapter II, Introduction. *In* "Environment and Cognition" (W. H. Ittelson, ed.), Seminar Press, New York.

Milgram, S. and Jodelet, D. (1976). Psychological maps of Paris. *In* "Environmental Psychology: People and their Physical Settings" (H. M. Proshansky, W. H. Ittelson, and L. G. Rivlin, eds), Holt Rinehart and Winston, New York.

Minsky, M. (1975). Frame-system theory. *In* "Theoretical Issues in Natural Language Processing" (R. C. Schank and B. L. Nash-Webber, eds), Preprints of a conference at MIT.

Moar, I. T. (1978). "Mental Triangulation and the Nature of Internal Representation of Space", Unpublished Ph.D. thesis, APU, Cambridge.

Newell, A. (1973). Productions systems: models of control structures. *In* "Visual Information Processing" (W. G. Chase, ed.), Academic Press, New York.

Russell, B. (1948). "Human Knowledge: Its Scope and Limits", Allen and Unwin, London.

Sadalla, E. K. and Magel, S. G. (1980). The perception of traversed distance. *Environment and Behavior*, **12**, 65–79.

Sadalla, E. K. and Staplin, L. J. (1980a). An information storage model for distance cognition. *Environment and Behavior*, **12**, 183–193.

Sadalla, E. K. and Staplin, L. J. (1980b). The perception of traversed distance: Intersections. *Environment and Behavior*, **12**, 167–182.

Schank, R. C. and Abelson, R. P. (1975). Scripts, plans and knowledge. *Proceedings of the Fourth International Joint Conference on Artificial Intelligence*. Tbilisi.

Siegel, A. W. and White, S. H. (1975). The development of spatial representations of large-scale environments. *Advances in Child Development and Behavior*, **10**, 9–55.

Smith, P. (1978). "The environmental schemata of the blind: an exploratory study",

University of Hull, Department of Psychology, unpublished report.

Sommer, R. (1969). "Personal Space: the Behavioral Basis of Design", Prentice-Hall, New Jersey.

Stea, D. (1967). Reasons for our moving. *Landscape*, **17**, 27–28.

Stevens, A. and Coupe, P. (1978). Distortions in judged spatial relations. *Cognitive Psychology*, **10**, 422–437.

Stevens, S. S. (1957). On the psychophysical law. *Psychological Reports*, **64**, 153–181.

Thorndyke, P. W. (1981). Spatial cognition and reasoning. *In* "Cognition, Social Behavior and the Environment" (J. H. Harvey, ed.), Lawrence Erlbaum Associates, New Jersey.

Thorndyke, P. W. and Hayes-Roth, B. (1978). "Spatial knowledge acquisition from maps and navigation", Paper presented at Psychonomics Society Meetings, San Antonio, Texas.

Thorndyke, P. W. and Stasz, C. (1980). Individual differences in procedures for knowledge acquisition from maps. *Cognitive Psychology*, **12**, 137–175.

Tolman, E. C. (1948). Cognitive maps in rats and men. *Psychological Review*, **55**, 189–208.

Tolman, E. C. (1959). Principles of purposive behavior. *In* "Psychology: A Study of a Science. Vol II. General Systematic Formulations, Learning, and Special Processes" (S. Koch, ed.), McGraw-Hill, New York.

Tulving, E. (1972). Episodic and semantic memory. *In* "Organization of Memory" (E. Tulving and W. Donaldson, eds), Academic Press, New York and London.

4

Using Cognitive Diaries to Investigate Naturally Occurring Memory Blocks

J. Reason and D. Lucas

I. INTRODUCTION

A recent development in cognitive psychology has been the increasing use of naturalistic data, derived from everyday life, to supplement and extend laboratory findings. In particular, there has been a marked growth in the number of studies employing diaries and other self-report methods to gather instances of minor cognitive failures as they occur in real-life settings (see Chapter 8 in this volume, Herrmann, 1984).

Slips of the tongue and pen have been profitably investigated in this way for nearly a century (Meringer and Mayer, 1895; Bawden, 1900; Fromkin, 1973, 1980). A more novel departure, however, has been the application of these techniques to the collection and analysis of mistakes in other cognitive domains, especially slips of action and lapses of memory (Herrmann and Neisser, 1978; Bennett-Levy and Powell, 1980; Norman, 1981; Broadbent *et al.*, 1982; Reason and Mycielska, 1982).

The rationale for studying these normally inconsequential errors is that they yield important insights into the operation of the largely covert control processes that govern our internal and external activities. In addition, systematic and relatively predictable error forms can reveal something of the underlying biases to which these cognitive mechanisms are prone.

One of the most pervasive of these biases has been labelled variously as "strong associate substitution" (Chapman and Chapman, 1973), "inert stereotypes" (Luria, 1973), or "banalization" (Timpanaro, 1976). Stated simply, it is that many cognitive failures tend to take the form of unintended words or actions that are, nevertheless, more commonplace, usual or expected under the prevailing circumstances than those demanded by the current plan. These "slips of habit" almost invariably appear as highly organized and intact sequences that are clearly recognizable as belonging to the present context or to some well-established routine, but which do not form part of our current intentions.

The impression gained from a close examination of these errors is that the more frequently and recently a particular routine is set in train and achieves its desired outcome, the more likely it is to recur uninvited as a slip of habit (Reason, 1977, 1979, 1982). William James (1890) likened habits to "great flywheels". Once set in motion, they require very little in the way of additional energy to keep them going. But the price we pay for this economy of conscious effort is the reluctance of these established routines to change when altered circumstances or revised plans make it necessary.

Strong habit intrusions are most likely to occur in the speech or actions of normal individuals when the greater part of their limited attentional capacity is claimed elsewhere, either by internal preoccupation or by an external distractor. They can also occur during moments of "free-wheeling" when present actions are not guided by any immediate intention, as in waiting for something to happen (Reason and Mycielska, 1982). Exaggerated forms of the same error type have been observed in schizophrenics, in whom attentional deficits are assumed to exist (McGhie and Chapman, 1961; Venables, 1963, 1964; Chapman and Chapman, 1973), and in frontal lobe patients whose ability to conceive and execute plans is impaired through brain damage (Luria, 1973).

The aim of the present study was to investigate the incidence and characteristics of strong habit intrusions as they occur in the deliberate and often laboured memory searches associated with the "tip-of-the-tongue" (TOT) experience. For the most part, familiar words or names spring to mind immediately without any sense of conscious effort. But, on occasions, these automatic retrieval mechanisms fail and we are forced to deploy, at least momentarily, the bulk of our intentional and attentional resources to recover the sought-for memory item (the *target*).

In attempting to resolve a TOT state, we usually begin by assembling the partial fragments of information we feel we know (see Hart, 1965) about the structural and semantic features of the target (the *initial attributes*). Beyond this, however, we are confronted by the "intensively active gap" in consciousness, described by James (1890). We are certain that somewhere within the "gap" lies the word we seek, but we are powerless to penetrate it directly. What seems to happen is that particular sections of the "word store", addressed in some way by the initial attributes, are stirred up remotely by our intention, causing partial or complete items to be propelled into consciousness. By some means of which we are largely unaware, these *intermediates* are matched against the "gap" unique to the target. If there is a fit, we feel an ill-defined sense of rightness and end the search. If there is not, we reject the intermediate solution and search for another. This process may be repeated many times over several hours or even days of intermittent searching, or it may be terminated almost immediately with the rapid discovery of the target word.

For our present purposes, it is useful to regard rejected intermediates as intrusion errors in the process of memory retrieval. As in other error forms, these intrusions constitute clear deviations from intention—in this case, that of recovering a specific memory item. We might reasonably expect, therefore, that they would show "strong associate substitutions" in a way comparable to that manifested by everyday slips of word or action (Reason, 1979; Reason and Mycielska, 1982). Freud (1901), for instance, noted that when we are searching for a forgotten name, we substitute names that ". . . although immediately recognised as false, nevertheless *obtrude themselves with great tenacity*." [our italics].

The first of our two diary studies was therefore designed to establish the existence of TOT states in which target recovery is impeded by the repeated calling to mind of the same incorrect intermediate(s), or what we have called "recurrent blockers". It also examined the effects that the presence of such a "blocker" had upon the mode of successful resolution and the number of deliberate searches made.

Our work with slips of action (see Chapter 7 of this volume) indicates that the "strong associate" bias is most evident when the conscious guidance of planned activity is diminished or temporarily absent. It has been noted, for example, that slips of habit usually occur during the mainly automatic execution of familiar routines when attention is "captured" by matters unrelated to the task in hand. Although, in contrast, TOT states are generally characterised by a high degree of conscious involvement, the memory searches that ensue are restricted by the inability of consciousness to reach directly into the word store. While the search may begin with an acute awareness of our failure to find a given item, it is subsequently carried out in a region beyond the reach of conscious guidance. Such conditions, it is believed, are likely to bring the "strong associate" bias into particular prominence.

II. METHODOLOGICAL ISSUES

A. Limitations of cognitive diaries

In addition to the problems inherent in any diary mode of data collection (see Oppenheim, 1966), our experience suggests that there are at least three kinds of bias involved in using diaries to elicit first-hand accounts of naturally occurring cognitive failures:

(i) *Volunteer bias* Individuals who undertake to keep a diary often do so on the assumption that they are unduly prone to the type of cognitive failure being investigated.

(ii) *Selection bias* Only the more noteworthy, amusing or memorable slips are likely to find their way into the diary.

(iii) *Recording bias* Less information will be recorded in the diary than was available at the time of the lapse. Moreover, what goes into the diary report is likely to be strongly influenced by the diarist's personal theory as to why the lapse occurred.

These difficulties clearly set limits upon the kinds of inference we can draw from diary studies. Not only would it be unwise to use diary material to obtain estimates of failure incidence in the general population, the selection and recording biases mean that we cannot even take these data as representative samples of the diarist's own memory lapse behaviour over the recording period.

So what are cognitive diaries good for? We believe they serve a valuable function as wide-gauge trawl nets, picking up the more salient types of lapse. If the trawls are extensive enough, we can reasonably expect to catch a qualitatively representative sample of these cognitive failures, even if the quantities of any particular error form cannot be taken as accurately reflecting their presence in the total error population.

In addition, we believe it is possible to circumvent some of these selection and recording problems by using an "extended" form of the cognitive diary (Reason, 1982) in which the subjects are required not only to provide the basic details of each lapse (i.e. what was intended, and what actually happened), but also to answer a series of standardized questions in regard to each recorded incident. In this way, diarists are cued to consider aspects of the lapse that might otherwise have been omitted. Furthermore, asking the same questions in relation to each lapse permits at least ordinal comparisons to be made across particular features of the recorded lapses.

Finally, it should be noted that this investigation was carried out in the naturalistic tradition of Woodworth (1929, 1934, 1938) and Wenzl (1932, 1936) as distinct from the more recent experimental studies of the TOT state (Brown and McNeill, 1966; Yarmey, 1973; Koriat and Lieblich, 1974; Rubin, 1975; Gruneberg and Sykes, 1978). Most of these experimental studies have used the technique of artificially inducing TOTs, pioneered by Brown and McNeill. Since the aim of our study was to investigate the real-life circumstances of TOT states and their resolution, the extended diary form was considered more suitable.

B. Using cognitive diaries to investigate TOT states

The first of the two diary forms to be discussed in this chapter was made up of three sections: (a) A front page requesting basic information from the diarist (name, sex, age, etc.); (b) a set of instructions on how to complete the standardized questions asked about each resolved TOT, together with two specimen protocols; (c) five sets of standardized questions, each set to be completed by the diarist in regard to a single resolved TOT experience. The diary thus made provision for recording the details of five resolved TOT states.

The standardized questions covered the following aspects of each resolved TOT state:

(a) The target word or name (i.e. the sought-for memory item);
(b) the number of "searching periods" (i.e. those periods in which the diarist's attention was directed towards retrieving the target), the date and the approximate time at which they occurred, the length of the searching period, and whether or not it resulted in the recovery of the target;
(c) the specific features of the target that were felt to be known prior to the resolution of the TOT state (i.e. first letter, number of syllables, position of the main stress, etc.);
(d) the intermediate solutions dredged up during the course of the search (i.e. words or names that came to mind but which were recognized as being incorrect);
(e) the strategies used in recovering the target (i.e. alphabetical search, generation of similar words or names, recall of contextual information, asking others, consulting a reference book, being prompted by external cues, etc.), and whether or not the target "popped up" when no conscious effort was being made to retrieve it;
(f) the familiarity of the target words.

In the first study, 32 volunteers kept a record of their *resolved* TOT states over a 4-week period. Fourteen men and eighteen women acted as diarists, their average ages being 33 and 36 years respectively. The diarists included university staff, postgraduate students and housewives. They were asked to carry the diaries around with them during the course of their everyday activities. They were required to take note of their TOT states as soon as they occurred, and to answer the standardized questions immediately after they had recovered the sought-for item. It was stressed that they should have resolved the TOT state to their own satisfaction before attempting to answer these questions. They were asked to return the diaries after 4 weeks regardless of whether they had experienced the full five states required to fill the diary.

III. RESULTS OF THE FIRST DIARY STUDY COMPARING "BLOCKED" AND "NON-BLOCKED" TOTs

A. Number of states recorded

This study netted a total of 75 resolved TOTs, an average of 2.5 per diarist over the 4-week period. This is likely to be less than the true incidence. In a questionnaire study (Reason, 1982), just over half the sample (85 undergraduates) claimed to experience TOT states at least weekly, and 14% suffered them at least daily. There was no significant difference between the sexes in the mean number of TOTs recorded (males, 2.1; females, 2.6).

B. Presence of "blocking" intermediates

Twenty-two of the 31 diarists (68.8%) reported having at least one TOT state in which a word or a name, other than the target, kept recurring. This intermediate item was known to be wrong, but proved very difficult to put out of mind. These intrusive and tenacious words were called "blocking" intermediates. Such a blocking intermediate was reported in 40 of the 75 recorded TOT states (53.3%). This high proportion of blocked states may have reflected the operation of the "selection bias" in which TOTs that are more memorable (by virtue of the recurrent blocker) are more likely to be recorded but we have no evidence to suggest this was the case.

Table I. Comparing methods of resolution in "blocked" and "non-blocked" TOT states (first diary study).

Method of resolution	Number of "blocked" TOT states	Number of "non-blocked" TOT states	Totals
Internal strategies	10	19	29
"Pop-ups"	13	11	24
External strategies	17	5	22
Totals	40	35	75

C. Difference between "blocked" and "non-blocked" states

The 40 blocked TOT states were found to differ from the remaining 35 in the following respects

(1) *Method of Resolution*
It can be seen from Table I that most non-blocked TOTs were resolved through the use of internal strategies such as alphabetical search, recall of contextual information, generation of similar items, and the like. The majority of blocked TOTs, however, were resolved through external factors such as accidentally hearing or seeing the target, asking others, or finding it in a reference book. In both TOT forms, approximately the same proportion of states were resolved through spontaneous "pop-ups" that occurred at some variable time after the last search period had been abandoned.

(2) *Effective internal strategy*
From Table II it can be seen that the only internal strategy used with any success in the resolution of blocked TOTs was, surprisingly, the generation of similar words or names. By contrast, a variety of consciously employed strategies proved effective in the case of the non-blocked TOTs.

(3) *The number of reported searches*
There was a significant difference between the blocked and the non-blocked

Table II. Comparing internal strategies used successfully in "blocked" and "non-blocked" TOT states (first diary study).

Internal strategy employed	Number of "blocked" TOT states	Number of "non-blocked" TOT states	Totals
Alphabetical search	0	2	2
Generating similar items	9	4	13
Contextual search	1	5	6
Generating images	0	2	2
Other	0	6	6
Totals	10	19	29

states in the number of searches the diarists reported making before recovering the sought-for item ($p<.01$). Sixty-eight per cent of the non-blocked TOTs were resolved after only one search, whereas 57.5% of the blocked TOTs required more than one conscious search before the item came to mind.

(4) *Features of the target known prior to resolution*
Diarists having blocked TOT states knew significantly more features of the eventual target than did those having non-blocked states ($p<.01$).

D. Familiarity of the target words

The sought-for words and names in these 75 TOT states were not necessarily rare or infrequently used items. In this study, 26 targets (34.7%) were rated by the diarists as being moderately familiar, and 29 targets (38.7%) as being very familiar. In only 20 cases (26.7%) were the targets rated as being only slightly familiar. There were no differences in the familiarity ratings assigned to targets between blocked and non-blocked states.

These findings established that a substantial proportion of naturally-occurring TOT states are characterized by the presence of recurrent blocking intermediates: wrong words or names that are called to mind whenever a deliberate attempt is made to retrieve the target. The next step was to investigate whether these recurrent blockers could be classed as strong habit intrusions; that is, words or names that are judged by the subjects to be more recently and frequently encountered than either the particular target or the non-blocking intermediates that arose during that TOT state.

To this end, a second study was carried out in which the extended diary form was essentially similar to that used in the first study, except for the addition of a section for obtaining relative recency and frequency ratings between blocked intermediates and (a) targets, and (b) non-blocking intermediates. Diarists were also asked to rate the degree of association between each intermediate (both blocking and non-blocking) and the target item.

Six men and ten women volunteered to keep this second extended diary over a 4-week period. Their mean ages were 39.3 and 41.2 years, respectively. Twelve of the subjects had taken part in the first diary study.

IV. RESULTS OF THE SECOND DIARY STUDY COMPARING "BLOCKING" AND "NON-BLOCKING" INTERMEDIATES

A. Number of states recorded

This study yielded 40 resolved TOT states, an average of 2.4 per diarist over the 4-week period. Fifteen of the 16 diarists (93.8%) reported having at least one blocked TOT state, and 28 of the 40 TOTs (70%) involved blocking intermediates. However, complete data were only available for 22 of these 28 blocked states.

B. Comparing recency, frequency and association ratings

The rankings for recency, frequency and degree of association were examined in two ways:

(a) Blocking intermediates were judged by the diarists as being more frequently and more recently used than *both* the related targets *and* the non-blocking intermediates (see Table III). The diarists also rated blocking intermediates as being more closely associated with the target than were the

Table III. Mean rankings for recency, frequency and degree of association in the 22 "blocked" TOT states for which complete data were available.

	Targets	"Blocking" intermediates	"Non-blocking" intermediates
Recency	2.77	1.91	2.76
Frequency	2.73	2.23	2.46
Degree of association with target	—	1.35	2.62

other intermediates generated during that particular TOT state. In addition, non-blocking intermediates were rated as being more frequently used than the target items.

(b) In 11 of the 22 blocked TOT states (50%), the blocking intermediate was ranked higher than the target for both frequency and recency. In 5 blocked TOTs (22.7%), the blocking intermediate was ranked as being more recently used than the target; and in 1 case (4.5%) as being more frequently used. Thus, in 17 out of the 22 states (77.3%), the blocking intermediate was ranked higher than the target on either frequency, recency or both.

In general, therefore, these data support the notion that blocking intermediates constitute strong habit intrusions in the process of deliberate memory retrieval. In other words, blocking intermediates are likely to be a more familiar item than the sought-for one. These findings conform to the general principal of error production observed in other cognitive domains (Reason and Mycielska, 1982); namely, that when our activities deviate from plan, there is a strong likelihood that they will do so in the direction of producing a response that is more probable, more expected, more in keeping with our knowledge structures and the prevailing circumstances than the one actually intended at that time. The possible factors contributing to these intrusions are discussed in detail below.

V. THEORETICAL CONSIDERATIONS

A. The "ugly sister" phenomenon

Our data indicate that a relatively high proportion of naturally occurring TOT states are characterized by the repeated calling to mind of a word or name that, though closely resembling the sought-for item in its structural, contextual and semantic features, is not the target. The recurrence of this item appears to act as a major impediment to the recovery of the target. We have also presented evidence to show that this blocking intermediate is usually judged as more recently and frequently encountered than the target, and as such can reasonably be regarded as a strong habit intrusion in the memory search process. As noted earlier, strong habit intrusions constitute the commonest error form among slips of action (Reason and Mycielska, 1982), and are also prevalent in other cognitive domains as well.

In view of the close similarity between blocking intermediates and other forms of strong habit intrusion, it is appropriate to look to the global model of cognitive control, presented in Chapter 7 of this volume (Reason, 1984) and constructed to account for absent-minded errors, to assess the extent to which the principles embodied there are helpful in explaining the occurrence of blocked TOT states. Two issues need to be considered. First, what factors cause the blocking intermediate (rather than the target or some other intermediate) to be propelled into consciousness in the first place? And, second, why does this blocking intermediate recur during subsequent deliberate attempts to resolve the TOT state? It is to provide a framework for answering these questions that we have invoked the ugly sisters.

When Cinderella fled from the ball on the stroke of midnight the only tangible clue to her identity left to the smitten prince was one diminutive glass slipper. Declaring his intention to make the possessor of the foot that fitted the slipper his princess, the impetuous prince dispatched heralds with instructions to invite all the eligible spinsters in the realm to try on the slipper for size. Getting wind of this, Cinderella's ugly and pushy sisters (in the more gruesome versions of the story) performed some impromptu surgery on their toes in order that their ample feet might stand some chance of fitting into the slipper. The ruse, of course, failed; but to the extent that their attempts at deception delayed the happy reunion, it could be said that they acted as blockers in the search process. And they were not just passive impediments who simply happened to get in the way; they actively sought to usurp Cinderella's rightful place. Furthermore, although they differed from her in looks and temperament, the ugly sisters, by virtue of their family connection and the shared address, had numerous features in common with the object of the search.

When our largely automatic mechanisms for retrieving known words or names fail, the Intention System (the prince) is forced to initiate a deliberate search on the basis of whatever information it can assemble (the slipper) regarding the target (Cinderella). The Intention System, however, does not have direct access to the word and name schemata (the eligible spinsters) held in the long term store (the realm). It is therefore forced to act through intermediaries (the heralds).

In Chapter 7 (Reason, 1984) we propose that schemata are called into action whenever their activation exceeds a given threshold level. In the case of words or names, being called into action could mean their appearance in speech, writing or in consciousness. It was also suggested that schemata activation is derived from both the Intention System and from various non-intentional factors (context, need, association and recency/frequency) which exert their influence across all cognitive domains. At any point in time, therefore, schemata will be at widely differing levels of activation (i.e. readiness to act). The more active schemata require only the smallest pretext to trigger them into operation.

In the case of the blocked TOT, our data indicate that the partial information about the sought-for item possessed at the outset of the search (the initial attributes) is delivered to approximately the right "address" in the word and name store (where this "address" is defined both semantically and phonologically). It is presumed that certain schemata in this neighbourhood are already close to their triggering thresholds (the ugly sisters), and that some feature of these initial attributes is sufficient to fire off one of these schemata, even though it is not the intended item. An image of this incorrect word or name will then appear in consciousness as an output from this schema. Once there, it is recognized as being similar to, but not actually the target (we shall consider how this recognition process might operate at a later point). This sense of being very "close" to the target indicates that the searcher is on the right track, so that the same initial attributes are likely to be used again in the next retrieval attempt. In the subsequent search there is likely to be an even greater chance of coming up with the same wrong intermediate, since the activation of this particular schema will have been further elevated by its recent emergence into consciousness. As the search cycle is repeated, the activation of the blocking intermediate (and hence its chances of being called to mind) will continue to increase due to the operation of the recency/frequency factor.

This state of affairs is likely to persist for as long as the same or very similar initial attributes are employed in a given search period. Only by abandoning the deliberate search process (thus allowing the activation level of the blocker to decline spontaneously), or by changing the initial attributes are we likely to circumvent this now established blocker. However, we are often disinclined to take the latter course because of the strong sense of "being warm" conveyed by the blocking intermediate.

We are proposing, then, that the blocker emerges initially for two reasons. The first is that it has a high level of activation at the time of the first search: high, that is, relative to the target or other schemata in the locality. The second is that its close phonological and/or semantic resemblance to the target make it compatible with some of the initial attributes which, in turn, contribute the additional activation necessary to call it to mind. Subsequently, the blocker is likely to recur due to the continued use of the same initial attributes, and, most importantly, to the incremental effects of the recency/frequency activating factor. This cycle gains added momentum from the continued sense of being "close" to the target that is engendered by the recurrent blocker.

Although this "ugly sister" explanation of the blocking phenomenon has been couched in terms of the cognitive control model elaborated in Chapter 7, the basic ideas have much in common with those advanced some 50 years ago by Wenzl (1932, 1936) and Woodworth (1929, 1938). Wenzl held that intermediate solutions to a TOT problem can be both helpful and misleading. They are useful in that they help to fix that part of the target word that is on the threshold of consciousness. Their negative effect is due to the fact that ". . . the greater availability of false content blocks the way to the correct content." Woodworth (1929), like Wenzl, regarded these intermediates as being a form of inhibition. He distinguished three types of interference: emotional (as, for example, in stage fright), that due to distraction, and that arising from conflicting responses. In a later account (Woodworth, 1938), he is more specific as to the way in which a competing response blocks retrieval:

The nimbleness of just formed associations is sometimes an inconvenience. When we have run off the track in trying to remember a name, the wrong name recalled acquires a recency value and blocks the correct name . . . a rest interval allows the recency value of the error to die away. (p. 38)

It should also be noted that both Wicklegren (1976) and Niemi (1979) have recently proposed blocking as a retrieval interference phenomenon in experiments using the paired-associate learning paradigm.

B. "Non-blocked" TOT states

While the blocked TOT states share the common characteristic of a recurrent intermediate, we have no grounds for assuming that non-blocked TOTs constitute anything but a heterogeneous remainder. Of the 115 TOT states recorded in *both* diary studies, 68 (59%) were blocked and 47 (41%) were non-blocked states. No intermediates were produced in 77% of these non-blocked TOTs. In these cases, presumably, the interval prior to the appearance of the target was occupied with incomplete fragments of words or names, rather than with clearly identifiable intermediates. Here, the TOT states appear to have been little more than a noticeable "hiccup" in the normal automatic retrieval process. And the fact that the target is the first intact word or name to be called to mind suggests that the initial attributes were correctly "addressed" to the appropriate location in the word and name store.

We are therefore left to explain the non-appearance of blockers in the 27% of these states in which intermediates were recorded. One possibility (borne out by personal experience) is that the initial attributes were predicated on a wrong hypothesis about the target. For example, in failing to retrieve the name "Joel", we might start by emphasising the latter rather than the former syllable, and hunt for a name beginning with "L" rather than for one beginning with "J".

Thus, we are suggesting that whereas blocked TOTs begin with a set of attributes that are "close" to but not precisely "on" the target, non-blocked states may be characterized by at least two different starting conditions. Either the initial attributes are even "closer" to the target than in the case of blocking TOTs. Or they may be aimed, in the first instance at least, at the wrong target altogether. In the latter case, the intermediates called to mind will not convey a sense of "being warm", so that subsequent searches are likely to be carried out with different initial attributes. Since this hypothesis-changing mode of search is unlikely to be repeatedly probing the same area of the word and name store, as we suppose is happening in the case of blocked TOTs, there is less chance of arousing and sustaining a recurrent inter-mediate.

C. The recognition paradox

Perhaps the most puzzling feature of TOT states is the means by which we recognize that an item dredged up in the course of the search is or is not the one we seek, and usually with a fair degree of confidence in either case. How can we accept or reject these items without more knowledge of the target than we apparently possess? St. Augustine confronted this "recognition paradox" in his *Confessions* around the end of the fourth century.

> When, therefore, the memory loses something—and this is what happens whenever we forget something and try to remember it—where are we to look for it except in the memory itself? And if the memory offers us something else instead, as may happen, we reject what it offers until the one thing we want is presented. When it is presented to us we say 'This is it,' but we could not say this unless we recognised it, and we could not recognise it unless we remembered it. (Pine-Coffin, 1961, p. 225).

William James in a much-quoted passage on the TOT phenomenon wrote of the gap in consciousness that is created by the failure to recall a well known name.

> It is a gap that is intensely active. A sort of wraith of the name is in it, beckoning us in a given direction, making us at moments tingle with the sense of our closeness, and then letting us sink back without the longed for term. If wrong names are proposed to us, this singularly definite gap acts immediately so as to negate them. They do not fit its mould. And the gap of one word does not feel like the gap of another, all empty of content as both might seem necessarily to be when described as gaps. (James, 1890, p. 251)

Implicit in James's timeless description of the TOT state is a separation of the recall and recognition functions. Names are summoned to mind and then matched against the "singularly definite gap". Details of neither the searching nor the matching processes are directly available to consciousness. All that we are aware of within this arena are their end-products: the image of a name and a sense of whether it is right or wrong. And, in the case of the latter, we also have a rough idea of how far off the mark it is.

Although our data do not inform us directly on the matter, the simplest (though perhaps not the most parsimonious) way to account for these processes within our cognitive control model is to postulate two distinct sets of parallel schemata (or two distinct aspects of the same schemata). One set is concerned with controlling the output of words and names in speech, writing and/or consciousness in response to instructions from the Intention System (see Chapter 7 of the present volume). Another corresponding set reacts to input data from vision, hearing, or, in the case of the contents of consciousness, to the "mind's eye" or the "mind's ear". The former set we call "output schemata", the latter "recognition schemata". Both are under the influence of the same general activating factors (context, need, association and recency/frequency). Such an arrangement would also be compatible with the usual advantages of recognition over recall, with other schema-based theories (see Schmidt, 1975) and with anomalous experiences such as *déjà-vu* (Hunter, 1957).

From these assumptions, we would argue that whenever a word or name is called to mind during a search period, it is tried out via the "mental ear" upon the appropriate recognition schema. The outcome of this matching forms the basis of our subsequent decision to accept or reject the word, and, when we decide upon the latter course, it gives us a sense of how "close" the intermediate was to the target. But this does not explain how the recognition schema for the target is selected as being the right "template" in the first place.

One possibility is that context, the underlying intentional activity and the initial attributes are sufficient to activate the appropriate recognition schema, but not its corresponding output schema. And without the parallel activity of the latter, the former is effectively "dumb". Such a notion would explain the "singularly definite" nature of the "gap" described by William James, and would also account for the agonizing sensation of having the missing item "on the tip of one's tongue", but not actually there.

Some aspects of our data also indicate that the TOT search is often conducted on the basis of attributes of which we are not consciously aware, but which become evident when the intermediates leading up to the successful retrieval of the target are examined. For example, one of us (JR) was unable to recall the film title, "Deliverance", even though a good deal was known about the cast and the plot. Two intermediates kept recurring during the course of the search: intemperance and intolerance. Both of them sounded very close when tried out on the "mental ear", and it was known that the second of the two (intolerance) was semantically close to the target, being a single word film title. But one thing that was not appreciated until the TOT was successfully resolved was that the target, like the intermediates, had an "-erance" ending. Yet this knowledge must have been available at some level of the search apparatus.

In short, the fact that we frequently are not conscious of all that we know about the target lends further credence to the idea that the appropriate recognition schema is at least partially activated at the outset. The strong sense of "proximity" evoked by the nearly-but-not-quite-matching intermediates encourages us to continue searching the same neighbourhood of the output schema store, even though we are not conscious of the precise grounds for our feelings of "warmth".

Another observation compatible with the idea of initial recognition schema activation is that we sometimes go wrong on the matching process. It happens, albeit fairly rarely, that we accept an incorrect intermediate as the target (false positive), and also reject the target as not being the item we are seeking (false negative). In both cases, these errors could arise either as the result of insufficient prior activation of the right recognition schema, or because the wrong schema has become energized, perhaps by the initial attributes or by non-intentional priming.

Underlying these arguments is the necessary assumption that input (recognition) schemata are intimately connected with their corresponding output (recall) schemata. And this clearly presents a problem for our theory. If the input schema is energized at the outset of the search, why is this not sufficient to trigger off the corresponding output schema automatically, as appears to be the case when we are externally cued by reading? Perhaps it is a matter of degree. It is possible that we only experience the TOT state on those occasions when the appropriate recognition schema is fired up enough to convey a strong "feeling of knowing" (see Hart, 1965), but not sufficiently to achieve the automatic calling to mind of the target item.

D. How do "pop-ups" occur?

Considering the pooled data, it was found that only 48% of all the TOT states netted in our two diary studies were successfully resolved through deliberate "internal" searches. Of the remainder, 27.8% were terminated by a variety of external means: either deliberately looking or asking for the target, or being accidentally cued by something in the environment; and 30.4% were resolved by "pop-ups". If nothing else, these findings clearly demonstrate that a deliberate intention to search for the missing item is not essential for its recovery. Such a conscious effort may be crucial at the outset to initiate the search process, but thereafter it seems neither necessary, nor even desirable. So how does this non-conscious retrieval process operate?

The short answer appears to be that the recognition schema, primed at an early stage of the TOT state, remains highly activated until it "finds" its appropriate input data. As we have seen, this period of sustained activation can last at least for as long as a month. Thus, we are proposing that the recognition schema behaves like an unresolved TOTE unit (Miller *et al.*, 1960). Until the right input data are available to match the image held by the "test" phase, the "operate" phase continues to cycle. In this case, "operating" would mean remaining vigilant for some auditory or visual representation of the missing item. Sometimes, as our data show, these representations are found accidentally in the outside world: on billboards, the printed page, or overheard on radio, TV, or in conversation. At other times, as in the case of pop-ups, the missing data are supplied from within: either in the stream of consciousness or in some preconscious verbal activity. In short, the unrequited schema, like Heathcliff, continues to scan both the inner and outer worlds until the target is found. When this happens, its level of activation is raised sufficiently to trigger the output from its corresponding schema, and the search ends.

VI. PRACTICAL IMPLICATIONS

What have we learned that could be of use to those frequently afflicted by the TOT state? The lessons would seem to be fairly straightforward. In the first instance, it is worth generating words or names that seem to be both semantically and structurally similar to the missing item. For this, it is necessary to have faith in ill-defined hunches. Should the intermediates so produced not evoke a sense of "being warm", then the initial hunch (attributes) must be modified—possibly by making a review of the context and forming a fresh hypothesis. Where these intermediates produce a feeling of "closeness" but are not the sought-for item, then there is a strong possibility that a recurrent blocker will appear, if it has not done so already. When this occurs, it is best to abandon the search for the time being. If the blocker reappears on subsequent searches, then do not pursue the hunt further. There is a reasonable chance that the item will appear spontaneously, either through accidental external prompting or in the form of a pop-up. Should this uncertainty prove too hard to bear, then it is best to seek the item in some reference source. Asking someone else may provide the answer, but there is also a fair likelihood that the other person will merely end up in the same condition. But two heads, as they say, are better than one.

VII. ACKNOWLEDGEMENTS

The authors gratefully acknowledge the support of the Social Science Research Council. The data were collected while the senior author was supported by research grant No. HR 6290, and the writing of the present chapter was supported by a further grant, No. HR 7755/1. During the period of the data collection, Mrs Lucas was funded by an SSRC Linked Studentship. We are also indebted to Dr Graham Hitch for his helpful and encouraging comments on earlier versions of this chapter.

REFERENCES

Bawden, H. H. (1900). A study of lapses. *Psychological Monographs*, **3**, 1–21.

Bennett-Levy, J. and Powell, G. E. (1980). The Subjective Memory Questionnaire (SMQ): An investigation into the self-reporting of "real-life" memory skills. *British Journal of Social and Clinical Psychology*, **19**, 177–188.

Broadbent, D. E., Cooper, P. F., Fitzgerald, P. and Parkes, K. R. (1982). The Cognitive Failures Questionnaire (CFQ) and its correlates. *British Journal of Clinical Psychology*, **21**, 1–16.

Brown, R. and McNeill, D. (1966). The "tip of the tongue" phenomenon. *Journal of Verbal Learning and Verbal Behaviour*, **5**, 325–337.

Chapman, L. B. and Chapman, J. P. (1973). "Disordered Thought in Schizophrenia", Prentice Hall, Englewood Cliffs, New Jersey.

Freud, S. (1901). "The Psychopathology of Everyday Life", Penguin, Harmondsworth.

Fromkin, V. (1973). "Speech Errors as Linguistic Evidence", Mouton, The Hague.

Fromkin, V. (1980). "Errors in Linguistic Performance: Slips of the Tongue, Ear, Pen and Hand", Academic Press, New York and London.

Gruneberg, M. M. and Sykes, R. N. (1978). Knowledge and retention: the feeling of knowing and reminiscence. *In* "Practical Aspects of Memory" (M. M. Gruneberg, P. E. Morris and R. N. Sykes, eds), Academic Press, London and New York.

Hart, J. T. (1965). Memory and the feeling of knowing experience. *Journal of Educational Psychology*, **56**, 202–216.

Herrmann, D. J. (1984). Questionnaires about memory. *In* "Everyday Memory, Actions and Absent-Mindedness" (J. E. Harris and P. E. Morris, eds), London: Academic Press, London, Orlando and New York;

Herrmann, D. J. and Neisser, U. (1978). An inventory of everyday memory experiences. *In* "Practical Aspects of Memory" (M. M. Gruneberg, P. E. Morris and R. N. Sykes, eds), Academic Press, London and New York.

Hunter, I. M. L. (1957). "Memory", Penguin, Harmondsworth.

James, W. (1890). "The Principles of Psychology", Holt, New York.

Koriat, A. and Lieblich, I. (1974). What does a person in a "TOT" state know that a person in a "don't know" state doesn't know? *Memory and Cognition*, **2**, 647–655.

Luria, A. R. (1973). "The Working Brain", Penguin, Harmondsworth.

McGhie, A. and Chapman, J. (1961). Disorders of attention and perception in early schizophrenia. *British Journal of Medical Psychology*, **34**, 103–116.

Meringer, R. and Mayer, K. (1895). "Versprechen und Verlesen: Eine Psychologische-Linguistische Studie", Goschensche Verlagsbuchhandlung, Stuttgart.

Miller, G. A., Galanter, E. and Pribram, K. (1960). "Plans and the Structure of Behavior", Holt, Rinehart and Winston, New York.

Niemi, P. (1979). A note on "blocking" as a retrieval interference phenomenon. *American Journal of Psychology*, **92**, 547–550.

Norman, D. A. (1981). Categorization of action slips. *Psychological Review*, **88**, 1–15.

Oppenheim, A. N. (1966). "Questionnaire Design and Attitude Measurement", Heinemann, London.

Pine-Coffin, R. S. (1961). "St Augustine's 'Confessions' ", Penguin, Harmondsworth.

Reason, J. T. (1977). Skill and error in everyday life. *In* "Adult Learning" (M. Howe, ed.), Wiley, London.

Reason, J. T. (1979). Actions not as planned: the price of automatization. *In* "Aspects of Consciousness, Vol. 1: Psychological Issues" (G. Underwood and R. Stevens, eds), Academic Press, London and New York.

Reason, J. T. (1982). Lapses of attention. *In* "Varieties of Attention" (W. Parasuraman, R. Davies, and J. Beatty, eds), Academic Press, New York and London.

Reason, J. T. (1984). Absent-mindedness and cognitive control. *In* "Everyday Memory, Actions and Absent-Mindedness" (J. E. Harris and P. E. Morris, eds), Academic Press, London, Orlando and New York.

Reason, J. T. and Mycielska, K. (1982). "Absent Minded? The Psychology of Mental Lapses and Everyday Errors", Prentice-Hall, Englewood-Cliffs, New Jersey.

Rubin, D. C. (1975). Within word structure in the tip of the tongue phenomenon. *Journal of Verbal Learning and Verbal Behavior*, **14**, 392–397.

Schmidt, R. A. (1975). A schema theory of discrete motor skill learning. *Psychological Review*, **82**, 225–260.

Timpanaro, S. (1976). "The Freudian Slip", New Left Books, London.

Venables, P. H. (1963). Selectivity of attention, withdrawl and cortical activation. *Archives of General Psychiatry*, **9**, 74–78.

Wenzl. A. (1932). Empirische und theoretische Beitrage zur Erinnerungsarbeit bei erschwerter Wortfindung, *Arch. ges. Psychol.* **85** 181–218.

Wenzl, A. (1936). Empirische und theoretische Beitrage zur Erinnerungsarbeit bei erschwerter Wortfindung. *Arch. ges. Psychol.* **97**, 294–318.
Wickelgren, W. A. (1976). Memory storage dynamics. *In* "Handbook of Learning and Cognitive Processes, Vol. 14: Attention and Memory" (W. K. Estes, ed.), Erlbaum, Hillsdale, New Jersey.
Woodworth, R. S. (1929, 1934). *cited in* Woodworth, R. S. and Schlosberg, H. (1954) *Experimental Psychology*, Methuen, London.
Woodworth, R. S. (1938). "Experimental Psychology", Holt, New York.
Yarmey, A. D. (1973). I recognise your face but I can't remember your name: Further evidence on the tip-of-the-tongue phenomenon. *Memory and Cognition*, **1**, 287–290.

5

Remembering to do Things: a Forgotten Topic

J. E. Harris

I. INTRODUCTION

To most people remembering to do things is just as much a use of memory as is remembering information from the past. Until recently psychological research on memory, from Ebbinghaus to Bartlett, has dealt, almost exclusively, with remembering information rather than remembering to do things.

In the typical memory experiment the subject does not have to remember to recall or recognize. What is being tested is the ability to reproduce or identify previously learned material or information. Therefore remembering to recall or recognize is made trivially easy with explicit instructions, or it is implicitly signalled, for example, by the end of the presentation list. In either case it is seldom, if ever, reported that any subjects forgot to try to recall. In everyday life the situation can sometimes be the reverse; the information to be recalled may be trivially easy, but remembering to recall at all may be the difficulty. A good example that differentiates *remembering to recall* from *remembering what to recall* is passing on a telephone message to someone that is out at the time of the call. On the one hand, it is possible to remember to tell the person that there has been a message but to forget what the message is. On the other hand, it is possible to forget completely to tell the person that there has been a message, but once prompted by "Were there any calls for me?", to recall the whole message without any further difficulty. If any readers are unconvinced about this distinction or feel that the topic of this chapter is not strictly one of memory or remembering, and that these terms should be reserved for the conventional type of memory research, they can find further philosophical discussion of these issues in Munsat (1966), Malcolm (1977) and Meacham (1982).

The importance of remembering to do things in everyday life is shown by the aids people use to help them with this aspect of memory. Indeed, it seems the aids that are used the most are those that remind people to do things rather than merely helping to store information (Harris, 1980a). Several authors have described this aspect of memory, but their varying contexts and viewpoints have led them to use different terms, such as *prospective* (as opposed to *retrospective*) remembering (Meacham and Leiman, 1975), remembering to remember (Reed, 1979; Schonfield and Stones, 1979), remembering to recall (Wilkins and Baddeley, 1978), remembering to do things (Harris and Wilkins, 1982), remembering intentions (E. Loftus, 1971), remembering future actions (Morris, 1979), and operational (as opposed to informational) remembering (Kantor and Smith, 1975). In Chapter 1 of this volume, Baddeley and Wilkins (1984) draw parallels between prospective and retrospective memory, a dichotomy they see as weak. But even without a sharp boundary between the two, *prospective* memories may be characterized as a "fuzzy set", typical members of the set having *actions* for content, these being *future* actions and *not* having obvious external *cues*.

Although the bulk of memory research deals with retrospective remembering, there have been a few studies of prospective memory. In these the information to be remembered is usually made trivial (i.e. what action to perform) and what is of interest is whether it is remembered at all (cf. Wilkins and Baddeley, 1978). Because these studies are outside the mainstream of memory research, access to the original reports is often difficult; one purpose of this chapter is to collect them together, and so I make no apology for referencing conference papers and unpublished work.

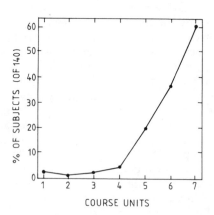

Fig. 1. Percentage of subjects forgetting to check petrol and radiator gauges. Reproduced from Drew (1940) with permission.

II. SOME EXPERIMENTAL STUDIES

A. A flight simulation

The earliest experiment I have found was performed by Drew (1940) using the Cambridge Cockpit (a simulator for instrument flying, built mainly by Kenneth Craik) to look at the effect of fatigue on pilot error. Apart from "flying" the simulator, 140 pilots were required to keep a check on six temperature and pressure gauges and also a fuel indicator. There were few omissions during the first four periods, but a sharply increasing number from the fifth (see Fig. 1). Welford (1958) interpreted this result in terms of a narrowing of attention in order to maintain performance on the main, flying task. Drew (1940) went on to report:

> A further difficulty about these pressure gauges is that, with the exception of the petrol gauge, none of them carry any indication of the correct reading, so that even when the subjects did look at these gauges when they were tired they were unable to remember what the correct temperatures and pressures should be, and so refused to react to them. They characteristically explained afterwards that they were not unduly worried by being unable to remember the correct readings, because they trusted themselves to be able to diagnose any change in the engine note sufficiently accurately to be able to tell which instrument was reading incorrectly. In other words they ignored their instruments almost completely, and used auditory cues to enable them to interpret the instrument panel. This seems to be a reversal of the designers' conception of the value of the panel.
>
> The undercarriage switches were also frequently overlooked by the fatigued pilot. It was, in fact, one of the most common of all faults for the pilot to land with his undercarriage up, and explain that he had completely forgotten about it. In fact, more than 80 of the 140 pilots tested landed with the undercarriage up. (p. 16)

It can be seen that Drew was describing three rather different types of failure to do things involving the fuel indicator, (which had an indication of the correct reading), the pressure and temperature gauges (which did not), and the undercarriage switches. The different types of task and of failure are discussed in the second part of this chapter, after accounts have been given of other experimental work.

B. Remembering to keep appointments

A number of studies have involved asking subjects to send back one or more postcards to the experimenter on particular dates (Levy et al., 1979; Meacham and Leiman, 1975; Meacham and Singer, 1977; Orne, 1970; Wilkins, 1976), or to telephone (Levy, 1977; Moscovitch and Minde, cited in Moscovitch, in press) or turn up for an appointment (Levy and Clark, 1980) at particular times and dates. As these tasks have much in common in terms of time scale, of strategies available, and of involving an appointment to recontact the experimenter after a period away from his control and observation, I shall deal with them collectively under the label "appointment keeping". Findings have included beneficial effects on appointment keeping of memory aids (Meacham and Leiman, 1975), of strong commitment (Levy, 1977; Levy et al., 1979), of incentive (Meacham and Singer, 1977) and of external* rather than internal remembering strategies (Meacham and Singer, 1977). Wilkins (1976) found no effect of retention interval, Orne (1970) found no correlation with level of hypnosis at instruction, and Moscovitch and Minde (Moscovitch, personal communications) have found that old people may perform better than young people, probably by using more effective remembering strategies.

(1) Appointment keeping and a memory aid

Meacham and Leiman (1975) performed two experiments in which a total of 71 students in ten groups were instructed to post a number of cards back to the experimenter on particular dates. The students were given either 4 or 8 cards to be posted back one by one on particular days up to either 32 or 16 days later, starting either soon after instruction or about 16 days later. In each pair of groups, the subjects in one group were given coloured tags to put on their key chains as a reminder, while the subjects in the other group were left to their own devices.

Unfortunately, ceiling effects, the large number of conditions, and the low number of subjects per condition (usually 7) combined to obscure the effects and interactions of the various manipulations. Taken together, however, the results did indicate that the tags increased the likelihood of the cards being posted on the correct date.

A follow-up questionnaire indicated that apart from the tag, 52% of subjects placed the cards in a conspicuous place, 32% used calenders as reminders, two subjects reported using internal methods and the remaining subjects reported no extra ways of remembering. This preference for external rather than internal aids for prospective remembering has also been found for everyday tasks in interviews with children (Kreutzer et al., 1975) and adults (Harris, 1980a).

Meacham and Leiman (1975) found no correlations between retrospective remembering (immediate recall of short word lists) and the prospective memory task (cf. negative association found by Wilkins and Baddeley, 1978), nor between subjects' predictions of their remembering abilities and their actual performance. It is not possible to tell whether ceiling effects may have been responsible.

---

* External strategies involve changing the world outside your head, such as writing in a diary or leaving something in a noticeable place, whereas internal strategies involve mental manipulation, as in the classical mnemonics.

(2) *Incentive, hypnosis and compliance*

Meacham and Singer (1977) examined the effect of incentive and of the regularity with which the cards had to be posted. All 48 student subjects had eight cards to post back, one per week for eight weeks. In the more regular condition, the cards had to be posted each Wednesday while in the less regular condition the day of the week varied randomly over the five weekdays. In the high incentive condition the subjects were instructed that four of the cards posted on time would be drawn and their senders given a maximum of $5.

There was no effect of, or interaction involving, the regularity condition or the sex of the subjects.

The effect of incentive was small but significant whether measured in terms of the number of cards returned late per subject (a reduction in mean from 2.13 to 1.41 cards/subject) or in terms of the mean number of days late per card (a reduction in mean from 0.84 to 0.33 days/card). It is not, of course, clear whether this represents improved memory performance or improved compliance once it has been remembered that a card should be posted. This applies to several of the following experiments and the issues connecting prospective memory and compliance are covered in Chapter 6 of this volume (Levy and G. Loftus, 1984). (Meacham and Kushner, 1980, have carried out a questionnaire study comparing Freudian repression with non-compliance as factors in failing to do anxiety-provoking things, such as missing a dentist's appointment.)

In a questionnaire sent at the end of the experiment, subjects were asked how they had remembered to post their cards on time and whether they had always done their best. Although the associations between these self-report variables, the level of incentive and lateness were in the expected directions, only the following reached conventional levels of significance. Being in the high incentive group was associated with the reported use of external aids and reports of always doing their best was associated with a lower number of days late.

Orne (1970) reported an experiment in which 34 subjects were paid in different ways to post back 56 postcards, one per day for eight weeks. Conditions involving a lump sum pre-payment of $2.50 (group A), of $8.10 (group B), or a pre-payment of $2.50 plus 10c. paid afterwards per card posted on time (group C), did not differ significantly. A fourth group (D) were given a prepayment of $2.50 plus a prepayment of 10c. for each of the 56 cards, the subjects being told that they were being paid in advance because the experimenters were confident that they would send the postcards. Group D sent back a significantly higher proportion (69%) of the cards on time than the other three groups (mean of 56%). Orne (1970) reported a further experiment, run by Jeremy Cobb at Brandeis University, in which postcard sending (52 subjects with 100 cards each) failed to correlate with depth of hypnosis at the time of instruction. Orne (1970) also described Damaser's (1964) finding that posthypnotic suggestion was no more effective than instructions given under waking conditions to return the cards, a similar result to those of

Kellogg (1929) and of Patten (1930), who used different tasks for post-hypnotic suggestion. Interested readers should refer directly to the Orne (1970) paper and also to Wagstaff (1981) who argued that experiments on posthypnotic suggestion had not managed to eliminate the possibility that subjects were simply complying with the experimenter's or hypnotist's instructions in a normal conscious manner (cf. Chapter 6 of this volume, Levy and Loftus, 1984).

(3) Commitment, compliance and ecological validity
Rona Levy (Levy, 1977; Levy and Clark, 1980; Levy et al., 1979) has carried out a series of experiments on commitment and compliance in a therapeutic or medical context. These are covered in more detail in Chapter 6 (Levy and G. Loftus, 1984), but it is appropriate to mention these studies here as they use tasks similar to the one just described and so involve remembering to do things. Subjects were required to telephone between 7 and 9 p.m. on a day up to a week later (Levy, 1977), to return a postcard after 48 h (Levy et al., 1979) or to come back for an appointment at a pre-arranged time within two weeks (Levy and Clark, 1980). In each case the level of commitment was varied; for example, Levy (1977) had three levels of commitment, with one group simply being asked to do the task, a second group were asked for an oral commitment, and a third for an oral and a written commitment. In a medical compliance experiment it is important that the task should be seen by the subject as relevant to the treatment rather than just as an experimenter's tool. So Levy's studies reach a level of ecological validity not sought in the similar experiments described above. Levy's (1977) subjects were mothers partici-pating in the behaviour therapy of one of their children, and they were asked to telephone for information on procedures for the next stage of treatment. The subjects of Levy et al. (1979) had received flu inoculations and were given preprinted cards as they left on which to record symptoms occurring over the following two days. Levy and Clark's (1980) subjects were patients making appointments to attend hospital outpatient clinics. In these experiments commitment did not always increase compliance (see Chapter 6 of this volume for more detailed results.)

(4) Appointment keeping and the retention interval
Arnold Wilkins (1976) was interested in the effect of the length of the interval between instruction and the correct time for the to-be-remembered action in a prospective memory task. It might at first seem as if this interval is comparable in some way to the retention interval in a conventional retrospective memory task. Wilkins instructed his 34 subjects to return their cards (just one each) from 2 to 36 days later. He found no effect of length of interval on performance (but he could not rule out a floor effect in that only 35% were not returned on time). In common with the studies described above, the experimenter had no control over the methods subjects used to remember to return the cards, indeed subjects were deliberately left to their own devices. It

is likely that external methods such as a note in a diary will be noticed as much a month later as a few days later. This experiment does not, therefore, rule out an effect of retention interval if subjects are forced to use internal methods. (Meacham and Leiman's, 1975, Experiment 2 indicated that later cards in a series may be less likely to be posted on time than the earlier cards.) Harris and Wilkins (1982) also failed to find a difference in performance between what can be regarded as 3- and 9-minute retention intervals in a prospective memory task (see below), while Loftus (1971) did find a drop in performance with more items in an interpolated task (see below). However, these were both very short-term compared with the card-posting task, and it seems likely that short-term prospective memory tasks, such as remembering to retrieve the toast from the grill before it burns, may be very different psychologically from long-term ones, such as remembering your mother-in-law's birthday in six month's time.

(5) *Appointment keeping and ageing*

Moscovitch and Minde (Moscovitch, personal communications and cited in Moscovitch, 1982) instructed a group of ten young subjects (students aged 22–37) and a group of 10 old subjects (graduates aged 65–75) to telephone once a day for two weeks at a fixed time of their choosing. A telephone answering service noted the day, time and caller. Subjects were told that if they were more than five minutes late for an "appointment" they would be considered to have missed it. Only one of the old people ever completely forgot one of these telephone appointments, whereas seven of the young group forgot a total of 14 appointments. The young subjects were also late more often than were the old ones. Old people live more regular lives than young people and may therefore find it easier to telephone at the same time each day. So in a second experiment two new groups of old and young subjects were asked to telephone at only three, randomly chosen times over the following two weeks. Only two of the 9 young subjects remembered all three appointments, as against 4 of the 6 old subjects; in addition one of the young subjects forgot *two* of the three appointments. Examination of the data and subsequent interviews with the subjects indicated that the critical variable might not be age but use of external cues. There was a tendency for those subjects who trusted their memories and made comments such as "I've got an internal alarm" to be more likely to miss an appointment. The old people may have learned to rely on external aids whereas the young were often a little "cocky" about their memories. In two subsequent experiments subjects were asked not to use any external aids; the older subjects were less likely than the students to comply with this instruction and when they did their performance was at a comparable level to that of the young subjects. Moscovitch pointed out that the older people might be more highly motivated so that, when left to their own devices, they would be more likely to use effective, external strategies, and to be more reluctant to give them up when instructed to do so.

The reversal found by Moscovitch and Minde of the usual result that young subjects perform better than older ones on memory tasks, may go some way towards explaining why older subjects often report having better memory for everyday tasks or fewer memory problems than do younger subjects (Bennett-Levy and Powell, 1980; Chaffin and Herrmann, 1983; Harris and Sunderland, 1981; McKenna, 1981). Harris and Sunderland (1981) reported two studies in which older subjects gave lower average frequencies than younger subjects for various everyday memory problems listed in a 28-item questionnaire. Young subjects were compared in the first study with retired people (mean ages were 27 and 74 years) and in the second with pre-retired people (mean ages 25 and 55 years). On six of the 28 items, young people complained far more consistently of frequent problems than did the groups of older people, three of these 6 being about remembering to do things. They were:

Completely forgetting to do things you said you would do and things you planned to do.

Completely forgetting to take things with you, or leaving things behind and having to go back and fetch them.

Forgetting to tell someone something important. Perhaps forgetting to pass on a message or remind someone of something.

These three items all refer to situations in which it would not be difficult to use external aids. It is possible to speculate why Moscovitch and Minde's young subjects and maybe young people in general are more "cocky" about their memories and use fewer memory aids. The most obvious possibility is that old people know or expect their memories not to be as good as they were (Perlmutter, 1978), and that they are therefore less likely to be cocky and more likely to be prepared to use an aid. Secondly, the over-confident youngsters may learn as they go through life that even when you expect to remember to do something you can easily forget, and it is safer to use an external aid. Thirdly, old people have had longer to acquire a repertoire of effective strategies, including external aids, and to develop a habit of using them. For example, Harris (1980a) found that the women (mean age 47 years) he interviewed regarded it as their role within the family to remember friends' and relatives' birthdays and social events such as meals with friends. To cope with this they used a variety of external aids including at least one diary, calendar or wall chart on which to keep reminders of things to be done. When their families have grown up and left home and their husbands are retired these women will have less of a prospective memory load but may continue to use effectively the aids they earlier needed so much. However, we shall see below that in other types of prospective memory task, performed in the laboratory and not involving appointment keeping, old people may not perform as well as young.

C. Remembering to do one thing before or after another

Another method of experimentation has required subjects to perform a special task at a particular stage during an experimental session (Loftus, 1971; Meacham and Colombo, 1980; Meacham and Dumitru, 1976; Schonfield and Shooter, described in Welford, 1958). The time scale for these prospective memory tasks is typically much shorter than for the appointment-keeping studies described in the last section. The experimenter also has control over such things as written reminders and can observe the subject over the whole period from instruction until the action is performed or forgotten.

As reported in Chapter 6 of this volume, (Levy and G. Loftus, 1984), E. Loftus (1971) conducted an experiment in the form of an opinion poll. Before answering a number of questions, subjects were asked to wait till they had answered all the questions and then to name the state in which they had been born. More subjects remembered after five intervening questions than after 15 (68% against 54%), (see discussion above of the effect of retention intervals). Warning subjects in advance that the last intervening question was about the Black Panther Party provided sufficient cueing effect to raise the proportion of subjects remembering from 53% to 69%. Loftus interpreted her results as suggesting that the same mechanisms that are responsible for forgetting in conventional memory paradigms are also responsible for forgetting intentions. The later studies that have followed Loftus's experiment and which are reviewed in this chapter have not been so clear cut.

(1) Children's use of memory aids

Meacham and Dumitru (1976) investigated the use of a memory aid by two groups of 41 children (mean ages 5 years 7 months and 7 years 7 months). The children were taken individually from the classroom to a testing room, passing on the way a bright orange posting box which was pointed out to them. Having drawn a picture in the testing room, each child was complimented on his picture and told that he could enter it in a contest by posting it in the orange box on his way back to the classroom. However, before leaving the test room the child spent another seven minutes doing a locus of control test in another part of the room, leaving the picture in an envelope near where he had drawn it.

There were three conditions for the remembering task. In a control condition no memory aid was available. In a "cue" condition and an "elaboration" condition, the children were allowed to choose one of three picture cards, showing a postbox, a lamp or a cup, to help them remember to post their own pictures. (They all successfully chose the card showing the postbox.) In the elaboration condition, but not in the cue condition, the children were coached in the use of the aid. Over all three conditions more of the older children (73%) than of the younger children (37%) remembered to post their pictures. However, the three cueing conditions did not differ significantly, though the trend was strongly in the right direction in the younger group (21%, 31% and 57% remembering in the control, cue and elaboration conditions respectively).

With a slightly changed task Meacham and Colombo (1980) found a significant difference between the control and elaboration conditions, using two groups of 38 children (mean ages 5 years 10 months and 7 years 8 months). The children were tested individually and shown a small, colourful "surprise" box. They were told that a surprise would happen when the lid was opened and that they should remind the experimenter to open it when they had finished and before they left the room. The experimenter checked that the children had understood and then he put the box out of sight. In the elaboration condition the children were given a clown to use as a reminder and were coached in its use till they understood. In the control condition there was no reminder, and in this experiment there was no simple cue condition. Half the children spent the intervening seven minutes doing a locus of control test and the other half played a card game with the experimenter. This time significantly more of the children in the elaboration condition (75%) than in the control condition (52%) remembered. No effects were found for age, sex or intervening task. It may be that the age difference Meacham and his co-workers used in these two experiments (2 years) was too small to give consistent effects. Kreutzer *et al.* (1975) showed how children's repertoires of strategies and their use of aids increases across four groups aged approximately 6, 7, 9 and 11 years.

(2) *Ageing and doing one thing before another*
An early experiment in which adults of various ages had to remember to do one thing before doing another was started by Schonfield in 1949 at the Cambridge Nuffield Unit. Shooter ran the final subjects and the experiment is described in Welford (1958). Curiously the experiment was performed to collect quite different data. The subjects had four flaps which they could raise, one at a time, to reveal a simple pattern of dots. The subjects' task was to discover in which pattern and position there was a dot that did not occur in any of the other three patterns. In order to obtain a measure of how long the

Table I. Number of times subjects forgot to press the key before giving judgments in Schonfield and Shooter's experiment.

Age Range	Mean omissions per subject
15–20	0.6
21–29	1.7
30–39	2.7
40–49	3.5
50–71	5.6

From Welford, A. T. (1958). "Ageing and Human Skill." Oxford University Press, London. Copyright A. T. Welford and reproduced by permission.

subjects spent on the task, they were instructed to press a morse key, placed to the right hand side of the flaps, before giving their answers. The mean number of key presses omitted per subject is given as a function of age in Table I. The increased forgetting with age in this laboratory study is in contrast with the results of Moscovitch and Minde's appointment-keeping studies described above. It seems that the availability of memory aids to their subjects may have been the crucial factor, though clearly there are other differences between the paradigms, which are discussed below.

(3) A potential task for test batteries

Before finishing this section on remembering to do one thing after another, it is worth noting a technique recently devised by Arnold Wilkins in collaboration with a group at the Montreal Neurological Institute headed by Dr Brenda Milner. A battery of tests is routinely given to patients with focal epilepsy; it has now been elaborated so that at the beginning of the session, the patients are instructed to use a red pencil for one of the subsequent tests (drawing a bicycle), a conventional "lead" pencil having been used for the earlier tests in the session. Although detailed results are not yet available, initial indications are that patients with large left hippocampal excisions forget to change pencils as previously instructed (Pajurkova and Wilkins, 1983). This result indicates the potential usefulness of such a technique as a simple laboratory test that can easily be incorporated into test batteries. For example, in a study currently being performed at the MRC Applied Psychology Unit, subjects do a battery of tests and are required to "post" special cards into a box after only those eight tests in which the box has been used.

D. Remembering to take medicines

Remembering to take medicines can be either of the *appointment-keeping* type of task (e.g. "Take every 8 hours" or "Take daily at 10.00 p.m.") or of the *remembering to do one thing before or after another* type (e.g. "Take before each meal"), and so it is covered separately in this section. I have already mentioned the topic of medical compliance in relation to Rona Levy's studies of the effect of commitment, and Chapter 6 of this volume (Levy and Loftus, 1984) deals specifically with compliance (see also Ley, 1978; Sackett and Haynes, 1976), but there are some issues concerned with remembering to take medicines that are worth raising here. Failing to take medicines seems more likely to be a matter of forgetting than in the case of failing to comply with a physician's instructions to stay in bed or to keep to a diet; it may also be easier to measure the level of compliance in the case of medicine taking. Usual methods of assessment include adding chemical tracers to the drugs for detection in the urine, and counting the pills left in the bottle. Several factors other than the amount of medicine taken, such as the patients' absorption of the tracer, affect the amount of tracer in the urine, so this is not an accurate method. Counting pills may be more accurate, but there is no way of checking when the pills were taken out of the bottle. They may even have all been removed at once, half an hour before the count, so as not to "disappoint" the doctor or researcher.

In collaboration with Professor Exton-Smith and staff at St Pancras Hospital, London, Arnold Wilkins is using a special *Dosett* pill-box with separate compartments for each dose of pills. The box has been adapted by Graham Bason so that it records electronically the times at which each compartment is opened. Although the subject can open the compartments correctly and still throw the pills away rather than take them, the opening of the box does confirm that the subject has *remembered* that it is time to take the pills. The same sort of remembering data can be collected by the apparatus Wilkins and Baddeley (1978) used as an analogue of a pill-taking task. Their 31 female subjects were instructed to press a button on a portable box at 8.30 a.m., 1.00 p.m., 5.30 p.m. and 10.00 p.m. each day for a week (the times being written on the outside of the box together with a reminder of the instructions). If the subjects forgot to press the button on time, they were instructed to press it as soon as they remembered unless the next response time had arrived, in which case they were instructed to record the omission on the label on the side of the box. Apparatus inside the box recorded the times at which the button was pressed.

The distribution of responses over time showed that the vast majority were within five minutes of the target time, with a short tail of earlier responses and a longer one of late responses. Analysis in terms of lateness showed significant effects of the day of the task (first to seventh), time of day (8.30 a.m. less late than 1.00 p.m. or 5.30 p.m.). Low scorers on a free recall task were less late than high scorers. The authors considered an interpretation of this result in terms of life-style, but additional data from activity diaries failed to support it. Lastly, lateness was not affected by the day of the week, nor by the day on which the subjects started (Monday *vs* Friday).

There were 30 complete omissions contributed by 15 of the 31 subjects, and 9 of these 15 subjects failed to record on the labels 11 of the 30 omissions. One might have also expected extra responses to occur when a subject, forgetting she had already responded, would make another, late response before the next target time. Such errors of "commission" did not seem to occur. So when subjects remembered to respond, they always remembered they had done so, but when they forgot to respond, they often failed to remember (record) their omissions.

(1) Wilkins's "random walk" model

Although I have tried to leave theoretical considerations to be discussed together in the second part of this chapter, it is appropriate to mention here a model that Wilkins (1979) has put forward in an attempt to account for the shape of the lateness distribution found by Wilkins and Baddeley (1978). The model involves the "train of thought", which is seen as moving about in a statistically random manner ("random walk") through a multi-dimensional semantic space. Some area of this space is associated with pill-taking (or button-pushing) in such a way that the closer the train of thought approaches to this area, the greater the likelihood that it will jump to the subject of taking the pill. If it is not too early the pill is now taken, but if it is too early the train of thought will move away until it again ventures close enough to the area associated with pill-taking.

III. THEORETICAL CONSIDERATIONS

A. Monitoring and TWTE tasks

The essence of remembering to do something is that it cannot be done straightaway; there is usually a relative cost associated with doing it too early (or, of course, too late). So in order for it to be done at the most appropriate time some process or signal has to be monitored or checked. In experiments I have considered in this chapter the monitoring has involved temperature and fuel gauges, checking the date, maybe with a calendar, to see if it is the right day to send a postcard, and monitoring a clock or watch for the time to push a button. In everyday life it could, for example, involve remembering to take a cake out of the oven, the costs of doing it too early or too late being a cake that is either undercooked or burnt. So either some sort of clock or the state of the cake (or at first one and later the other) has to be checked so that the cake is removed at the appropriate time (unless an alarm timer is used to eliminate the memory component of the task).

In a recent collaborative paper with Arnold Wilkins (Harris and Wilkins, 1982), I have given a detailed description of this process. At first a series of tests may reveal that it is too early to make the main response (posting the card etc.). Between these tests the monitored process must be allowed to proceed, resulting in a "wait" period. Eventually a test will reveal that it is appropriate to make the main response, resulting in an "exit" from the test-wait loops, which completes a procedure that can be described as test-wait-test-exit (TWTE; cf. Miller *et al.*, 1960, and see Fig. 2a). TWTE tasks vary in a number of ways, such as in the nature of the information that the test provides, the control the rememberer has over the speed of the process he is monitoring, and the duration and "shape" of the "critical period" during which it is appropriate to respond (see Figs 2b and 2c). Interested readers can find a detailed description of these variations, with examples, in Harris and Wilkins (1982). In summary, a TWTE task can be defined as one in which (a) responding early or late results in a cost relative to responding at the correct time, i.e. there is a hump in the function that relates the benefit of responding to time; (b) information can be obtained about the current value of this function; and (c) the cost of obtaining this information is small compared to that of responding early or late, although sufficient to discourage continuous monitoring.

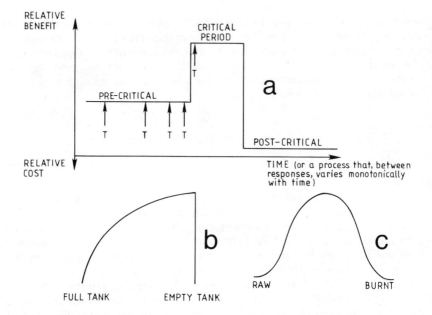

Fig. 2. Functions relating relative benefit/cost of responding to time (or the monitored process) in a TWTE task.

(a) An idealized function showing tests (T); the final test is shown to occur during the critical period when the test reveals that it is time to respond.

(b) A function shape that might represent remembering to fill a car with petrol. The cost of filling it too early (making unnecessary trips to a petrol station) gradually declines. The cost of leaving it too late arrives very suddenly when the car runs out of petrol.

(c) A function that might represent remembering to retrieve food from the oven. The cost of an early response would be undercooking it and of a late response overcooking or burning it. (Note that an "early response" followed by returning it to the oven represents monitoring rather than a genuine early response.)

(1) *Types of Forgetting*

Using the TWTE description it is possible to separate three types of failure in tasks involving remembering to do things. The first involves complete failure to make a test during the critical period, so that the information that it is now appropriate to proceed to exit is never received. The second type is not to include the appropriate test for the particular TWTE task, despite monitoring during the critical period; for example, checking the clock at 4.30 and only testing whether it is time to collect a child from school and forgetting to test whether it is also time to retrieve a cake from the oven. The third type of failure involves forgetting the test criterion, despite remembering that a test should be made; for example, when timing the boiling of an egg using an ordinary clock, it is possible to forget how long the egg should be boiled or at what time it was put in the water. It is this last type of failure that Drew's

(1940) pilots suffered when they forgot the correct reading of their pressure and temperature gauges (see above quotation from Drew, 1940).

B. Types of prospective memory task

(1) Habitual and episodic prospective memory

Meacham and Leiman (1975) distinguished what they called *habitual* and *episodic* prospective remembering. Habitual remembering involves re-membering to do things that are done routinely, such as brushing one's teeth before going to bed. Episodic remembering involves remembering to do things that are done "infrequently or on an irregular basis", such as stopping to buy bread on the way home from work. Although very fuzzy in the middle (is buying bread once a week or once a month on the way home episodic or habitual?), the distinction is clear at the extremes. Meacham and Leiman (1975) argued that habitual tasks are easier to remember than episodic because of the extra cues from the environment and from preceding activities. Another way of expressing it, in terms used by Reason (1977, 1979), is that sequences of actions that are most frequently and recently performed (habitual) can be run off in "open loop" operation (not involving control at the level of conscious attention), while less frequently and recently performed actions (episodic) require "closed loop" operation if they are not to be forgotten.

Meacham and Singer (1977) pointed out that constructing lists of episodic tasks and regularly checking the list conveys the advantages of habitual tasks to episodic ones. As we have seen, Meacham and Singer (1977) tried to experiment with this habitual-episodic distinction (referred to in the des-cription above as varying "regularity"), by instructing some subjects to return postcards on Wednesdays each week, while others had varying target days. This minor manipulation does not seem to capture the richer distinction they were aiming at and indeed it had no detectable effect on responding.

(2) Number of activities and type of monitoring

In the review of experiments in the first half of this chapter, some experiments were classified as appointment-keeping and others as remembering to do one thing before or after another. In this section I shall try to draw some fundamental distinctions between such groups of tasks, groups that probably require different paradigms for investigation and that may require different models.

(i) Single-activity and dual-activity prospective memory. Both the follow-ing tasks involve remembering to do something; (a) remembering to put tea leaves into the tea pot when making tea, and (b) remembering to buy some bread on the way home from work. In (a), the to-be-remembered action is part of the main, ongoing activity and there is a single goal (a pot of tea); it can therefore be regarded as involving a *single* activity. In (b) the journey home has to be interrupted in order to buy the bread and there are two goals

(arriving home and obtaining bread); it can therefore be regarded as involving two activities. This distinction is not a logical one because it relies on an arbitrary choice of levels of analysis and at a lower level making tea involves multiple sub-goals; however these sub-goals are habitually part of making tea, whereas it is assumed in the example that buying bread is not habitually part of going home from work. So this distinction is a psychological one and similar to that made by Meacham and Leiman (1975) between episodic and habitual remembering.

(ii) Simple and compound prospective memory tasks. Dual-activity prospective memory tasks can be further split into two psychological types according to what has to be monitored (see above section on Monitoring and TWTE tasks). This time the contrast can be illustrated by comparing the dual-activity task (b) used in the last section, remembering to buy bread on the way home from work, with (c) remembering to set off at 4.30 p.m. to fetch a child from school (some other activity such as cooking, writing, watching TV or resting will·therefore have to be interrupted at 4.30). In (b) *the progress on the interrupted activity itself is monitored*, because this determines when the interruption should occur (i.e. when progress on the way home has reached the bread shop). Since it is the interrupted activity itself that must be monitored, this type of task can be referred to as *simple*. In (c) *something unrelated to the interrupted activity has to be monitored* (i.e. in order to set off at 4.30 for the school, the writing, TV watching etc. has to be punctuated by checking a clock or a watch). Since an independent process (the progress of the hands around the clock) has to be monitored, this type of task can be regarded as *compound*. (Single-activity tasks such as making a pot of tea involve monitoring progress on that task and are therefore regarded as simple.)

The appointment-keeping experiments described above can now be classified as compound dual-activity tasks, while those that were described as doing one thing before or after another are simple dual-activity tasks. However, single-activity tasks also involve remembering to do one thing before or after another, like remembering to put tea in the pot, but no experiments of this type were included in the review. Such tasks have, of course, been the object of psychological study, but are usually thought of as part of skilled performance, action slips and absent-mindedness, topics that are particularly associated with Reason (1975, 1976, 1977, 1979), though his analysis covers many other aspects of the tasks as well as those involving remembering to do things (see also Chapter 7 of this volume for Reason's, 1984, three-component model of cognitive control).

Although it has been argued that all types of prospective remembering must involve monitoring some process, only compound tasks involve monitoring a process that is independent of the ongoing activity, and therefore it is only in these tasks that the monitoring can be overt and the TWTE description applied. In a TWTE task such as remembering to take something from the oven when it looks cooked, the reason for the wait stage between tests (looks) is that the cooking continues autonomously, without the participation of the tester, who is therefore free to engage in an unrelated activity from which he may forget to return to perform the next test. In such tasks the tests are often overt and yield objective data. For example, Wilkins (Harris and Wilkins, 1982) had the idea of placing a clock that subjects needed to monitor behind them; in order to make "tests", the subjects had to turn their heads, an overt and recordable response (see below). In simple tasks where it is the ongoing activity that is monitored, the TWTE description is inappropriate and the monitoring usually covert.

To conclude this section on types of prospective memory task, I should refer the reader to Chapter 1 of this volume, in which Baddeley and Wilkins (1984) apply the short-term *vs* long-term and semantic *vs* episodic distinctions, so familiar in studies of retrospective memory, to those of prospective memory.

C. Collecting data on monitoring

In most of the prospective memory experiments reviewed in this chapter the main data collected have concerned whether subjects eventually remembered to do what they were instructed. However, it is important to know what leads up to remembering or forgetting. Some experiments have included a subsequent interview or questionnaire asking the subjects about the methods they had used (Meacham and Leiman, 1975; Meacham and Singer, 1977; Moscovitch, personal communication). The main conclusion has been that external aids and methods are more effective than internal strategies. However, people do not and cannot always use external aids and they sometimes forget even when they do use them. In this section I describe an initial attempt to investigate what happens when external memory aids are not available (Harris and Wilkins, 1982), and then, in the next section, discuss what underlies the effectiveness of external aids.

It has been argued above and in Harris and Wilkins (1982) that monitoring prior to responding is a crucial aspect of remembering to do something. Theorizing about the internal processes that mediate between instruction and response is unlikely to be profitable in the absence of data on this monitoring. Apart from the strategy questionnaires, however, investigators have ignored what leads up to remembering or forgetting to do something.

Returning to the TWTE description, the period of monitoring is represented by test-wait cycles, and the tests, being potentially observable, can provide data. In an experiment designed to collect these data, we (Harris and Wilkins, 1982) chose to simulate the task of having to do something at a particular time and in the meantime watching TV. Subjects watched a two-hour film about a hijack and also had to perform another task at particular times. These times (e.g. 2.30) were separated by 3 or 9 min and each one was written on one of a series of sheets of paper, which were in temporal order with the earliest time on the top sheet. The only clock that the women subjects had available was placed behind them so that they had to turn their heads to consult it. It displayed the time in hours, minutes and seconds. The subjects were instructed that they could respond (by holding up the sheet) at any time between that written on the sheet and 15 s later; any response outside this period would be considered to be early or late. Using this procedure it was possible to observe and record both the subjects' final responses and their observations of the clock.

Most of the final responses were made in the first few seconds after the target times written on the sheets, though the distribution had a long tail of late responses, over 12% occurring after the allowable period. The observation rate immediately preceding the target time was correlated with the response latency, reaching a rate of over 9 observations per minute in the last few seconds before a prompt response, but not rising beyond 2 observations per minute before a late response. Surprisingly, on over a quarter of those occasions on which subjects forgot to respond on time, they had nevertheless looked at the clock within the last 10 s before the target time. Apparently people can forget to do things very quickly, at least in this situation.

We discussed (Harris and Wilkins, 1982) the similarity of our experiment to those that involve fixed-interval reinforcement schedules and in which a clock is available for timing the interval (see Lowe, 1979). While the demands of the tasks are similar, it was argued that the behaviourist approach does not address the most interesting questions; these deal with the cognitive events that intervene between observations of the clock, and in particular with how the subject decides when to look again. One aspect of this question concerns what information the subject uses, potentially what she remembers of the time at the last observation and her estimate of how long has passed since then (or some combination of the two). Another aspect concerns how the information is used, for example, to avoid dropping below a certain level of confidence that the target time has not yet passed. A third aspect concerns whether there is competition for cognitive resources between this decision and the ongoing activity, and if so which of several possible ways it is resolved. If such competition is resolved by occasional "switching" of attention (rather than some form of parallel processing, cf. Reason's, 1984, "attentional blob" in Chapter 7 of this volume), it raises the question of what determines the occasions, in particular whether a cue arising from the ongoing activity is needed to divert attention to the monitoring decision (cf. Wilkins's, 1979, random walk model outlined above.) It was argued (Harris and Wilkins, 1982) that several models would be consistent with the results of this initial experiment, but hopefully some could be eliminated by further experimental investigation of the three aspects of the decision I have outlined. However, the exact processes involved are likely to depend on strategies that vary from task to task and even from subject to subject.

IV. THE EFFECTIVENESS OF REMINDERS TO DO THINGS

In two interview studies I asked Southampton University students and female members of the Cambridge Applied Psychology Unit subject panel how frequently they used various types of memory aid (Harris, 1980a). It turned out that in both groups the aids that were reported to be used most frequently were those that act as reminders to do things (e.g. appointment diaries) rather than merely helping to store information (e.g. the method of loci mnemonic). Although this result may have been partly due to the selection of aids about which subjects were asked specific questions (Neisser, 1982, has pointed out that I confounded external *vs* internal with prospective *vs* retrospective), it is clear that considerable use is made of a wide range of external reminders to do things. These reminders can be regarded as cueing devices, and I have argued (Harris, 1978, 1980b) that the effectiveness of the cues that they provide depends on certain attributes.

> For a cue to be maximally effective it should (a) be given as close as possible before the time the action is required — it may be no good reminding someone as he leaves home to buy some bread on his way home from work, (b) be *active* rather than *passive* — a passive reminder in a diary may fail if the user forgets to consult it, and (c) be a specific reminder for the particular action that is required — a knotted handkerchief may only remind its user that something must be remembered but not what that something is (Harris, 1978, p. 178).

The need for a reminder to be timely is well illustrated by the Esselte "Electronic Diary", which can only be set to ring at 15 minute intervals. If set, for example, at 2.45 as a reminder of a meeting 10 minutes later, it is easy to become reabsorbed in work during the interval and still to forget the meeting (I write from bitter experience!). A more striking example was the speed with which subjects in the film-watching experiment (Harris and Wilkins, 1982) sometimes forgot to hold up their sheets (see preceding section). Within 10 s of having looked at the clock they could apparently become sufficiently reabsorbed in the film to forget to respond.

An active reminder obviates the need for monitoring (provided it is also timely), because it eliminates the prospective aspect of the memory task leaving just the retrospective one; it is now just a matter of recalling information about what it is that should be done. An efficient reminder will also provide a cue or hint to aid this recall.

V. CONCLUDING REMARKS

In this chapter I have argued that remembering to do things is an important aspect of memory, I have given an account of the studies that have been performed, and I have discussed some embryonic theoretical notions. If the account seems to be like a list, it is because the studies have been performed in the absence of any encompassing theory and the researchers have performed their investigations for various, sometimes applied reasons, with little knowledge of each other's work. I hope, however, that the reader will agree that prospective memory is an interesting topic, worthy of study and accessible to experimentation.

Note

It has been difficult tracking down studies on remembering to do things and there may be some that I have omitted: I should be pleased to have them brought to my attention. I am particularly grateful to Professor David Schonfield, Dr John Meacham, Dr Martin Binks and Dr Brian Fellows who pointed me towards studies I might otherwise have missed.

REFERENCES

Baddeley, A. D. and Wilkins, A. J. (1984). Taking memory out of the laboratory. *In* "Everyday Memory, Actions and Absent-Mindedness" (J. E. Harris and P. E. Morris, eds), Academic Press, London, Orlando and New York.

Bennett-Levy, J. and Powell, G. E. (1980). The subjective memory questionnaire (SMQ). An investigation into the self-reporting of "real-life" memory skills. *British Journal of Social and Clinical Psychology*, **19**, 177–188.

Chaffin, R. and Herrmann, D. J. (1983). Self reports of memory performance as a function of age in adulthood. *Human Learning*, **2**, 17–28.

Damaser, E. C. (1964). Experimental study of long-term posthypnotic suggestion. Unpublished doctoral dissertation. Harvard University. Cited by Orne (1970).

Drew, G. C. (1940). An experimental study of mental fatigue. British Air Ministry, Flying Personnel Research Committee Paper No. 277. Re-issued 1960 and reprinted in E. J. Dearnaley and P. J. Warr (eds) (1979), "Aircrew Stress in Wartime Operations", Academic Press, London, and New York.

Harris, J. E. (1978). External memory aids. *In* "Practical Aspects of Memory" (M. M. Gruneberg, P. E. Morris and R. N. Sykes, eds), Academic Press, London, and New York.

Harris, J. E. (1980a). Memory aids people use: two interview studies. *Memory and Cognition*, **8**, 31–38.

Harris, J. E. (1980b). We have ways of helping you remember. *Concord: Journal of the British Association for Service to the Elderly*, **17** (May), pp. 21–27.

Harris, J. E. and Sunderland, A. (1981). Effects of age and instructions on an everyday memory questionnaire. Paper presented to the British Psychological Society Cognitive Psychology Section Conference on Memory, Plymouth.

Harris, J. E. and Wilkins, A. J. (1982). Remembering to do things: a theoretical framework and an illustrative experiment. *Human Learning*, **1**, 123–136.

Kantor, J. R. and Smith, N. W. (1975). *The Science of Psychology: An Interbehavioral Survey*. Principia Press, Chicago.

Kellogg, E. R. (1929). Duration and effects of post-hypnotic suggestions. *Journal of Experimental Psychology*, **12**, 502–514.

Kreutzer, M. A., Leonard, C. and Flavell, J. H. (1975). An interview study of children's knowledge about memory. *Monographs of the Society for Research in Child Development*, **40** (1, Serial No. 159).

Levy, R. L. (1977). Relationship of an overt commitment to task compliance in behavior therapy. *Journal of Behavior Therapy and Experimental Psychiatry*, **8**, 25–29.

Levy, R. L. and Clark, H. (1980). The use of an overt commitment to enhance compliance: a cautionary note. *Journal of Behavior Therapy and Experimental Psychiatry*, **11**, 105–107.

Levy, R. L. and Loftus, G. R. (1984). Compliance and memory. *In* "Everyday Memory, Actions and Absent-Mindedness" (J. E. Harris and P. E. Morris, eds), Academic Press, London, Orlando and New York.

Levy, R. L., Yamashita, D. and Pow, G. (1979). The relationship of an overt commitment to the frequency and speed of compliance with symptom reporting. *Medical Care*, **17**, 281–284.

Ley, P. (1978). Memory for medical information. *In* "Practical Aspects of Memory" (M. M. Gruneberg, P. E. Morris and R. N. Sykes, eds), Academic Press, London, and New York.

Loftus, E. F. (1971). Memory for intentions. *Psychonomic Science*, **23**, 315–316.

Lowe, C. F. (1979). Determinants of human operant behaviour. *In* "Advances in Analysis of Behaviour, Vol. 1: Reinforcement and the Organization of Behaviour" (M. D. Zeiler and P. Harzem, eds), Wiley, Chichester.

Malcolm, N. A. (1977). "Memory and Mind", Cornell University Press, Ithaca, N.Y.

McKenna, F. P. (1981). Unpublished project report. MRC Applied Psychology Unit, Cambridge.

Meacham, J. A. (1982). A note on remembering to execute planned actions. *Journal of Applied Developmental Psychology*, **3**, 121–133.

Meacham, J. A. and Colombo, J. A. (1980). External retrieval cues facilitate prospective remembering in children. *Journal of Educational Research*, **73**, 299–301.

Meacham, J. A. and Dumitru, J. (1976). Prospective remembering and external retrieval cues. *JSAS Catalog of Selected Documents in Psychology*, **6**, No. 65 (Ms. No. 1284). Also ERIC Document Reproduction Service No. 119 859.

Meacham, J. A. and Kushner, S. (1980). Anxiety, prospective remembering, and performance of planned actions. *Journal of General Psychology*, **103**, 203–209.

Meacham, J. A. and Leiman, B. (1975). Remembering to perform future actions. Paper presented at the meeting of the American Psychological Association, Chicago, September. Also in U. Neisser (ed.) (1982), "Memory Observed: Remembering in Natural Contexts", W. H. Freeman and Company, San Francisco.

Meacham, J. A. and Singer, J. (1977). Incentive in prospective remembering. *Journal of Psychology*, **97**, 191–197.

Miller, G. A., Galanter, E. and Pribram, K. H. (1960). "Plans and the Structure of Behavior", Holt, Rinehart and Winston, New York.

Morris, P. E. (1979). Strategies for learning and recall. *In* "Applied Problems in Memory" (M. M. Gruneberg and P. E. Morris eds), Academic Press, London and New York.

Moscovitch, M. (1982). A neuropsychological approach to memory and perception in normal and pathological aging. *In* "Aging and Cognitive Processes" (F. I. M. Craik and S. Trehub, eds), Plenum Press, New York.

Moscovitch, M. (personal communications). 15 January 1981 and 1 April 1982.

Munsat, S. (1966). "The Concept of Memory", Random House, New York.

Neisser, U. (1982). "Memory Observed: Remembering in Natural Contexts", W. H. Freeman and Company, San Francisco.

Orne, M. T. (1970). Hypnosis, motivation, and the ecological validity of the psychological experiment. In "Nebraska Symposium on Motivation Vol. 18" (W. J. Arnold and M. M. Page, eds), University of Nebraska Press, Lincoln.

Pajurkova, E. M. and Wilkins, A. J. (1983). Prospective remembering in patients with unilateral temporal or frontal lobectomies. Paper presented at the Sixth European Conference of the International Neuropsychological Society, Lisbon.

Patten, E. F. (1930). The duration of post-hypnotic suggestion. *Journal of Abnormal and Social Psychology*, **25**, 319–334.

Perlmutter, M. (1978). What is memory aging the aging of? *Developmental Psychology*, **14**, 330–345.

Reason, J. T. (1975). How did I come to do that? *New Behaviour*, 24 April, pp. 10–13.

Reason, J. T. (1976). Absent minds. *New Society*, 4 November, pp. 224–245.

Reason, J. T. (1977). Skill and error in everyday life. In "Adult Learning: Psychological Research and Applications" (M. Howe, ed.), Wiley, London.

Reason, J. T. (1979). Actions not as planned: the price of automation. In "Aspects of Consciousness, Vol. 1" (G. Underwood and R. Stevens, eds), Academic Press, London, and New York.

Reason, J. T. (1984). Absent-mindedness and cognitive control. In "Everyday Memory, Actions and Absent-Mindedness" (J. E. Harris and P. E. Morris, eds), Academic Press, London, Orlando and New York.

Reed, G. (1979). Everyday anomalies of recall and recognition. In "Functional Disorders of Memory" (J. F. Kihlstrom and F. J. Evans, eds), Lawrence Erlbaum Associates, Hillsdale, N.J.

Sackett, D. L. and Haynes, R. B. (1976). "Compliance with Therapeutic Regimens", Johns Hopkins University Press, Baltimore.

Schonfield, A. E. D. and Stones, M. J. (1979). Remembering and aging. In "Functional Disorders of Memory" (J. F. K. Kihlstrom and F. J. Evans, eds), Lawrence Erlbaum Associates, Hillsdale, N.J.

Wagstaff, G. F. (1981). "Hypnosis, Compliance and Belief", Harvester Press, Brighton.

Welford, A. T. (1958). "Ageing and Human Skill", Oxford University Press, London.

Wilkins, A. J. (1976). A failure to demonstrate effects of the "retention interval" in prospective memory. Unpublished manuscript.

Wilkins, A. J. (1979). Remembering to remember. Paper presented at Department of Experimental Psychology, Cambridge University.

Wilkins, A. J. and Baddeley, A. D. (1978). Remembering to recall in everyday life: an approach to absent-mindedness. In "Practical Aspects of Memory" (M. M. Gruneberg, P. E. Morris and R. N. Sykes, eds), Academic Press, London, and New York.

6

Compliance and Memory

R. L. Levy and G. R. Loftus

I. INTRODUCTION TO COMPLIANCE

One of us has defined compliance elsewhere as "carrying out an assignment in the way described by the assignment giver(s)" and has added that "ideal compliance would then mean carrying out the assignment at the time, in the place, and in the manner prescribed" (Shelton and Levy, 1981, p. 37). We concern ourselves here with the special situation in which (a) a person is requested to carry out some assignment after a delay in time and (b) the assignment giver is not present at the time of the required action.

This kind of situation differs from that typically required in laboratory research where the subject is cued by the experimenter to remember something. Indeed, some research has already demonstrated that remembering to do something is a different memory phenomenon than memory as measured by conventional verbal test (Wilkins and Baddeley, 1978). This point is made elsewhere in this book (Harris, 1984 Chapter 5). Very little research has been carried out on uncued remembering relative to cued remembering, yet uncued remembering is required all the time in everyday life. We constantly ask colleagues, friends and family members to do things. Clinical psychologists and social workers frequently emphasize activities the client should perform such as contacting someone for employment, monitoring daily behaviour reading, or certain educational material.

Throughout this paper we shall concentrate our illustrations on the medical profession. The medical profession is a sphere in which compliance is critical, since the vast majority of medical patients need to participate actively in their treatment programme in order that the treatment be effective. Patients need to take pills, monitor bodily functions, rest and perform a host of other activities in response to health requirements. Some of these regimens can be extremely complex. Consider, as an example, the diabetic, who may need to eat a prescribed diet at regular times throughout the day. Urine and/or blood glucose levels may need to be monitored as many as four times each day, and the results recorded in a record book. If glucose levels so indicate, the patient may need to adjust insulin according to a specified formula. Exercise and food also may need to be altered. In short, the patient is required to remember to perform a wide variety of behaviours throughout the day.

The next three sections are organized as follows. First, we describe the rather scanty research that is directly concerned with the relationship between memory and compliance. Second, we describe the much more extensive literature on factors that affect compliance *per se*. We suggest that some or all of these factors may have their effects on compliance through mediating memory factors; however, research on compliance has typically not been carried out with memory factors in mind, and memory mediation hypotheses must therefore remain the provence of the proverbial future research. Finally, we offer a mathematical framework within which the relationship between memory and compliance might potentially be couched. Such a framework may prove useful for organizing such future research.

II. FORGETTING AND NON-COMPLIANCE

There are three necessary requirements for compliance. First, one must remember that something is to be done at a particular time. Second, one must remember what the thing is. And third, one must carry out the action. Failure of any of those requirements will result in failure to comply. Failure of either of the first two requirements constitutes forgetting of one sort or another and will be the focus of this section.

There is a body of literature that implicates forgetting as an important source of non-compliance. Haynes *et al.* (1979) reported several studies in which non-complying patients, interviewed some time after compliance was to have occurred, reported forgetting as the reason for their failure. A major problem with these studies, however, is the validity of self-report data. It is quite likely that saying "I forgot" is socially more acceptable as a reason for missing an appointment than saying "I didn't feel I had anything to gain by coming", or "I couldn't be bothered". Additionally, patients may not accurately recall what was going on at the time compliance was to have occurred.

More convincing evidence regarding the role of forgetting in compliance comes from studies that measure remembering independent of compliance. In such a study, the patient is asked to recall his or her instructions immediately after the instructions have been provided. Ley (1979), in the most comprehensive review of the work of this area, has pointed out that much of the research in compliance and memory has attempted to determine the correlates of forgetting. In his review, he concludes that:

(1) patients fail to recall much of what they are told;
(2) the number of statements not recalled is a linear function of the number presented;
(3) ageing is not consistently related to recall;

(4) intelligence is not related to recall;
(5) medical knowledge is related to recall; with greater knowledge associated with greater compliance
(6) anxiety is related to recall in a curvilinear fashion with intermediate levels of anxiety leading to optimal recall. Recall of medical information can also be manipulated. Recall was good in one study where information was placed first and its importance stressed (Ley, 1972). Amount of information recalled was also affected by such variables as word and sentence length, categorization of interview topics, degree of ·repetition (although these findings are not consistent) and the degree to which advice was couched in concrete *vs* abstract or specific rather than general language (Ley, 1979).

Although these manipulations affected compliance (Ley *et al.*, 1976; Ley, 1977, 1978), it is not clear whether the effect was mediated by memory factors or by some other mechanism, such as perceived value of complying or comprehension of the task, or by some combination of factors. For example, tasks perceived as important might be remembered more frequently and thus be complied with more often. However, without supporting data that bore specifically on remembering under varying conditions at the time compliance was to occur, it is inappropriate to assume that compliance was enhanced by memory in these particular studies.

In a paradigm that examines memory factors more directly, subjects are supplied with memory aids. Reminding subjects of their assignment provides a technique for isolating memory factors that potentially affect compliance. In some experiments, for example, the effects of reminders on appointment keeping have been assessed. Shepard and Moseley (1976) and Gates and Colborn (1976) compared compliance rates for subjects who received mail or phone reminders to compliance rates for control subjects who received no reminders. Both types of reminders improved the appointment-keeping rates for these subjects over the rates for subjects in the control condition. In the Shepard and Moseley study, subjects in the mailed reminder group kept 56% of their appointments (n = 198); those in the telephone reminder kept 61.8% (n = 377); and the controls kept 43.3% (n = 367). Data were also collected for subjects without telephones: here, the mail-reminder group had a 50% rate (n = 34) *vs* 33.3% (n = 63) for the no-reminder controls. In the Gates and Colborn study, a letter reminder produced 83.7% compliance (n = 92), a telephone reminder resulted in 80% compliance (n = 80), while the no-reminder group only kept 55% of its appointments (n = 100).

Other research has similarly examined the joint effects of cueing and the type of cue. Nazarian *et al.* (1974) compared the effect of two types of reminder cards on appointment keeping for appointments made 12 days to eight weeks in advance. Both cards indicated the date and time of the appointment, and one card also noted the physician or nurse, and the reason for appointment. No difference in compliance was found with the type of card that was used. The appointment keeping rates for these groups were 61%

and 67% (n = 219 and n = 216, respectively). However, both groups receiving cards had a significantly higher appointment-keeping rate than the control group at 48% (n = 228). The reminders also had greater effect as the interval between appointments increased.

In a study by Levy and Claravell (1977), the effect of reminders which patients received two days before their appointments on compliance was assessed for appointment intervals as low as three days. This study, together with that of Nazarian et al. (1974) allows a comparison of the effect of reminders over a wide range of interval periods. In the Levy and Claravall study, 68.2% of the patients with appointments more than 15 days away (n = 22) who received a call complied. Of the patients who did not receive the call (n = 32), 37.5% complied. In the group with appointments 14 or fewer days away, compliance in the called group (n = 20) was 60%, vs 54% in the no-call group (n = 24). A significant outcome worth noting here is the likely decrease of medical staff, inconvenience and cost resulting from the increase in compliance rates between those patients receiving reminders in the longer interval group.

Some studies have failed to show that reminders enhance appointment-keeping rates (Barkin and Duncan, 1975; Kidd and Euphrat, 1971; Krause, 1966). In a review of this literature, Frankel and Hovell (1978) suggested that the negative results may be due to variations in the clinics or in the selection of patients to be reminded (for example, Kidd and Euphrat, 1971, only look at subjects who previously failed). Of course, these findings may also be due to low statistical power or poor designs.

In one laboratory experiment, E. Loftus (1971) examined the joint effect of cueing and retention interval on compliance. In this experiment, subjects were asked either five or 15 general-interest, survey questions. Prior to being asked the questions, each subject was asked to tell the experimenter the name of the state in which he or she was born, but was cautioned to delay providing this information until after all the survey questions had been asked. In addition, half of the subjects were provided a cue (". . . the last question will be about the Black Panthers . . .") whereas the other half were not provided a cue. The probability of compliance (remembering to report the birth information) was higher with fewer survey questions (means of .68 and .54 with five and 15 questions, respectively) and was higher when a cue was provided (means of .69 and .53 in the cue and no-cue conditions respectively). In this experiment, only very short retention intervals were used (of the order of 10–15 min), but the data are at least suggestive of the general importance of the standard memory factors of retention interval and memory cues as determinants of compliance.

Despite this one laboratory study, little is known about cues, including their timing (even time of day may be relevant: see Folkard, 1979), content and the effects of repetition on cueing (see Harris's Chapter 5 of this volume for a further discussion on how different types of cues may affect compliance). Beyond research in which cueing is manipulated, we are still left with little information regarding the mediating role of memory on compliance. The memory researcher interested in compliance has several factors to consider which we cover in the next section. The effects of these factors on compliance may, as noted earlier, be mediated at least to some degree by their effects on such memory factors as depth of initial encoding (Craik and Lockhart, 1972), amount of rehearsal (Rundus, 1969) or encoding specificity (Tulving and Thomson, 1973).

III. BEYOND REMINDING: OTHER COMPLIANCE ENHANCERS

Shelton and Levy (1981) provided three categories of reasons for non-compliance. First, the individual may not have the skills or knowledge to comply. Second, compliance may not be supported by the individual's belief system. A medical patient, for example, who does not believe in the value of the to-be-complied with behaviour, or who does not believe in the competency of the assignment giver may well fail to comply. Third, compliance may fail if it were likely to be associated with aversive events such as disrupting the person's regular schedule or annoying a spouse.

These concerns and the compliance literature suggest several compliance enhancement strategies. Cueing has already been discussed; nine others are discussed below. These strategies may affect compliance directly or compliance may be enhanced, using these strategies, through the mediation of memory. As with the series of studies by Ley mentioned earlier, these studies were not designed to determine which was the case.

A. Specificity

Studies in the medical literature indicate considerable variation in interpretation of instructions regarding timing and sequencing of to-be-complied-with behaviours such as medication taking (Malahy, 1966). In one study, for example, Mazzulo et al. (1974) found that patients had very different interpretations of a simple instruction such as "take four times a day". Written instructions specifying the desired behaviour in detail may decrease the variance in interpretation and may also serve as cues (Leventhal, 1967; Thomas and Carter, 1971) therefore enhancing the likelihood of compliance.

Understanding of instructions has been shown to be related to compliance (Kincey, et al., 1975; Ley et al., 1976; Ley et al., 1976), and a substantial amount of research indicates that specific instructions are more likely to be followed than less specific instructions (Doster, 1972; Kanfer, et al., 1974; Liebert et al., 1969; Rappaport et al., 1973; Svarstad, 1976). The success of contracting procedures (Steckel and Swain, 1977) may also be taken as evidence of the value of explicitness, since, to meet all contingencies, contracts require clear and specific descriptions of the required behaviour.

B. Skill training

A substantial body of research has demonstrated that use of participant modelling and behaviour rehearsal enhances learning behaviour (Bandura, 1969; Lewis, 1974; McFall and Marston, 1970). Feedback and reinforcement during practice sessions may also augment the learning experience (Locke et al., 1978; Leitenberg, 1975). In medical programmes, supervised practice of assigned tasks also has been used as a compliance enhancer (Bowen et al., 1961).

C. Reinforcements

The systematic application of rewards, such as money or praise has been shown to alter behaviour in a variety of settings. For example, positive reinforcement has been incorporated into several weight-treatment programmes. Mahoney et al. (1973) found that positive reinforcement had more effect than punishment and self-monitoring in their weight-reduction programme, and Agras et al. (1974) showed the power of positive reinforcement in the treatment of anorexia nervosa. In an antihypertension programme, Haynes et al. (1976) combined positive reinforcement with monitoring, home visiting, and tailoring a regimen to a client's daily activities to increase compliance in medication taking. In the area of dentistry, Reiss et al. (1976) demonstrated that a monetary incentive increased the number of parents who brought their children in for dental care, and Iwata and Becksfort (1978) demonstrated that home dental care improved when monetary reinforcement was used.

Data also exist attesting to the value of a contract technique. Eyberg and Johnson (1974) demonstrated the effect of promising rewards in advance, and then delivering such rewards contingent on successful performance. Experimentation in other clinical areas has supported the use of written contracts (Kanfer et al., 1974), and many of the positive reinforcement programmes in obesity have also been based on a contract structure (Harris and Bruner, 1971; Leon, 1976; Mann, 1972).

Many treatment programmes (Becker and Green, 1975; Blackwell, 1979; Brownlee, 1978; Christensen, 1978; Stokols, 1975; Stuart and Davis, 1972) utilize mediators existing in the client's natural environment for both monitoring and delivering reinforcement. For example, Stuart and Davis (1972) suggested that spouses of overweight persons need to be involved throughout any weight reduction programme. Several studies also demonstrate a relationship between some measure of "social support" and compliance (Caplan et al., 1976; Earp and Ory, 1979; Haynes, 1976; Kar, 1977; Mahoney and Mahoney, 1976; Nessman et al., in press). Unfortunately, it is difficult to draw conclusions from this research, as "social support" is often defined in different ways across studies. For example, it may simply mean having a support system in the home, or it might mean having subjects report that their spouse supported them in the treatment programme in which they participated (Levy, 1983).

There are also experimental studies that actually manipulate some form of social support to determine its effect on compliance. In two reports on a weight reduction programme and its follow-up results, Israel and Saccone (1979) and Saccone and Israel (1978) found that monetary reinforcement delivered by spouse was more effective than experimenter delivered reinforcement for producing and maintaining weight loss. Zitter and Freemouw (1978) investigated whether subjects complied more if consequences were delivered to them or to a partner (whom they had chosen). Subjects in one group received a reward for compliance. Subjects in a second group lost money if their partner did not lose weight. Weight was kept off more when subjects received their own reward for compliance than when their partner received it. The authors suggested that partners may actually have mediated against compliance. Attention, for example, may actually have reinforced non-compliance, as partners might talk to each other about how nice it might be to eat, and so on.

Environmental mediators have been used in several programmes. Dapcich-Miura and Hovell (1979) sued a multiple baseline/reversal single-subject experimental design to demonstrate that a token reinforcement contingently administered by the subject's granddaughter could be used to increase juice and medication consumption and walking. Tokens were redeemable for the subject's dinner selection. Lowe and Lutzker (1979) also used a multiple baseline design to demonstrate that a programme using points as rewards (which could then be redeemed for items such as games, etc.) was effective in motivating a nine-year-old female diabetic to comply with dieting, urine-testing, and foot-care regimens. The child's mother both monitored compliance and delivered prompts and reinforcement.

In another study Brownell et al. (1978) compared three groups of subjects in training for weight reduction. Twenty-nine subjects with co-operative spouses (i.e. spouses who agreed to participate in the programme) were placed in either an individual training group (where subjects alone participated) or a couples-training group where spouses took part in the training along with the subjects. Subjects with an unco-operative spouse (those who refused to participate) were placed in another contrast group where the subjects received training but the spouses did not. This contrast group provided controls for possible confounding due to spouse co-operation. In the couples training group, spouses were present at all meetings and were given the Partner's Weight Reduction Manual (Brownell, 1975). They also were instructed in specific behaviours such as reinforcement, mutual monitoring, and stimulus control. After six months, subjects in the couples-training group had done significantly better than the subjects in the other two groups, with a mean weight loss of 29.6 lbs as compared to 19.4 lbs in the no training, co-operative spouse group and 15.1 pounds in the non-co-operative spouse group (but see Wilson and Brownell, 1978, for a failure to replicate this finding).

This study had two strengths. First, the authors always used the same type of social support (the spouse). Second, this study provided the couples with several behavioural suggestions and a monitoring system that the experimenter could use to determine if the suggestions were met.

D. Shaping

Three experiments have strongly supported the effectiveness of what has come to be known as the "foot-in-the-door" effect. In two experiments, Freedman and Fraser (1966) showed that suburban housewives were more likely to submit to a major request (such as allowing a large unattractive billboard to be placed on their front lawn, or allowing a survey team to enter their homes and catalogue their household produces) if they had first complied with a simple request like signing an innocuous petition, answering a few survey questions, or placing a sign in the window. Lepper (1973) extended the generality of this effect in an experiment on 7-year-old children's ability to resist temptation: children who resisted the temptation to play with an attractive toy under minimal-threat conditions resisted the temptation to cheat in a game played three weeks later more than children who were not exposed to the initial situation or who were exposed to it under high-threat conditions. Lepper stressed the importance of the initial compliance being obtained under relatively low-demand conditions. Minimal initial demand may be related to one of the processes involved in creating cognitive commitment. If the client is an active participant in determining the therapeutic activities rather than a respondent to heavy demands from the therapist, the chances for compliance are increased.

E. Public commitment

Levy has conducted a series of experiments to test the effect of public commitment on compliance. In the first (Levy, 1977), clients in an outpatient behaviour therapy setting were asked to phone the therapist in a few days to set up a subsequent appointment. Subjects in a "verbal commitment" condition, given the assignment and asked if they would comply, indicated their willingness with a verbal statement and a head nod. Subjects in a second condition (the "verbal and written commitment" group) were asked to sign a form indicating that they would comply, in addition to providing verbal assurance. Subjects in the control condition were merely given the assignment. Subjects complied more in the commitment conditions than the control condition, with the highest compliance rates in the verbal and written commitment condition. (Compliance in the verbal and written condition = 76.9%, verbal alone = 50% and no commitment = 36.8% χ^2 = 5.007, df = 2, p <.08). In a second study (Levy et al. 1979), patients reporting for a flu inoculation were asked to return a postcard within 48 h that indicated whether they were experiencing any symptoms. Experimental subjects again were asked to indicate verbally (or by nodding) their intention to comply. Again, experimental subjects returned more cards (72.9% to 59.4%; $\chi^2 = 13.1$, df = 1, p<.01) and at a faster rate (6.9 days to 7.9 days; t = 3.197, df = 444, p<.001.) than control subjects. The rate of return includes time in post which may be estimated at 2 or 3 days thus making the one day time saving proportionately more significant.

In a final study (Levy and Clark, 1980), however, the effect of a public commitment was not replicated. Subjects given a reappointment time and randomly placed in a commitment experimental or a no-commitment control condition were compared on appointment keeping rates. No differences between the experimental and control conditions were found (62.3% of the experimental, N = 61, and 54.8% of the controls, N = 62 complied; $\chi^2 = .701$, df = 1, N.S.). They hypothesized that an overt commitment may be sufficient to promote some behaviour change, but may not have been enough to affect compliance rates in situations when the "cost" of the behaviour was high.

Wurtele *et al.* (1980) also found that both verbal and verbal plus written commitment resulted in increased compliance. Patient return rate for a skintest reading during a TB detection drive was the major dependent variable. In a subsequent replication of the commitment condition, however, Roberts *et al.* (1981) were unable to show the effect of various commitment conditions on return rates in a TB detection drive. Since the procedure seems, at times, to bring about a desirable outcome at a low cost, it seems that its use is merited even with these mixed research findings. However, knowledge about the specific variables controlling these inconsistent findings will have to wait for further research. The cost of carrying out the behaviour, or the makeup of the subject population, or other factors may all interact with the effects of commitment.

F. Private commitment

The Health Belief Model, developed by Rosenstock (1966), outlined several areas of patient beliefs that are thought to affect compliance with medical regimens. Several studies have demonstrated relationships between health beliefs and medical compliance, that might be applicable in the therapy situation (Becker and Maiman, 1975; Maiman and Becker, 1974; Maiman *et al.*, 1977). Included in health beliefs are perceptions about one's own sense of control, the priority one puts on health in one's life, the perceived severity of an illness, and the cues for action that are available to the client. Again, although several studies support the Health Belief Model, a large number have not found relationships between compliance and health beliefs (Haynes *et al.*, 1979). Variation across situations may be a critical factor here.

Several writers in the behaviour therapy literature have discussed the role of expectation in treatment (e.g. Wilson and Evans, 1972). Expectations, as these authors point out, may keep clients active participants in treatment during the early, difficult stages of the therapeutic process. Finally, it appears that clients who do not get what they expect to get in therapy are less likely to be compliant with therapeutic recommendations (Davis, 1968; Francis *et al.*, 1969).

Some studies have supported the value of client participation in decision making. Kanfer and Grimm (1978) found that subjects who were given a choice of several behavioural methods designed to increase reading performance did significantly better than those who were given no choice. Lovitt and Curtiss (1969) found that children showed higher rate of academic behaviours, such as studying, when they were allowed to participate in their own treatment plan. A similar study by Brigham and Bushell (1972) revealed that children would work to earn control over their own rewards. In this particular study, the authors found that individual response rates were higher even when the self-imposed reinforcement conditions were identical to those imposed by a teacher. Likewise, Phillips (1966) was able to demonstrate that clients who helped in the design of their own treatment were more motivated to change.

Schulman (1979) developed a measure of Active Patient Orientation (APO) that determined the extent to which patients perceived themselves to be "addressed as active participants, involved in therapeutic planning and equipped to carry out self-care activities". High APO was associated with greater blood pressure control, adherence, and understanding, and fewer medication errors. Since contracts, as a tool for establishing a contingency relationship, may also be effective because they give patients an opportunity to discuss treatment options and participate in treatment decision, it is not surprising that patients assigned to a contracting group in a larger study showed higher APO scores. Furthermore, from a memory perspective, one might consider that active participation may lead to more or deeper processing, both of the fact that various things must be remembered and of what those things are.

G. Cognitive rehearsal

Several studies have demonstrated that cognitive rehearsal improves targeted behaviours. In one study Nesse and Nelson (1977) used between-session rehearsals of covert modelling scenes to examine the effectiveness of several variations of covert modelling on cigarette smoking reduction. In covert modelling, the client is asked to imagine a competent model engaging in the behaviours he or she wishes to develop. In this particular study subjects were asked to imagine themselves feeling an urge to smoke, making an alternative non-smoking response, and then receiving a favourable consequence for not smoking. This study found that covert rehearsal combined with self-reinforcement was more effective than covert rehearsal alone in reducing cigarette smoking.

During the Twelfth Winter Olympics, Suinn (1977) worked with the athletes of the United States' cross-country skiing and biathlon teams. Suinn developed a package composed of his Visual Motor Behavior Rehearsal, thought stopping, and covert positive reinforcement to counteract pain sensations. The athletes' self-report indicated that this behavioural-cognitive treatment package improved their performance. However, because of the lack of objective controls, the conclusions of this research should be taken as suggestive rather than definite.

Other research has confirmed the importance of using covert rehearsal as a means of enhancing subject behaviours outside the therapeutic session. For example, this technique has been shown to be effective in reducing fear (Cautela et al., 1974; Kazdin, 1973, 1974a, 1974b, 1974c), in increasing assertive behaviour (Kazdin, 1974d, 1975, 1976a, 1976b), and in decreasing alcoholic and obsessive-compulsive behaviour (Hay et al., 1977).

H. Reduction of negative consequences for compliances

The basis for the suggestion that compliance will be enhanced if negative consequences for compliance are reduced is derived primarily from client self-report data. Self reports have identified various barriers to compliance as reasons for not complying. These barriers include finances (Alpert, 1964; Caldwell et al., 1970), transportation (Abernathy, 1976; Alpert, 1964), and employment (Abernathy, 1976). However, studies utilizing experimental manipulations to test the effect of these reasons have been less than overwhelming. In one of the few, Sackett et al. (1975) found no increase in compliance when client treatment centres were located on the worksite as opposed to some distance from it. Further experimental work is needed to test their findings in a variety of settings with different patient populations.

Support for enhancing compliance by counteracting potential punishers is derived from the almost self-evident position that punished behaviour is likely to decrease. Again, a vast number of studies support this position. Clients complain of punishment following assertive responses of cite side-effects as another reason for non-compliance with medical regimens (Ballweg and McCorquodale, 1974; Caldwell et al., 1970). Exactly how much reinforcement, of what kind, and in what situations can offset punishment has yet to be investigated.

The medical literature also provides some data supporting the idea that fitting a regiment into a client's daily activities, or "tailoring" increases compliance. One effect of tailoring may be the reduction of undesirable disruptions in the patient's life and hence the reduction of potential negative consequences for complying (Fink, 1976; Haynes et al., 1976; Logan et al., in press).

I. Monitoring

Monitoring has been used extensively as a component of successful treatment programmes in several studies in both therapy and medicine. Books by Ciminero et al. (1977), Cone and Hawkins (1977), Haynes (1978), Haynes and Wilson (1979), and Keefe et al. (1978), as well as the journals *Behavioral Assessment* and the *Journal of Behavioral Assessment*, provide documentation of its use. For example, self-monitoring has been used in studies for medication taking (Carnahan and Nugent, 1975; Deberry et al., 1975; Epstein and Masek, 1978; Haynes et al., 1976; Moulding, 1961) and in obesity treatment programmes (Bellack, 1976; Kingsley and Shapiro, 1977).

Other examples of monitoring by others to enhance compliance have been reported in both the behaviour therapy and medical literature. All of the non-observational methods of assessment of compliance in medicine, such as pill counts, prescription filling, blood and urinary levels and therapeutic outcomes are examples of ways health care providers have monitored compliance (Gordis, 1979). Clinician monitoring of blood pressure, for example, has been a part of some strategies to enhance compliance with antihypertension regimens (Logan et al., in press; McKenney et al., 1973; Takala et al., 1979). In addition, direct observation of desirable behaviours has been reported in the behaviour therapy literature for eating (Epstein and Martin, 1977), drinking (Miller, 1978), and sexual behaviours (Zeiss, 1978), using colleagues, friends or relatives, and spouses, respectively. While many studies have incorporated monitoring into an intervention package or investigated the effect of monitoring as an intervention itself, more research is needed on the implementation of monitoring to enhance compliance and the variables that influence the effects of monitoring on compliance.

IV. IMPLICATIONS FOR MEMORY RESEARCH: AN INTEGRATING FRAMEWORK

If memory researchers wish to make contributions to compliance enhancement, several features must be included in their research. First, experimental settings must be constructed in ways that parallel everyday demands. Specifically, unlike the conventional verbal learning task, subjects should be asked to comply in a situation where the experimenter is not present to cue compliance and where other factors may influence compliance.

Second, in designing studies attention must be paid to separating out compliance due to remembering and compliance due to other factors. For example, a public commitment has often been shown to enhance compliance. Is this because a public commitment enhances recallability or because a public commitment exposes one to public consequences for non-compliance, or because of some other as yet unknown feature? Does an incentive work because someone is more likely to remember something for which they are rewarded, or does it work simply because of the basic behavioural principle that positive reinforcement increases behaviour that it follows? Or are both principles operating, the latter being mediated by the former? Perhaps an incentive works because of a person's increased willingness to comply *given that* the person has remembered what to do.

Earlier, we noted that three events are necessary if compliance is to occur: first, the person must self-generate a cue; that is, he or she must remember at some given time that there is something to be remembered. Second, the person must remember what is to be done. And third, the person must carry out the required action as a function of a variety of reasons discussed before. We formalize these notions as follows. Let us first make the following definitions.

(1) Let G be the probability that a cue that some action need be carried out is generated at the proper time.

(2) Let R be the probability that the action itself is remembered, given that the cue is successfully generated.

(3) Let A be the probability that the action is actually carried out given that the cue is generated and the action remembered.

Since R and A are defined to be conditional probabilities, it follows that the probabilities of compliance, C is

$$C = RGA$$

Traditional studies in memory have typically been concerned with the probability that we have defined as R: that is, the probability of remembering something given some cue. Many researchers, starting with Ebbinghaus (1885) have assumed forgetting to be exponential over the time, t, between initial learning and test, that is

$$R = e^{-k_1 t}$$

Such a function would follow from the reasonable assumption that information in memory, like the contents of many other physical systems is lost at a rate that is proportional to the amount remaining in the system. It likewise seems reasonable to assume that G declines exponentially over time, that is,

$$G = e^{-k_2 t}$$

There is, however, no reason to expect that A would change over time. Thus, we can write the equation for compliance probability as,

$$C = e^{-k_1 t} e^{-k_2 t} A \tag{1}$$

This simple model could be quite useful in predicting compliance in a variety of situations, as well as providing a framework for organizing research in the area of memory and compliance. At present, however, the model is speculative and untested. We suggest the following tests and applications.

(1) Isolation of G, R and A. Experimental techniques to isolate the three principal components of the model readily suggest themselves. For instance, in a laboratory setting, A could be set to 1.0 by using compliant subjects. This would allow examination of G (by, for example, having the subject telephone an experimenter or otherwise record at a specified time, that he or she was supposed to carry out some action) and of R (using traditional memory techniques such as asking the subject at various times what it is that he or she is supposed to be doing at that time).

(2) The exponential model. Testing the assumed exponential decay of the

components may easily be done by plotting the logarithm of compliance probability as a function of the retention interval, t, since the compliance instructions were administered. Linear functions should result, since from Equation 1,

$$\text{Log } C = -(k_1 + k_2)t + \log A$$

(3) Use of the framework. Given this framework, the factors listed above, known to affect compliance (e.g., cognitive rehearsal, commitment) could be examined in terms of which components of the system they affect.

V. CONCLUSIONS

In 1967, Jack Adams wrote one of the first books on modern conceptions of human memory. The cover of Adams's book depicted a finger with a string tied around it. The odd thing about this cover was that it represented a type of memory, memory for intentions, about which virtually no research had been done and to which Adams himself did not devote a single word. Now, 15 years later, very little has changed. Despite the widespread prevalence and importance of this type of memory (the origins of the string-around-the-finger technique are lost in the mists of antiquity, but probably go back to the invention of string) psychologists have mysteriously shunned it as a topic of research. We hope that Harris's Chapter 5 and our attempted integration of memory and compliance research, along with the framework that we have offered, might provide at least a start at rectifying this unfortunate and puzzling state of affairs.

Note

Preparation of this chapter was supported in part by NIH Grant No. 1F33-HL06506 and NSF Grant BNS79-06522.

REFERENCES

Abernathy, J. D. (1976). The problem of non-compliance in long-term antihypertensive therapy. *Drugs*, **11**, 86–90.

Adams, J. (1967). "Human Memory", McGraw-Hill, New York.

Agras, W. S., Barlow, D. H., Chapin, H. N., Abel, G. C. and Leitenberg, H. (1974). Behavior modification of anorexia nervosa. *Archives of General Psychiatry*, **30**, 279–286.

Alpert, J. J. (1964). Broken appointments. *Pediatrics*, **34**, 127–132.

Ballweg, J. A. and McCorquodale, D. W. (1974). Family planning method change and dropouts in the Phillippines. *Social Biology*, **21**, 88–95.

Bandura, A. (1969). *Principles of Behavior Modification*. Rinehart & Winston, New York.

Barkin, R. M. and Duncan, R. (1975). Broken appointments: Questions, not answers. *Pediatrics*, **55**, 747–748.

Becker, M. H. and Green, L. W. (1975). A family approach to compliance with medical treatment. *International Journal of Health Education*, **18**, 175–182.

Becker, M. H. and Maiman, L. A. (1975). Sociobehavioral determinants of compliance with health and medical care recommendations. *Medical Care*, **13**, 10–24.

Bellack, A. S. (1976). A comparison of self-reinforcement and self-monitoring in a weight reduction program. *Behavior Therapy*, **7**, 68–75.

Blackwell, B. (1979). Treatment adherence: A contemporary overview. *Psychosomatics*, **20**, 27–35.

Bowen, R. G., Rich, R. and Schlatfeldt, R. M. (1961). Effects of organized instruction for patients with the diagnosis of diabetes mellitus. *Nursing Research*, **10**, 151–155.

Brigham, G. and Bushell, D. (1972). Notes on autonomous environments: Student-selected versus teacher-selected rewards. Unpublished manuscript, Brown University.

Brownell, K. D. (1975). Partner's weight control manual. Unpublished manuscript, University of Kansas.

Brownell, K. D., Heckerman, C. L., Westlake, R. J., Hayes, S. C. and Monti, P. M. (1978). The effects of couples training and partner cooperativeness in the behavioral treatment of obesity. *Behaviour Research and Therapy*, **16**, 323–333.

Brownlee, A. (1978). The family and health care: Explorations in cross-cultural settings. *Social Work in Health Care*, **4**, 179–198.

Caldwell, J. R., Cobb, S., Dowling, M. D. and DeJongh, D. (1970). The dropout problem in antihypertensive therapy. *Journal of Chronic Diseases*, **22**, 579–592.

Caplan, R. D., Robinson, S. A. R., French, J. R. P., Caldwell, J. R. and Shinn, M. (1976). "Adhering to medical regimen: Pilot experiments in patient education and social support", University of Michigan Press, Ann Arbor, Michigan.

Carnahan, J. E. and Nugent, C. A. (1975). The effects of self-monitoring by patients on the control of hypertension. *American Journal of Medical Sciences*, **269**, 69–73.

Cautela, J., Flannery, R. and Hanley, S. (1974). Covert modeling: An experimental test. *Behavior Therapy*, **5**, 494–502.

Christensen, D. B. (1978). Drug-taking compliance: A review and synthesis. *Health Services Research*, **13**, 171–187.

Ciminero, A. A., Calhoun, K. S. and Adams, H. E. (1977). "Handbook of Behavioral Assessment", John Wiley and Sons, New York.

Cone, J. D. and Hawkins, R. P. (1977). "Behavioral Assessment: New Directions in Clinical Psychology", Brunner/Mazel, New York.

Craik, F. I. M. and Lockhardt, R. S. (1972). Level of processing: A framework for memory research. *Journal of Verbal Learning and Verbal Behavior*, **11**, 671–684.

Dapcich-Miura, E., and Hovell, M. F. (1979). Contingency management of adherence to a complex medical regimen in an elderly heart patient. *Behavior Therapy*, **10**, 193–210.

Davis, M. S. (1968). Variations in patients' compliance with doctors' advice. An empirical analysis of patterns of communications. *American Journal of Public Health*, **58**, 274–288.

Deberry, P., Jefferies, L. P. and Light, M. R. (1975). Teaching cardiac patients to manage medications. *American Journal of Nursing*, **75**, 2191–2193.

Doster, J. A. (1972). Effects of instructions, modeling, and role rehearsal on interview verbal behavior. *Journal of Consulting and Clinical Psychology*, **39**, 202–209.

Earp, J. A. and Ory, M. G. (1979). The effects of social support and health professional home visits on patient adherence to hypertension regimens. *Preventive Medicine*, **8**, 155.

Epstein, L. H. and Martin, J. E. (1977). Compliance and side-effects of weight reduction groups. *Behaviour Modification*, **1**, 551–558.

Epstein, L. H. and Masek, B. J. (1978). Behavioral control of medicine compliance. *Journal of Applied Behavior Analysis*, **11**, 1–9.

Eyberg, S. M. and Johnson, S. M. (1974). Multiple assessment of behavior modification with families: Effects of contingency contracting and order of treated problems. *Journal of Consulting and Clinical Psychology*, **42**, 594–606.

Fink, D. L. (1976). *In* "Compliance with Therapeutic Regimens" (D. L. Sackett and R. B. Haynes, eds), Johns Hopkins University Press, Baltimore.

Flanders, J. P. and Thistlethwaite, D. L. (1970). Effects of informative and justificatory variables upon imitation. *Journal of Experimental and Social Psychology*, **6**, 316–328.

Folkard, S. (1979). Time of day and level of processing. *Memory and Cognition*, **7**, 247–252.

Francis, V. F., Korsch, B. M and Morris, M. (1969). Gaps in doctor-patients communication: Patients' response to medical advice. *New England Journal of Medicine*, **280**, 535–540.

Frankel, B. S. and Hovell, M. F. (1978). Health service appointment keeping. *Behaviour Modification*, **2**, 435–464.

Freedman, J. L. and Fraser, S. C. (1966). Compliance without pressure: The foot-in-the-door technique. *Journal of Personality and Social Psychology*, **4**, 195–202.

Gates, S. J. and Colborn, D. K. (1976). Lowering appointment failures in a neighborhood health center. *Medical Care*, **14**, 263–267.

Gordis, L. (1979). *In* "Compliance in Health Care" (R. B. Haynes, D. W. Taylor and D. L. Sackett, eds), Johns Hopkins University Press, Baltimore.

Harris, J. E. (1984). Remembering to do things: a forgotten topic. *In* "Everyday Memory, Actions and Absent-Mindedness" (J. E. Harris and P. E. Morris, eds), Academic Press, London, Orlando and New York.

Harris, M. B. and Bruner, C. G. (1971). A comparison of a self-control and a contrast procedure for weight control. *Behavior Research*, **9**, 347–354.

Hay, W., Hay, L. and Nelson, R. O. (1977). The adaptation of covert modeling procedures to the treatment of chronic alcoholism and obsessive-complusive behavior: Two case reports. *Behavior Therapy*, **8**, 70–76.

Haynes, R. B. (1976). A critical review of the determinants of compliance with therapeutic regimens. *In* "Compliance with Therapeutic Regimens" (D. L. Sackett and R. B. Haynes, eds), Johns Hopkins University Press, Baltimore.

Haynes, R. B., Sackett, D. L., Gibson, E. S., Taylor, D. W., Hackett, B. C., Roberts, R. S. and Johnson, A. L. (1976). Improvement of medication compliance in uncontrolled hypertension. *Lancet*, **i**, 1265–1268.

Haynes, R. B., Taylor, D. W. and Sackett, D. L. (1979). "Compliance in Health Care", Johns Hopkins University Press, Baltimore.

Haynes, S. N. (1978). "Principles of Behavior Assessment", Gardner Press, New York.

Haynes, S. N. and Wilson, C. C. (1979). "Behavioral Assessment", Jossey-Bass, San Francisco.

Israel, A. C. and Saccone, A. J. (1979). Follow-up effects of choice of mediator and target of reinforcement on weight loss. *Behavior Therapy*, **10**, 260–265.

Iwata, B. A. and Becksfort, S. M. (1978). Behavioral approaches to preventive dentistry: Contingent fee reductions. Paper presented to the Annual Conference of the American Psychological Association, Toronto.

Kanfer, F. H. and Grimm, L. G. (1978). Freedom of choice and behavioral change. *Journal of Consulting and Clinical Psychology*, **46**, 873–876.

Kanfer, F. H. and Karoly, P. (1972). Self-control: A behavioristic excursion into the lion's den. *Behavior Therapy*, **3**, 398–416.

Kanfer, F. H., Karoly, P. and Newman, A. (1974). Source of feedback, observational learning, and attitude change. *Journal of Personality and Social Psychology*, **29**, 30–38.

Kar, S. B. (1977). Community interventions in health and family planning programmes: A conceptual framework. *International Journal of Health Education*, **20**, 2–15.

Kazdin, A. E. (1974). Comparative effects of some variations of covert modeling. *Journal of Abnormal Psychology*, **81**, 87–95.

Kazdin, A. E. (1974). Covert modeling, model similarity and reduction of avoidance behavior. *Behavior Therapy*, **5**, 624–635.

Kazdin, A. E. (1974). Effects of covert modeling and model reinforcement on assertive behavior. *Journal of Abnormal Psychology*, **83**, 240–252.

Kazdin, A. E. (1974). Reactive self-monitoring: The effects of response desirability, goal setting, and feedback. *Journal of Consulting and Clinical Psychology*, **42**, 704–716.

Kazdin, A. E. (1974). Covert modeling, imagery assessment and assertive behavior. *Journal of Consulting and Clinical Psychology*, **43**, 716–724.

Kazdin, A. E. (1976). Assessment of imagery during covert modeling of assertive behavior. *Journal of Behavior Therapy and Experimental Psychology*, **7**, 213–219.

Kazdin, A. E. (1976). Effects of covert modeling, multiple models, and model reinforcement on assertive behavior. *Behavior Therapy*, **7**, 211–222.

Keefe, F. J., Kopel, S. A. and Gordon, S. B. (1978). *A Practical Guide to Behavioral Assessment*. Springer, New York.

Kidd, A. H. and Euphrat, J. L. (1971). Why prospective outpatients fail to make or keep appointments. *Journal of Clinical Psychology*, **27**, 394–395.

Kincey, J., Bradshaw, P. and Ley, P. (1975). Patients' satisfaction and reported acceptance of advice in general practice. *Journal of the Royal College of General Practitioners*, **25**, 558–566.

Kingsley, R. G. and Shapiro, J. (1977). A comparison of three behavioral programs for the control of obesity in children. *Behavior Therapy*, **8**, 30–36.

Kothandapani, V. (1971) Validation of feeling, belief, and intention to act as three components of attitude and their contribution to prediction of contraceptive behavior. *Journal of Personality and Social Psychology*, **19**, 321–333.

Krause, M. S. (1966). Comparative effects on continuance of four experimental intake procedures. *Social Casework*, **47**, 515–519.

Leitenberg, H. (1975). Feedback and therapist praise during treatment of phobia. *Journal of Consulting and Clinical Pyschology*, **43**, 396–404.

Leon, G. R. (1976). Current dimensions in the treatment of obesity. *Psychological Bulletin*, **83**, 557–578.

Lepper, M. R. (1973). Dissonance, self-perception and honesty in children. *Journal of Personality and Social Psychology*, **25**, 65–74.

Leventhal, H. (1967). Fear communications in the acceptance of preventive health practices. *In* "Experiments in Persuasion" (R. L. Rosnow and E. J. Robinson, eds),

Academic Press, New York and London.

Levy, R. L. (1977). Relationship of an overt commitment to task compliance in behavior therapy. *Journal of Behavior Therapy and Experimental Psychology*, **8**, 25–29.

Levy, R. L. (1983). Social support and compliance. A selective review and critique of treatment integrity and outcome measurement. *Social Science and Medicine*, **17**, 1329–1338.

Levy, R. L. and Carter, R. D. (1976). Compliance with practitioner instigations. *Social Work*, **21**, 188–196.

Levy, R. L. and Claravell, V. (1977). Differential effects of a phone reminder on patients with long and short between-visit intervals. *Medical Care*, **15**, 435–438.

Levy, R. L. and Clark, H. (1980). The use of an overt commitment to enhance compliance: A cautionary note. *Journal of Behavior Therapy and Experimental Psychiatry*, **11**, 105–107.

Levy, R. L., Yamashita, D. and Pow, G. (1979). Relationship of an overt commitment to the frequency and speed of compliance with decision making. *Medical Care*, **17**, 281–284.

Lewis, S. (1974). A comparison of behavior therapy techniques in the reduction of fearful avoidance behavior. *Behavior Therapy*, **5**, 648–655.

Ley, P. (1972). Primacy, rated importance and recall of medical information. *Journal of Health and Social Behavior*, **13**, 311–317.

Ley, P. (1977). Psychological studies of doctor-patient communication. *In* "Contributions to Medical Psychology" (S. Rachman, ed.), No. I, Pergamon Press, Oxford.

Ley, P. (1978). Psychological and behavioral factors in weight loss. *In* "Recent Advances in Obesity Research No. II" (G. A. Gray, ed.), Newman, London.

Ley. P. (1979). Memory for medical information. *British Journal of Social and Clinical Psychology*, **18**, 245–255.

Ley, P., Jain, V. L. and Skilbeck, C. E. (1976). A method of decreasing patients' medical errors. *Psychological Medicine*, **6**, 599–601.

Ley, P., Jain, V. and Skilbeck, C. *Psychiatry in Medicine*, **5**, 599–601.

Ley, P., Whitworth, M., Skilbeck, C., Woodward, R., Pinsent, R., Pike, L., Clarkson, M. and Clark, P. (1976). Improving doctor-patient communication in general practice. *Journal of the Royal College of General Practitioners*, **26**, 720–724.

Liebert, R. M., Hanratty, M. and Hill, J. H. (1969). Effects of role structure and training method on the adoption of a self-imposed standard. *Child Development*, **40**, 93–101.

Locke, E. A., Cartledge, H. and Koeppel, J. (1968). *Psychological Bulletin*, **70**, 478–485.

Loftus, E. F. (1971). Memory for intentions. *Psychometric Science*, **23**, 315–316.

Logan, A. G., Milne, B. J., Achber, C., Campbell, W. P. and Haynes R. B. (1979). Worksite treatment of hypertension by specially trained nurses: A controlled trial. *Lancet*, **ii**, 1175–1178.

Lovitt, T. C. and Curtiss, K. (1969). Academic response rate as a function of teacher- and self-imposed contingencies. *Journal of Applied Behavior Analysis*, **2**, 49–53.

Lowe, K. and Lutzker, J. R. (1979). Increasing compliance to a medical regimen with a juvenile diabetic. *Behavior Therapy*, **10**, 57–64.

Mahoney, M. J. and Mahoney, J. (1976). Treatment of obesity: A clinical exploration. *In* "Obesity" (B. T. Williams, S. Martin and J. P. Foreyt, eds), Brunner/Mazel, New York.

Mahoney, M. J., Moura, N. G. and Wade, T. C. (1973). Relative efficacy of self-reward, self-punishment, and self-monitoring techniques for weight loss. *Journal of Consulting and Clinical Psychology*, **40**, 404–407.

Maiman, L. A. and Becker, M. H. (1974). The health belief model: Origins and correlates in psychological theory. *Health Education Monograph*, **2**, 455–469.

Malahy, B. (1966). The effects of instruction and labeling on the number of medication errors made by patients at home. *American Journal of Hospital Pharmacy*, **23**, 283–292.

Mann, R. A. (1972). The behavior-therapeutic use of contingency contracting to control an adult behavior problem: Weight control. *Journal of Applied Behavior Analysis*, **5**, 99–109.

Mazzulo, S. M., Lasagna, L. and Griner, P. F. (1974). Variations in interpretation of prescription assignments. *Journal of the American Medical Association*, **227**, 929–931.

McFall, R. M. and Marston, A. R. (1970). An experimental investigation of behavior rehearsal in assertive training. *Journal of Abnormal Psychology*, **76**, 295–303.

McKenney, J. M., Slining, J. M., Henderson, H. R., Devins, D. and Barr, M. (1973). The effect of clinical pharmacy services on patients with essential hypertension. *Circulation*, **48**, 1104–1111.

Miller, W. R. (1978). Behavioral treatment of problem drinkers: A comparative outcome study of three controlled drinking therapies. *Journal of Consulting and Clinical Psychology*, **46**, 74–86.

Moulding, T. (1961). Preliminary study of the pill calendar as a method of improving self-administration of drugs. *American Review of Respiratory Disease*, **84**, 284–287.

Nazarian, L. F., Machuber, J., Charney, E. and Coulter, M. D. (1974). Effects of a mailed appointment reminder on appointment keeping. *Pediatrics*, **53**, 349–351.

Nesse, M. and Nelson, R. O. (1977). Variations of covert modeling on cigarette smoking. *Cognitive Therapy and Research*, **1**, 343–354.

Nessman, D. G. and Carnahan, J. C. (1980). Improving compliance: Patient operated hypertension groups. *Archives of Internal Medicine*, **140**, 1427–1430.

Phillips, R. (1966). Self-administered systematic desensitization. *Journal of Consulting and Clinical Psychology*, **18**, 491–501.

Rappaport, J., Gross, T. and Lepper, C. (1973). Modeling, sensitivity training and instruction. *Journal of Consulting and Clinical Psychology*, **40**, 99–107.

Reiss, W., Piotrowski, W. and Bailey, J. S. (1976). Behavioral community psychology: Encouraging low-income parents to seek dental care for their children. *Journal of Applied Behavior Analysis*, **9**, 387–397.

Roberts, M. C., Wurtele, S. K. and Leeper, J. D. (1981). Experiments to increase return in a medical screening drive: Two futile attempts to apply theory to practice. Unpublished manuscript, University of Alabama.

Rosenstock, I. M. (1966). *Milbank Memorial Fund Quarterly*, **44**, 94–124.

Rundus, D. (1971). Analysis of rehearsal processes in free recall. *Journal of Experimental Psychology*, **89**, 63–77.

Saccone, A. J. and Israel, A. C. (1978). Effects of experimenter versus significant other-controlled reinforcement and choice of target behaviors on weight loss. *Behavior Therapy*, **9**, 271–278.

Sackett, D. L., Haynes, R. B., Gibson, E. S., Hackett, B. C., Taylor, D. W., Roberts, R. S. and Johnson, A. L. (1975). Randomized clinical trial of strategies for improving medication on compliance in primary hypertension. *Lancet*, **i**, 1205–1207.

Schulman, B. (1979). Active patient orientation and outcome in hypertensive treatment. *Medical Care*, 17, 267–280.

Shelton, J. L. and Levy, R. L. (1981). "Behavioral Assignments and Treatment Compliance", Research Press, Champaign, Illinois.

Shepard, D. S. and Moseley, T. A. (1976). Mailed *vs* telephoned appointment reminders to reduce broken appointments in a hospital outpatient department. *Medical Care*, 14, 268–273.

Steckel, S. B. and Swain, M. A. (1977). Contracting with patients to improve compliance. *Hospitals*, 51, 81–84.

Stokols, D. (1975). The reduction of cardiovascular risk: An application of social learning perspectives. *In* "Applying Behavioral Science to Cardiovascular Risk" (A. J. Enelow and J. B. Henderson, eds), American Heart Association, Dallas.

Stuart, R. B. and Davis, B. (1972). "Slim Chance in a Fat World", Research Press, Champaign, Illinois.

Suinn, R. M. (1977). Behavioral methods at the Winter Olympics Games. *Behavior Therapy*, 8, 283–284.

Svarstad, B. (1976). Physician-patient communication and patient conformity with medical advice. *In* "The Growth of Bureaucratic Medicine" (D. Mechanic, ed.), John Willey & Son, Inc., New York.

Takala, J., Niemela, N., Rosti, J. and Sivers, K. (1979). Improving compliance with therapeutic regimens in hypertensive patients in a community health centre. *Circulation*, 59, 540–543.

Thomas, E. J. and Carter, R. D. (1971). Instigative modification with a multiproblem family. *Social Casework*, 52, 444–455.

Tulving, E. and Thomson D. M. (1973). Encoding specificity and retrieval processes in episodic memory. *Psychological Review*, 80, 352–373.

Wilkins, A. J. and Baddeley, A. D. (1978). Remembering to recall in everyday life: An approach to absent-mindedness. *In* "Practical Aspects of Memory" (M. M. Gruneberg, P. E. Morris and R. N. Sykes, eds), Academic Press, London and New York.

Wilson, G. T. and Brownell, K. D. (1978). Behavior therapy for obesity including family members in the treatment process. *Behavior Therapy*, 9, 943–945.

Wilson, G. T. and Evans, I. M. (1972). The therapist-client relationship in behavior therapy. *In* "The Therapist's Contribution to Effective Psychotherapy: An Empirical Approach" (A. S. Gurman and A. M. Razin, eds.), Pergamon Press, Elmsford, New York.

Wurtele, S. K., Galanos, A. N. and Roberts, M. C. (1980). Increasing return compliance in a tuberculosis detection drive. *Journal of Behavioral Medicine*, 3, 311–318.

Zeiss, R. A. (1978). Self-directed treatment for premature ejaculation. *Journal of Consulting and Clinical Psychology*, 46, 1234–1241.

Zitter, R. E. and Freemouw, W. J. (1978). Individual vs. partner consequation for weight loss. *Behavior Therapy*, 9, 808–813.

7

Absent-mindedness and Cognitive Control

J. Reason

I. INTRODUCTION

As many of the contributions to this volume will testify, the past few years have seen a marked renewal of interest in naturally occurring cognitive failures (see also Broadbent *et al.*, 1982; Norman, 1981; Herrmann and Neisser, 1978; Bennett-Levy and Powell, 1980; Reason, 1975, 1976, 1977, 1979, 1982; Reason and Mycielska, 1982). Of particular concern in the present chapter are the minor yet by no means random deviations of our thoughts, words and deeds from the paths that we had (at least consciously) intended them to take. Freud (1901) described these mistakes collectively as "the psychopathology of everyday life," and, in another felicitous phrase, as "the refuse of the phenomenal world" (Freud, 1922). More commonly, though, we call them absent-minded errors.

A practical reason for this revival has been a growing awareness that man-made disasters, such as the Tenerife runway collision of 1977, or the catastrophe that so nearly happened at Three Mile Island in 1979, were not, as their horrendous consequences (actual or potential) might initially suggest, the product of a rare species of monumental blunder. Rather, they tend to be due to quite commonplace slips and lapses which in more forgiving circumstances would pass largely unremarked. In short, catastrophic lapses make up a small sub-group of the total error population, and are distinguished more by environmental factors than by truly psychological ones. That being so, it clearly behoves us to study *all* the more or less predictable varieties of human fallibility, irrespective of whether their consequences are damaging or merely embarrassing.

Another reason has been the dissatisfaction expressed by some cognitive psychologists (e.g. Neisser, 1978) in the artificiality of laboratory studies, and their frequently demonstrated inability to generalize to real-life settings, especially in the clinical context (Bennett-Levy and Powell, 1980). But, for the present, the most important factor is the recognition that these normally inconsequential and banal slips reveal a high degree of uniformity, regardless of the particular domain in which they show themselves (i.e. perception, concept formation, problem-solving, memory retrieval, language production and skilled action). Such regularities strongly suggest that a close study of these everyday errors will yield valuable clues to the nature of the underlying control processes, and to the role of attention in the guidance of planned action (where the term "action" embraces both internal and external activities). Furthermore, the fact that these apparently lawful errors crop up in very similar guises across a wide variety of mental processes forces us to formulate more global theories of cognitive control than could hitherto be derived from laboratory studies focussing upon necessarily restricted aspects of memory, attention, recognition and the like.

This chapter presents one possible model of cognitive control. In particular it addresses the question: *What goes absent in absent-mindedness?* Before outlining the model, however, it is necessary to summarize the main findings of the everyday error studies upon which it was largely founded.

II. SUMMARIZING THE ERROR DATA

The theoretical ideas considered later are designed to take account of two kinds of evidence: (1) the nature and circumstances of absent-minded slips of action, as revealed for the most part by cognitive diary studies (Reason, 1977, 1979, 1982; Reason and Mycielska, 1982); and (2) questionnaire studies of individual differences in liability to minor cognitive failures (Broadbent *et al.*, 1982; Reason, 1982; Reason and Mycielska, 1982). Only the main findings are given here. Further details concerning methodology, data analysis and the like can be obtained from the primary sources.

A. Slips of action

The principal characteristics of absent-minded slips of action, and the circumstances of their occurrence can be summarized as follows.

(1) They are most likely to occur in highly familiar surroundings during the performance of frequently and recently executed tasks in which a considerable degree of automacity has been achieved.

(2) Their occurrence is very commonly associated with states of either preoccupation or distraction. Stressors such as being upset, feeling unwell, time pressure and the like, may contribute, but they are judged (by those who make the errors) to be relatively unimportant factors.

(3) A large proportion of the absent-minded slips (40% in one study) involve strong habit intrusions. That is, the errors take the form of intact action sequences that are judged as recognizably belonging to some activity other than the one currently intended. This "other activity" was consist-

ently rated as being recently and frequently engaged in, and as sharing similar locations, movements and objects with the intended actions (on the occasion that the slips occurred).

(4) In addition to the general disposing conditions indicated above, there were at least four, more specific, situations in which strong habit intrusions were likely to occur: (a) when a change of goal demands a departure from some well-established routine (e.g. "I had decided to cut down my sugar consumption and wanted to have my cornflakes without it. But I sprinkled sugar on my cereal just as I had always done."); (b) when changed circumstances require a modification of an established action pattern (e.g. "We now have two fridges in our kitchen, and yesterday we moved our food from one to the other. This morning I repeatedly opened the fridge that used to hold our food."); (c) when we enter a familiar environment (associated with a variety of habitual routines) in a reduced state of "intentionality" (e.g. "I went into my bedroom intending to fetch a book. Instead, I took off my rings, looked into the mirror and came out again without the book."); and (d) when features of our present circumstances contain elements common to those in highly familiar environments (e.g. "I found myself on a friend's front doorstep trying to fit my latchkey into the lock.").

(5) Two further classes of action slip (other than strong habit intrusions) can also be identified from the corpus: (a) *place-losing errors*, mostly involving omissions and repetitions, where the slips result from a wrong assessment of the present position in a sequence of actions; and (b) *blends and reversals*, in which mistakes arise from "crosstalk" between two currently active tasks (blends), or between elements of the same task (reversals or behavioural spoonerisms). In the latter case, the actions are correct, but the objects for which they were intended become partially or completely reversed.

B. Individual differences in error proneness

(1) People differ widely and consistently in their liability to minor cognitive failures. Self-reports in this regard are largely confirmed by the assessments of marital partners (Broadbent *et al.*, 1982). Moreover, these self-ratings remain relatively stable over periods of 16 months or so.

(2) This liability is not specific to any one cognitive domain, but appears to operate uniformly across the mental board (more of which later). Thus, those people who acknowledge, say, that they have many lapses of memory also report making frequent action slips and recognition errors, and conversely. Susceptibility to cognitive failure appears to be determined by some *general* control factor that exerts its influence over all aspects of mental function.

(3) Different forms of these error proneness questionnaires correlate highly one with another, regardless of the particular cognitive domain to which they are directed (see Broadbent *et al.*, 1982). No relationship of any importance

has yet been established between liability to cognitive failure and standard psychological tests of intelligence, neuroticism, trait-anxiety and the like. In short, these measures of error proneness appear to be tapping a dimension that is not readily assessed by existing psychometrics.

(4) There is evidence to suggest that a relatively high incidence of everyday slips and lapses is associated with an increased vulnerability to stress. The implication here is not so much that stress induces a high rate of failure (though it may indeed be so), but that the same general control factor that appears to determine liability to error is also involved in coping with the adverse effects of stress. At the other end of the scale, there are also hints that unusually low levels of error constitute a feature of the obsessional personality (Reason, 1982; Broadbent *et al.*, 1982).

III. A MODEL OF COGNITIVE CONTROL

The model proposes three closely related levels of cognitive control. Two of them are fairly uncontroversial, at least in their basic forms. They are the *schemata*, relatively permanent knowledge structures which also provide the detailed guidance for largely automatic (preprogrammed) sequences of speech, thought, action or perception; and the *Intention System*, which specifies goals and decides, in general terms, how they are to be achieved. In addition, the error data summarized above indicates the existence of a third agency: the *attentional control resource*. The functions of each of these controlling agencies are discussed below under separate headings.

A. Schemata

Since its introduction into the psychological literature by Bartlett (1932), the schema concept has had a chequered history. This is not the place to review that history, nor to trace the linkages between Bartlett's notion of "... an active organisation of past experiences, which must always be supposed to be operating in any well adapted organic response" (Bartlett, 1932, p. 201) and its more recent variants such as plans (Miller *et al.*, 1960), demons (Selfridge, 1959; Lindsay and Norman, 1972), scripts (Abelson, 1976), frames (Minsky, 1975), prototypes (Cantor and Mischel, 1977), personae (Nisbett and Ross, 1980) and stories (Bower *et al.*, 1979). For this, the reader is directed to the many theoretical discussions of schemata and their close relatives that have recently appeared (Neisser, 1976; Norman and Bobrow, 1975; Schmidt, 1976; Fiske and Linville, 1980; Taylor and Crocker, 1981; Hastie, 1981). For our immediate purposes, it is sufficient to assert that the presence in our error corpus of a substantial number of slips taking the form of intact, well-organized sequences of skilled or habitual activities provides ample justification for the assumption that the fine-grained control of such tasks is largely under the control of autonomous local "experts" or action schemata.

We shall take it as axiomatic that such organizing and controlling knowledge structures exist within some form of permanent and apparently limitless long-term store, and focus here upon the operating characteristics of schemata that are revealed by unintended actions.

It is assumed that schemata activity is experienced in consciousness as images, words, perceptions and feelings, but that their precise operation is usually beyond the reach of direct awareness. Thus, we are conscious of the schemata outputs, but not of the schemata themselves. During the preliminary stages of acquiring a skill, we are aware of the prime ingredients of what later become schemata, but this awareness diminishes with increasing proficiency.

Schemata vary widely in their current level of activation; that is, in their readiness to execute their various specialist functions. They require a certain minimum or threshold level of activation to trigger them into operation. In other words, they need some form of "priming" before they go to work.

They derive this activation from many different sources. These can be subsumed under two general headings: *domain-specific* and *universal* activating factors.

Usually, the most critical of these triggering agents are domain-specific. Thus, action and word schemata receive their primary activation from particular intentions to say or do something (we must not lose sight of the fact that errors are the exception rather than the rule; most of the time we do the things we intended). Recognition schemata, on the other hand, are called into operation primarily by the sensory input (see Selfridge, 1959; Bruner, 1957; Neisser, 1967).

Universal activating factors exert their influence across all cognitive domains quite independently of the Intention System. These factors include: (a) the environmental context; (b) the current need state or prevailing emotion; (c) influences from other schemata, particularly those groups of schemata sharing common operations (for example, making tea and coffee, filling hot water bottles, cooking vegetables, preparing certain brands of instant soup all share the initial common pathway of boiling a kettle—it is assumed that carrying out (or even simply intending to carry out) any one of these tasks will increase the activation of all the other schemata linked to the kettle-boiling routine); and (d) the recency and frequency of successful schema operation: the more recently/frequently a schema has been energized (either in action or in mental rehearsal), the greater will be its activation level. It will be noted that this list of schema activating factors has much in common with Bruner's (1957) determinants of perceptual readiness, and also with the agencies presumed to affect category accessibility in the social cognition literature (see Srull and Wyer, 1979, 1980).

B. Intention system

This comprises two closely related components: a central processor and a storage unit (Intention Store). Together they constitute the chief executive (or BOSS, see Morris, 1981) within the hierarchy of cognitive control. And, as we shall see later, it is not conceived of as a separate entity, but as an emergent property of the schemata.

The principal functions of this system are the assembly of plans for future action, the monitoring and guidance of ongoing activity, coping with changed circumstances and the detection and recovery of errors when they occur. At any moment in time, its operations coincide very closely with the current contents of consciousness.

Planning involves making a series of jottings on the mental scratchpad. These jottings are usually short verbal tags identifying some future action ("I must buy some fish on the way home.") and the approximate time at which it should be carried out. Each of these tags stands for a large number of automated action sequences that are not specified consciously, but whose guidance is directed by specialized schemata. There is no need to fill in the "small print" of each detailed operation. These are implicit in the brief headings on the scratchpad. The more we engage in relatively fixed routines, the fewer are the number of tags or jottings required at the conscious level. In short, repetition reduces the number of low level control statements that need to be made by the Intention System.

The Intention Store has much in common with Working Memory (Baddeley and Hitch, 1974). It acts as a temporal extension to the central processor. Its contents are limited, short-lived and subject to interference or loss. In many ways, the Intention Store is rather akin to a cluttered desk top where we throw the scraps of paper and old envelopes upon which we have scribbled down our lists of things to do. Mostly, we remember to consult our lists at the right time and execute our plans as intended. But on occasions we forget about the list altogether. At other times, we remember it is there, but fail to find it among the clutter, and we are left with the feeling: "I know I should be doing something, but I can't remember what it is". Or we may retrieve the memo at the right time and start on the planned activity, but then part way through we lose it—as when we find ourselves confronted by an open drawer or cupboard without the least idea of what we are searching for: the "what-am-I-doing-here?" experience. And there are also occasions when we start working our way down the list of things to do, but at some point fail to check the list and "wake up" to discover that our actions have become locked into some familiar but unintended routine. Intentional problems of one kind or another are among the most common of our everyday memory lapses (Reason, 1982).

The Intention System has two important properties. First, it has limited capacity so that only one plan at a time is usually maximally active (Shallice, 1972, 1978). Since the system functions serially, items waiting for consideration have to be held in store until the central processor is free to deal with them. Second, the system is always busy, at least during waking hours. Once it has initiated a set of routine actions and handed over detailed control to the appropriate schemata, it switches to some new concern which, in the case of largely habitual activities, may be quite unrelated to the task in hand. Like Nature, therefore, it abhors a vacuum. These two characteristics, in particular, render us vulnerable to absent-mindedness.

C. The attentional control resource

Three short quotations from William James will help to set the scene for our discussion of attentional control. With characteristic clarity they state the agreed features of attention, while omitting to specify its exact functions or the means by which they are achieved. Despite the passage of nearly a century, these statements continue to reflect the level at which we understand this mysterious entity. There is little or no dispute among either laymen or psychologists as to what the experience of attending feels like, but we are not much wiser about what attention does or how it does it. And it is with these last two issues that the remainder of the chapter is primarily concerned.

Attention, wrote James

... is the taking possession of the mind in clear and vivid form of one of what seem several simultaneously possible objects or trains of thought. Focalization, concentration, of consciousness are of its essence. It implies withdrawal from some things in order to deal more effectively with others. (James, 1890, pp. 403–404.)

Elsewhere, he commented upon the reciprocity that exists between attention and interest.

When we are studying an uninteresting subject, if our mind tends to wander, we have to bring back our attention every now and again by using distinct pulses of effort, which revivify the topic for a moment, the mind then running for a certain number of seconds or minutes with spontaneous interest, until again some intercurrent idea captures it and takes it off. (James, 1899, p. 101)

The third quotation relates to the phenomenon of automaticity:

Habit diminishes the conscious attention with which our acts are performed. (James, 1890, p. 114)

Thus, James tells us that attention is *selective*; that it is a *limited* commodity; that a large part of it is intimately bound up with the state of *consciousness*; that it is an extremely *mobile* entity over which we can only exercise *intermittent voluntary control*; and that the demands made upon its conscious component *decrease* the more we execute relatively invariant sequences of action, perception or thought.

Nothing that we have learned from studying everyday slips and lapses would cause us to reject or even modify any of the attentional characteristics listed by James. But as they stand they are merely descriptions, not explanations. What exactly does this limited attentional resource control, and how? In order to offer some answers to these questions, we must first

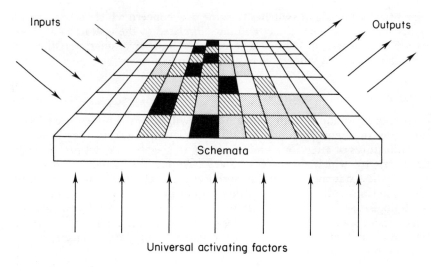

Fig. 1. The "cognitive board".

introduce the metaphor of the "cognitive board". This is shown in Fig. 1.

(1) *The cognitive board*
In order to distinguish and describe the hypothetical control functions of the attentional resource (A) and those residing within the schemata, it is convenient to regard the latter as being laid out in the form of an immense squared board (of which only a small part can be shown in Fig. 1). Each square is a separate schema (or closely related schema family), concerned with executing specialist functions in any of the various cognitive domains: recognition, language, memory retrieval, thinking, action and the like. No attempt has been made to differentiate these domains in Fig. 1, since it is assumed that notwithstanding the immense variety of expertise embodied in these knowledge structures, they share common operating features and are subject to the same universal activating factors (need, context, recency, frequency, etc.). Different levels of schema activation are shown in Fig. 1 by varying densities of shading.

A number of other important features of the "board" are also not represented in Fig. 1. The first is that all input–output relations with the outside world go through the board. Thus, recognition schemata act directly upon the appropriate effector systems. Second, all schemata can receive inputs from the Need System (see Reason, 1979, 1982; Reason and Mycielska, 1982). This is implicit in the fact that motivational factors constitute an important source of activation that can be quite independent of the Intention System. Third, all schemata are actually or potentially linked one with another by a complex nexus running laterally through the board. Finally, schemata are assumed to vary in their level of complexity. If, as a first approximation, we regard all schemata as being in the form of nested TOTE units (Miller *et al.*, 1960; Reason and Mycielska, 1982), then complexity is a function of the number of hierarchical levels contained within the schema.

These, then, are the basics of the cognitive board. Other features will become evident when we consider the interaction between it and the attentional control resource. For the present, however, it is important to make clear that (a) all the stored knowledge and all the potential processing power of which the mind is capable are contained within the schemata; (b) the extent to which this processing power can be realized depends upon the current level of schema activation; and (c) schema activation is determined both by universal factors and by the attentional control resource (beneath which lies the Intention System). It is this latter influence that will now be elaborated further.

(2) *Adding the attentional control resource to the board*
Although it is *potentially* capable of all possible modes of cognitive control, the "board" *by itself* has two very serious limitations. The first is that without some superordinate selective agency, the control of action in all domains would fall more or less at random to those schemata whose current activation exceeds the triggering threshold. In other words, those schemata presently energized by the combined influence of the universal (non-intentional) activating factors would compete for control of the effectors, and those that were initially successful would probably continue to dominate the system outputs due to the cumulating influence of the recency/frequency factors. In short, a curious kind of self-limited anarchy would prevail in which actions are likely to become increasingly repetitive. The second problem is that the universal activating factors working alone would be insufficient to elicit the full processing capabilities of the schemata in any sustained manner. Thus, the cognitive board as it stands would be incapable of generating the higher mental functions, of which consciousness is perhaps a necessary adjunct.

Evidently some additional control device is needed to overcome these deficiencies. It is to serve these purposes that the attentional control resource must be added to the cognitive board. This resource (to be referred to as the "blob" for reasons that its representation in Fig. 2 make obvious) is depicted at various momentary deployments in Figs 2a, 2b and 2c. Before presenting the control properties of the attentional "blob", we need first to consider its formal characteristics.

The first thing to notice about the blob is that it is highly mobile. It skids from point to point like a drop of quicksilver on a surface that is being gently and continually tilted in all directions.* Its second and equally important feature is its limited and fixed quantity. The blob can only cover a minute

---

* Although presented as being added to the "board", it is perhaps better thought of as a shifting deformation of its surface.

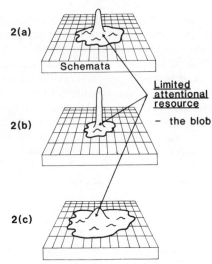

2(a)

Schemata

Limited
attentional
resource

2(b)

- the blob

2(c)

Fig. 2. Adding the attentional resource to the cognitive board. 2a, b and c represent momentary configurations of attentional resource upon the "cognitive board".

proportion of all the possible schemata on the board. (Actually, the respective sizes of the blob and the board as shown in Fig. 2 are grossly out of scale; the board is infinitely greater relative to the blob than is illustrated in these diagrams.) Although the blob can assume many different shapes, there is usually only a single "peak". This can vary both in its position within the blob and in its height. When the peak is high and narrow, the "skirts" of the blob are drawn in to a corresponding degree, and the total number of schemata covered is reduced (see Fig. 2b). Conversely, when the peak is relatively low and squat in shape (see Fig. 2c), the outlying skirts of the blob are extended accordingly.

(3) *What does the blob do?*
The blob's specific function is to modulate the level of activation within the schemata located beneath it at any moment in time. That is, it can either increase activation to any level up to that required to elicit the full processing potential of the underlying schemata (a level not normally achieved by the universal activating factors alone), or it can reduce an existing high level of activation temporarily. Thus, it can both selectively *energize* and selectively *suppress* particular schemata. These selective properties are conferred, obviously enough, by the fact that the blob can only cover a very restricted number of the available schemata. The *extent* to which the blob can carry out these modulating functions is dependent upon the *amount* of the attention resource (A) located immediately above a given schema. In order to achieve the most exacting levels of processing, high concentrations of A are needed. Hence, the principal peak of the blob is likely to be situated over those

schemata whose outputs constitute the present contents of consciousness. This relationship between *states* of consciousness, *levels* of processing and the amount of the associated attentional resource is spelled out in further detail below.

(4) *Attentional resource, levels of processing and states of consciousness*
The complex interaction between these three entities can be represented most simply by taking a partial cross-section through the blob and its underlying schemata. This is done in Fig. 3.

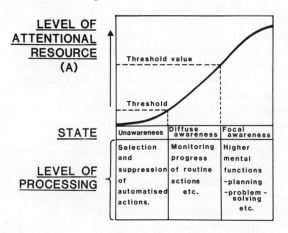

Fig. 3. Relating attentional resource, states of consciousness and levels of processing.

Let us assume that both the current level of processing and the extent to which we are aware of these operations are dependent in very large measure upon the amount of additional schemata activation contributed by the presence immediately above them of a given quantity of A. In this way, we can relate both levels of processing and states of consciousness to the amount of attentional resource in the vicinity. For simplicity, let us consider the correlates of three distinct amounts of A: low, intermediate and high.
(a) *Low amounts of A.* One of the implications of what has been presented so far is that absent-minded errors emerge out of areas of the cognitive board in which activated schemata are either not covered, or are insufficiently covered by the attentional blob. Now, if our highly routinized activities depart from the plan because the attentional resource was being deployed elsewhere, it follows that a larger quantity of A was necessary on those occasions to ensure the desired outcome. On this basis, it can be argued that some measure of A, no matter how small, is essential for the guidance of all ongoing physical and mental activities, even the most apparently automatic ones. This is not to

suggest that a fixed quantity is needed throughout. The error data indicate that the optimal amount varies according to the particular phase of the task. Some points in a sequence of actions actually suffer from too much attention (e.g. place-losing mistakes). But there are other occasions (particularly those "nodes" where a familiar sequence of schemata operations branches into a number of alternative paths) when a larger allocation of A is desirable.

It seems likely that well organized and closely associated schemata, of the kind used in the management of routine tasks, require only a small quantity of the attentional resource for their effective control. In other words, these schemata only need to be thinly covered by the "skirts" of the attentional blob. At these low levels of concentration, there would be no direct awareness of the detailed operations, and the attentional resource would serve two related functions. Firstly, it would confer the additional activation necessary to bring the appropriate schemata into play at the right times. Secondly, it would restrain those locally active but unwanted schemata that would otherwise try to grab a piece of the action. To keep a sequence of words, thoughts or movements on the right track, it is important not only to *select* the next intended schema, but also to *suppress* those that would seek to usurp this position. If schemata were merely passive structures, this problem would not arise. As it is, they can be both energetic and competitive, continually striving to display their expertise on the smallest pretext. The fact that strong habit intrusions represent the most common error form in all cognitive domains suggests that it is the suppressive rather than the selective function of the attentional resource that is more likely to fail.

(b) *Intermediate amounts of A.* A number of writers have distinguished between *focal* and *diffuse* awareness (James, 1890; Polanyi, 1958). We would argue that the latter state, the penumbra of consciousness, is associated with intermediate levels of the attentional resource. These are found either on the lower reaches of the blob's (usually) single peak, or in the various "bumps" that appear in the skirts of the blob (shown in Figs 2a–2c).

There are a number of ways in which this diffuse level of awareness could be related to cognitive processing. It could, for example, be involved in the "pre-attentional" processes, described by Neisser (1967), in which the figural properties of objects are first detached from the surrounding "ground" before being subjected to more rigorous perceptual analysis. It is also likely that this intermediate level of attention is used in the cursory checks we make upon the progress of some relatively habitual task. Certainly, much of the velocity and directional information we derive from peripheral vision while driving is likely to be processed at this level, or even at a lower one. The findings from visual kinaesthesis studies (Dichgans and Brandt, 1978; Reason et al., 1981) indicate that large-scale moving patterns falling upon the extreme periphery of the retina are the most influential in determining both body posture and the illusory displacement of the vertical. From the observer's point of view, such dynamic visual stimulation lies on the outermost fringes of awareness. The list could continue, but enough has been said to sketch out the general features of this penumbral region.

(c) *High amounts of A.* One of the central assumptions of the model is that the higher mental functions—decision-making, planning, problem-solving, concept formation, deliberate information retrieval and the wherewithal to create new schemata (skill acquisition)—are all emergent properties of the schemata comprising the cognitive board. The Intention System does not exist as a separate, superordinate entity. At any moment in time, the Intention System comprises those schemata lying beneath the peak of the attentional blob; that is, at the point subjected to the highest levels of attentional investment. Earlier, the Intention System was identified with the current contents of consciousness. Just as these are continually changing, in the manner of the "flights" and "perchings" described by James (1890, p. 243), so also are the board locations of the Intention System and the schemata that temporarily constitute it. Knowledge and processing are inextricably linked. Some cognitive model-makers find it convenient to represent them in separate boxes, but we should not allow this expository device to deceive us into believing that they are ever truly separable.

Obviously, it would not be sensible to claim that all schemata on the board are potentially capable of the most sophisticated levels of processing. The kettle-boiling schema, for example, has many uses, but as a vehicle for higher mental function it has its limitations. But all mental activities, no matter how demanding or complex, can and do become automatized to some degree. To put it another way: they eventually become well-developed schemata in their own right if they are successfully employed sufficiently often. The extent to which even the most strenuous of mental activities can be schema-driven has been elegantly demonstrated by de Groot (1965) in his studies of chess players. A chess master can accurately reproduce the entire disposition of meaningfully arranged pieces after a brief glance. No amateur can do as well. Through extensive experience and application, the chess master has developed a very great number of schemata for "chunking" recurring constellations of pieces. Chase and Simon (1973) have estimated that the master has a "vocabulary" of chess schemata of much the same order as most people's word vocabulary.

In the light of these and related observations, it is reasonable to assume that the cognitive board contains schemata specifically concerned with high level functions. Where these are developed to a high degree, as in the case of the chess master, they confer expert status upon their possessor. In addition, it seems probable that there will also be *metaschemata* that are responsible for the optimal deployment of the attentional blob in a given skilled activity.

Where does something like Working Memory fit into this model? How are intentions stored and later acted upon? One way to accommodate these functions is to suggest that, during the course of planning, the attentional blob moves rapidly and extensively about the board touching upon various alternative courses of action. Once a given sequence of actions has been decided upon, the plan exists on the board as a collection of critically active schemata. This activation is refreshed by periodic reviews of the plan. But in the absence of this review procedure, it is assumed that the activation of these schemata will decay spontaneously (at a rate dependent, among other things, upon the extent to which they are energized by universal activating factors). This decay of activation is one reason for forgetting planned items. Another is through interference from earlier or later planning. A great number of our plans are in themselves schematized routines. The error corpus indicates that planned items are most likely to be omitted when they exist as recent additions to, or variations from, well-established sequences. Unless we repeatedly remind ourselves to divert from our normal route home to buy the fish, we are liable to return fishless.

In the past, it has been more usual to regard attention as a subset of consciousness. James Sully (1884), for example, asserted that: "The field of Consciousness . . . is wider than that of Attention." (p. 73). The present model turns this argument on its head. The boundaries of consciousness are here defined by a given value of the attentional resource, and its contents are the outputs of the associated schemata. Focal consciousness therefore emerges from a restricted set of schemata that have been invested with a peak concentration of the A resource. Thus, in this conception, consciousness is a subset of the attentional resource.

The question of whether the state of consciousness is a necessary condition for the higher levels of processing, or whether it is simply an epiphenomenon as certain behaviourists have claimed, cannot be entirely resolved on the basis of the present evidence. And even for the model itself it is something of a side issue. The error data do, however, support Mandler's view of consciousness as a "trouble-shooter" (Mandler, 1975). The slips and lapses netted within our corpus owe their recorded existence to the fact that the individuals concerned *became aware* that their actions had deviated from intention. Consciousness does appear to play an important role in detecting inadvertent departures from plans.

(5) *What shifts the blob around the board?*

It is implicit within the model that introspection can provide only limited access to mental function (see also Nisbett and Wilson, 1977; White 1980; Ericsson and Simon, 1980; Morris, 1981). But since we have defined focal consciousness as being located beneath the peak of the attentional blob, the logic of the model would permit us fairly privileged subjective information concerning the progress of the blob around the board. On this basis, it is apparent that the blob can be guided, at least intermittently, by intentional activity. It is also evident, however, that control is frequently snatched from us by the relentless tendency of the blob to move or return to pressing concerns on the board that were not on the planned itinerary. In short, the blob is both active and reactive.

In order to avoid the homuncularity of postulating some further controlling agency hovering over both the blob and the board, it is argued that the blob can direct itself by the processing occurring immediately beneath it. The rich network of connections that are assumed to exist between the knowledge structures make it possible for distant schemata to be activated remotely, and thus acquire the potential for attracting the blob towards them at some later point in a planned sequence of moves. It is also likely that much of the blob's movements are determined by metaschemata that have developed to control its optimal deployment for a given task.

It must be admitted, however, that although the structural properties of the model allow for some measure of active control over the moment-to-moment location of the blob, the model does not tell us precisely how this control is achieved. In avoiding the perils of infinitely regressive arguments, we face the trap of creating circular ones. This dilemma becomes especially acute if we look to something like William James's (1890) ideomotor theory of volition to help us out. What directs the voluntary component of attentional control?: the effort required to hold some image of the desired goal before the mind. What form does this act of will take?: the ability to sustain attention upon the desired outcome. Round and round it goes.

The question of how the blob responds reactively is somewhat easier to answer. The blob is drawn inexorably to "hot spots" on the board. That is, to super-heated schemata that have been energized by the universal activating factors, by significant changes in the sense data, and most probably by earlier visits of the blob. In this way, we can account for the intrusive and painful ruminations that plague us in states of grief and depression. Although we repeatedly resolve not to brood upon these distressing issues further, they continue to dominate the mental stage no matter how hard we strive to direct the blob to more pleasing performances. This obsessive tendency to return to the scene of the emotional crime is further exacerbated by the fact that miserable people are inclined to dredge up unhappy memories (Bower, 1981; Teasdale, 1982). The primary aim of cognitive therapy is to cut through this positive feedback loop (Beck et al., 1979).

(6) *Making new connections*
It was suggested earlier that voluntary control of the attentional blob could be achieved through the rich lateral network of associations between schemata, and with the help of metaschemata. Yet if this were the case, the blob would inevitably follow pathways around the board that correspond to already established connections. How then are new linkages forged? From whence spring our creative leaps of imagination? A possible answer is that they are an incidental product of the reactive wanderings of the blob. In short, they occur largely by accident. Just as Alexander Fleming's genius is said to lie in his realization of the full implications of the chance invasion of his petrie dish by penicillin spores, so also could the act of creation simply involve recognizing the significance of unintentionally associated schemata outputs.

William James, of course, got there first. Discussing the relationship between attention and genius, he wrote:

One friend who does a prodigious quantity of work, has in fact confessed to me that, if he wants to get ideas on any subject, he sits down to work at something else, his best results coming through his mind-wanderings. . . . Our mind may enjoy but little comfort, may be restless and feel confused; but it may be extremely efficient all the same. (William James, 1908, pp. 114–115).

(7) Cognitive limits

Boiled down to its working essentials, the model has two major components: the board and the blob. The board is potentially limitless. The blob is a restricted commodity. It therefore follows that all cognitive limitations (in Working Memory, the Intention System, etc.) stem ultimately from the finite nature of the attentional blob. Related to this, however, is the fact that uncovered schemata tend to lose activation spontaneously if not recharged by either a return visit of the blob, or by the universal activating factors.

(8) The Freudian slip

Provision for "motivated errors" is present within the model in the form of the inputs from the Need System to potentially all schemata. The current status of the Freudian slip has been discussed in detail elsewhere (Timpanaro, 1976; Reason and Mycielska, 1982).

IV. SPECULATIONS CONCERNING INVOLUNTARY ATTENTIONAL FIXEDNESS

In summarizing the empirical evidence earlier, it was noted that individual differences in error proneness appeared to be determined by some general control factor that operated independently of cognitive domains. Moreover, Broadbent and his colleagues (Broadbent et al., 1982) observed that a pronounced liability to minor slips and lapses is associated with an increased vulnerability to stress. It was found that student nurses with high scores on the Cognitive Failures Questionnaire (CFQ) manifested a greater number of minor psychiatric symptoms following a six-week spell on a high-stress ward than did those with lower scores. The period assessed by the CFQ was the preceding six months and did not include the ward duty itself. In other words, those nurses with a consistently high liability to minor errors bore more "scars" as the result of their stressful experience than did those with low susceptibility.

One inference that can be drawn from these questionnaire findings as a whole is that people vary characteristically in the efficiency with which they deploy their limited attentional resource. We can go one step further and suggest that *both* consistently high rates of minor cognitive failure *and* increased vulnerability to stress are likely to be found in those individuals subject to *involuntary attentional fixedness*; or, in plainer language, who suffer from "sticky blobs". Cognitive strategies for coping with stress are liable to make heavy demands upon the limited attentional resource. For those people in whom a high incidence of error indicates a less than adequate disposition of attention between competing demands, the pressure on these coping devices may well exceed the ability to sustain them *and* to deal effectively with all that needs to be done. And, as Lazarus (1966) pointed out, psychiatric symptoms begin to emerge as coping strategies start to crumble.

So far we have considered evidence for the existence of trait-like differences in the effectiveness of attentional deployment. But this factor is also likely to show considerable *state* variation as well. One possible representation of both trait and state variation is along a dimension ranging from extreme attentional fixedness at one end to a high degree of flexibility at the other. There are two further assumptions. First, that people differ in their typical position along this dimension. Second, that the stresses engendered by (usually) negative life events (see Hamilton and Warburton, 1980) will act to shift all individuals some way towards the fixedness end of the dimension. In other words, major stresses (e.g. bereavement, separation, discovery of a breast lump, being made redundant) will cause, among other things, a reduction in the adaptive mobility of the attentional blob. The extent of this effect and its duration will depend upon a complex interplay of many factors that are likely to include the perceived severity of the stress, the success of the coping strategies brought to bear and the person's characteristic position along the dimension.

From various experimental and clinical observations (Hockey and Hamilton, 1970; Hockey, 1973; Horowitz, 1980; Bowlby, 1981), it would seem that one of the effects of stress is to cause the attentional blob to allocate a large part of its capacity to a very limited number of schemata, thus restricting its mobility. In short, it produces a rather exaggerated version of the situation depicted in Fig. 2b. This sticky, witch's hat configuration of the blob will reveal itself, according to the model, in a number of ways: by the presence of recurrent thought patterns, by an increase in the base rate of minor cognitive failures, and by a greater degree of "routinization" in the performance of mental and physical activities. This latter feature may be manifested as a diminution in the flexibility of information processing, by an increasing conservatism of thought and action, and by a relatively greater number of slips of habit or perseverative errors, both indicative of control rigidity.

V. CONCLUDING REMARKS

At the beginning we noted that Freud likened the banal and usually trivial errors of daily life to the contents of a psychological dustbin. By themselves, they do not amount to very much. But as archeologists know, the intricacies of remote civilizations may be pieced together by poking around in their buried rubbish; a large heap of refuse can be very revealing. Particularly when the discarded fragments originate from many different parts of the total organization.

In this chapter, I have concentrated on the recurrent aspects of our pile of errors, and especially the slips of habit. It has been emphasized that these and other error forms crop up in all domains of mental life. Though the model of cognitive control presented here may seem an excessively ambitious one to build on such dubious foundations, it is nonetheless the *kind* of model, even if it is not the actual model, that the evidence demands. Nothing less could cope with either the scope or the regularities of the data. Although the board and blob model has many obvious deficiencies, not the least of which being the vagueness of the schema concept and the difficulty of testing the model empirically, it is nonetheless hoped that by offering a limited set of general explanatory principles it will draw together into some meaningful whole that which had hitherto existed as a widely scattered collection of psychological oddments. If nothing else, it does attempt to meet the demand expressed by Claxton (1980) and others for a lingua franca of cognitive psychology that is applicable to all of its constituent areas.

The author gratefully acknowledges the support of the Social Science Research Council. The greater part of the error data was collected during the period covered by research grant No. HR 6290; while the writing of the present chapter was supported by a further grant, No. HR 7755/1.

REFERENCES

Abelson, R. P. (1976). Script processing in attitude formation and decision-making. *In* "Cognition and Social Behaviour" (J. S. Carroll and J. Payne, eds), Erlbaum, Hillsdale, N.J.

Baddeley, A. D. (1976). "The Psychology of Memory", Harper & Row, New York.

Baddeley, A. D. and Hitch, G. (1974). Working memory. *In* "The Psychology of Learning and Motivation", vol. 8. 47–90 (G. H. Bower, ed.), Academic Press, New York and London.

Bartlett, F. C. (1932). "Remembering", Cambridge University Press, Cambridge.

Beck, A. T., Rush, A. J., Shaw, B. F. and Emery, G. (1979). "Cognitive Therapy of Depression", Wiley, Chichester.

Bennett-Levy, J. and Powell, G. E. (1980). The Subjective Memory Questionnaire (SMQ). An investigation into the self-reporting of "real-life" memory skills. *British Journal of Social and Clinical Psychology*, **19**, 177–188.

Bower, G. H., Black, J. B. and Turner, J. T. (1979). Scripts in text comprehension and memory. *Cognitive Psychology*, **11**, 177–220.

Bower, G. H. (1981). Mood and Memory. *American Psychologist*, **36**, 129–148.

Bowlby, J. (1980). "Attachment and Loss Vol. 3: Loss" (Sadness and Depression), Penguin, Harmondsworth.

Broadbent, D. E., Cooper, P. F., Fitzgerald, P. and Parkes, K. R. (1982). The Cognitive Failures Questionnaire (CFQ) and its correlates. *British Journal of Clinical Psychology*, **21**, 1–16.

Bruner, J. S. (1957). On perceptual readiness. *Psychological Review*, **64**, 123–152.

Cantor, N. and Mischel, W. (1977). Traits as prototypes: Effects on recognition memory. *Journal of Personality and Social Psychology*, **35**, 38–48.

Chase, W. G. and Simon, H. A. (1973). The mind's eye in chess. *In* "Visual Information Processing" (W. G. Chase, ed.), Academic Press, New York and London.

Claxton, G. (1980). "Cognitive Psychology: New Directions", Routledge & Kegan Paul, London.

De Groot, A. D. (1965). "Thought and Choice in Chess", Mouton, The Hague.

Dichgans, J. and Brandt, T. (1978). Visual-vestibular interactions. *In* "Handbook of Sensory Physiology" (R. Held, Leibowitz and H-L. Teuber, eds), Vol. VIII, Springer-Verlag, Berlin.

Ericsson, K. A. and Simon, H. A. (1980). Verbal reports as data. *Psychological Review*, **87**, 215–251.

Fiske, S. T. and Linville, P. W. (1980) What does the schema concept buy us? *Personality and Social Psychology Bulletin*, **6**, 543–557.

Freud, S. (1901) "The Psychopathology of Everyday Life", Penguin, Harmondsworth.

Freud, S. (1922). "Introductory Lectures on Psychoanalysis", George Allen & Unwin, London.

Hamilton, V. and Warburton, D. (1980). "Human Stress and Cognition", Wiley, Chichester.

Hastie, R. (1981). Schematic principles in human memory. *In* "Social Cognition — The Ontario Symposium Vol. I" (E. T. Higgins, P. Herman, and M. P. Zanna, eds), Erlbaum, Hillsdale, N.J.

Herrmann, D. J. and Neisser, U. (1978). An inventory of everyday memory experiences. *In* "Practical Aspects of Memory" (M. M. Gruneberg, P. E. Morris and R. N. Sykes, eds), Academic Press, London and New York.

Hockey, G. R. J. (1973). Changes in information selection patterns in multi-source monitoring as a function of induced arousal shifts. *Journal of Experimental Psychology*, **101**, 35–42.

Hockey, G. R. J. and Hamilton P. (1970). Arousal and information selection in short-term memory. *Nature* (London), **226**, 866–867.

Horowitz, M. J. (1979). Psychological response to serious life stress. *In* "Human Stress and Cognition" (V. Hamilton and D. M. Warburton, eds), Wiley, Chichester.

James, W. (1890). "The Principles of Psychology", Holt, New York.

James, W. (1899). "Psychology: The Briefer Course", Harper & Brothers, New York.

James, W. (1908). "Talks to Teachers on Psychology: and to Students on some of Life's Ideals", Longmans, Green & Co, London.

Lazarus, R. S. (1966). "Psychological Stress and the Coping Process", McGraw Hill, New York.

Lindsay, P. H. and Norman, D. A. (1972). "Human Information Processing", Academic Press, New York and London.

Mandler, G. (1975). "Mind and Emotion", Wiley, New York.

Miller, G., Galanter, E. and Pribram, K. (1960). "Plans and the Structure of Behaviour", Holt Rinehart & Winston, New York.

Minsky, M. (1975). A framework for representing knowledge. *In* "The Psychology of Computer Vision" (P. H. Winston, ed.), McGraw Hill, New York.

Morris, P. (1981). The cognitive psychology of self-reports. *In* "The Psychology of Ordinary Explanations of Social Behaviour" (C. Antaki, ed.), Academic Press, London and New York.

Neisser, U. (1967). "Cognitive Psychology", Appleton-Century-Crofts, New York.

Neisser, U. (1976). "Cognition and Reality", W. H. Freeman, San Francisco.

Neisser, U. (1978). Memory: what are the important questions? In "Practical Aspects of Memory" (M. M. Gruneberg, P. Morris, and R. N. Sykes, eds), Academic Press, London and New York.

Nisbett, R. and Ross, L. (1980). "Human Inference: Strategies and Shortcomings of Social Judgement", Prentice-Hall, Englewood Cliffs, N.J.

Nisbett, R. E. and Wilson, T. D. (1977). Telling more than we know: verbal reports on mental processes. *Psychological Review*, **84**, 231–279.

Norman, D. A. and Bobrow, D. G. (1975). "Representation and Understanding: Studies in Cognitive Science", Academic Press, New York and London.

Norman, D. A. (1981). Categorization of action slips. *Psychological Review*, **88**, 1–15.

Polanyi, M. (1958). "Personal Knowledge", Routledge & Kegan Paul, London.

Reason, J. T. (1975). How did I come to do that? *New Behaviour*.

Reason, J. T. (1976). Absent minds. *New Society*, **4**, 244–245.

Reason, J. T. (1977). Skill and error in everyday life. In "Adult Learning" (Howe, M., ed.), Wiley, London.

Reason, J. T. (1979). Actions not as planned: the price of automatisation. In "Aspects of Consciousness vol. I: Psychological Issues" (G. Underwood and R. Stevens, eds), Academic Press, London and New York.

Reason, J. T. (1982). Lapses of attention In "Varieties of Attention" (R. Parasuraman, R. Davies, and J. Beatty, eds), Academic Press, New York and London.

Reason, J. T. and Mycielska, K. (1982). "Absent-Minded? The Psychology of Mental Lapses and Everyday Errors", Prentice-Hall, Englewood Cliffs, N.J.

Reason, J. T., Wagner, H. L. and Dewhurst, D. (1981). A visually-driven postural after-effect. *Acta Psychologica*, **48**, 241–251.

Schmidt, R. A. (1976). The schema as a solution to some persistent problems in motor learning theory. In "Motor Control: Issues and Trends" (G. E. Stelmach, ed.) Academic Press, New York and London.

Selfridge, D. (1959). Pandemonium: A paradigm for learning. In "Symposium on the Mechanization of Thought Processes", H.M. Stationery Office, London.

Shallice, T. (1972). Dual functions of consciousness. *Psychological Review*, **79**, 383–393.

Shallice, T. (1978). The dominant action system: an information-processing approach to consciousness. In "The Stream of Consciousness" (J. L. Singer and K. Pope, eds), Plenum Press, New York.

Srull, T. K. and Wyer, R. S. (1979). The role of category accessibility in the interpretation of information about persons: some determinants and implications. *Journal of Personality and Social Psychology*, **37**, 1660–1672.

Sully, J. (1884). "Outlines of Psychology", Longmans, Green and Co., London.

Taylor, S. E. and Crocker, J. C. (1981). Schematic bases of social information processing. In "Social Cognition: The Ontario Symposium. Vol. I" (E. T. Higgins, P. Herman, and M. P. Zanna, eds), Erlbaum, Hillsdale, N.J.

Teasdale, J. D. (1982). Negative thinking in depression. Unpublished paper.

Timpanaro, S. (1976). "The Freudian Slip", New Left Books, London.

White, P. (1980). Limitations on verbal reports of internal events: a refutation of Nisbett and Wilson and of Bem. *Psychological Review*, **87**, 105–112.

8

Questionnaires about Memory

D. J. Herrmann

I. INTRODUCTION

Over the last two decades, the questionnaire has increasingly come into use to study memory in everyday life. Questionnaires have been adopted to investigate memory ecologically because they provide an efficient way to gather information about memory functioning, information that would be considerably more difficult to acquire by field or laboratory research. Nevertheless, in the course of using questionnaires to study memory, it has become clear that the interpretation of questionnaire results is not as simple as it initially appeared.

The purpose of this chapter is to examine a crucial factor in the interpretation of questionnaire results in memory. This factor is the content of questionnaires. Previous reviews (Erber, 1981; Herrmann, 1982b) paid little attention to the implications of questionnaire content since they concentrated on reviewing the reliability and validity of these questionnaires. Questionnaire content is crucial because the soundness of the interpretation of questionnaire data depends on a proper understanding of content and the match between content and the memory issues of interest. Although sound research depends on such an understanding, it is rarely manifested in the literature. Investigators usually report the results for one questionnaire; they do not explain why the questionnaire used was selected over others; and they do not consider whether the questions unique to the questionnaire's results were critical to the results (e.g. Sunderland et al., 1983). Clearly, if the literature is to avoid being filled with ambiguous questionnaire findings (i.e. ones due to unique questions of questionnaires), greater attention has to be paid to questionnaire content.

This chapter addresses questionnaire content in four sections. The first section describes the two major kinds of questionnaires used to study memory. The second and third sections break down questionnaire content for each kind. Finally, discussion is devoted to the utility of questionnaires in memory research, taking acount of the present content analysis and of previous research.

Everyday Memory

II. KINDS OF QUESTIONNAIRES

At the most general level, there are two kinds of questionnaires. *Memory questionnaires* (MQ) ask people to recognise or recall knowledge or events. *Metamemory questionnaires* (MMQs) ask people to indicate how well they recognize or recall knowledge or events. Although these two kinds of questionnaires may seem to be similar, further consideration reveals that they differ in important ways. MQs ask about world knowledge or events; MMQs ask about memory functioning. MQs assess a person's memory performance; MMQs assess a person's beliefs about his or her memory performance. Since MQs assess what a person remembers, MQs are tests. In contrast, MMQs covered in this chapter are not tests since scoring does not involve comparing answers against a sample of relevant behaviour (MMQs could, of course, be treated as tests by using a behavioural standard for scoring; cf. the developmental literature, such as Flavell and Wellman, 1977). Instead, MMQs amount to a kind of opinion survey where the opinions pertain to a respondent's own memory performance. Because of these current scoring practices, a score on a MQ reflects how good a person's memory is, whereas an MMQ reflects how good a person *thinks* his or her memory is.

Since both MQs and MMQs are concerned with memory performance, either directly or indirectly, it will be useful to consider the relations between MQs, MMQs and the conventional laboratory memory tasks (LMTs) that most memory researchers have used. Consider, first, the relation between MQs and LMTs. Both are tests in that they draw upon memory for knowledge and for events. In the case of MQs, however, the researchers use one of the cases where natural memories acquired *outside* the laboratory may be tested and scored, i.e. episodic or semantic (see Table I for examples).

This distinction between MQs and LMTs becomes important when standardized measurement of individual differences is considered. Traditionally, clinical assessment of memory problems has been carried out with a standardized LMT (such as the Wechsler Memory Scale, 1945; see also Erickson and Scott, 1977; and Carroll and Maxwell, 1979), which consists of a series of tests in several intentional verbal learning paradigms, whereas MQs typically test for material learned in an incidental manner. MQs test for knowledge, i.e. established facts; standardized LMTs usually test for memory of presentations of verbal items. Thus, MQs and standardized LMTs may draw upon different memory skills and they should not be regarded as equivalent measures of a single memory aptitude.

III. MEMORY QUESTIONNAIRES (MQs)

MQs are of two types. One type tests semantic memories and the other type, episodic memories (Tulving, 1972; Baddeley and Wilkins, 1984, Chapter 1 this volume; Bahrick and Karis, 1982). An example of a semantic question is "What year did World War I end?" An example of an episodic question is "When did you last dine out?"

Within each of the two types of MQs, there are several different kinds of questions which each address, in the one case, a different body of knowledge (e.g. historical facts, names of TV shows) or, in the other case, personal experiences (past illnesses, high school acquaintances). Table I lists the contents of MQs, semantic and episodic, and for each content, a list of investigations concerned with that content. Most of the citations in the table consist of questionnaire studies, but some of them consist of laboratory studies, included because their findings suggest interpretations of MQs of the same content.

A good deal is known now about MQs and what they measure. Their psychometric properties are summarized next according to the two types of MQs.

A. Semantic MQs

Since this kind of MQ asks about established knowledge, scoring is relatively straightforward (Sanders, 1972). While reliability usually has not been reported for these instruments, it appears to be satisfactory since studies involving them are very replicable. The validity of these instruments, i.e. as a measure of long-term meory, is shown by findings concerning how relevant variables affect MQ scores. For example, a person's age has been found to be inversely related to the likelihood of recalling historical information (e.g. Warrington and Sanders, 1971) and trivia (Squire and Slater, 1975; Squire et al. 1975), although this relationship may vary according to the age at which the information was supposedly acquired (Botwinick and Storandt, 1974, 1980; Storandt et al., 1978; Perlmutter et al., 1980; Poon et al., 1979; for an excellent review of this research see Erber, 1981). In the recall of novels, memory differs for abstract and concrete statements (Neisser and Hupcey, 1974). In addition, the amount of knowledge revealed by responses to a football questionnaire correlated substantially (.8) with ability to learn new scores (Morris et al., 1981). Finally, expected individual differences have been found: e.g. amnesics and schizophrenics show less knowledge of historical facts than do controls (Squire, 1982; Johnson et al., 1977); memory of TV programmes for patients with brain atrophy is inversely related to the extent of atrophy (Wu et al., 1981). These findings and others obtained by investigators cited in Table I indicate that semantic MQs represent a valid way to investigate memory.

B. Episodic MQs

While semantic MQs may be easily scored, this is not always true of episodic MQs. In some cases, there are means for assessing the accuracy of responses,

Table I. Topics of memory questionnaire

Semantic MQs

Historic public events
   Warrington and Sanders (1971); Warrington and Silberstein (1970); Riegel (1973); Botwinick and Storandt (1974; 1980); Johnson and Klingler (1976); Perlmutter *et al.* (1980); Poon *et al.* (1979); Squire and Slater (1978); Cohen and Squire (1981).
Trivia
   Race Horses
      Squire and Slater (1975)
   TV Shows
      Squire and Slater (1975); Squire *et al.* (1975); Squire *et al.* (1975); Harvey and Crovitz (1979); Levin *et al.* (1977); Squire and Cohen (1979); Squire and Fox (1980); Cohen and Squire (1981)
   Football knowledge
      Morris *et al.* (1981)
   Entertainment
      Storandt *et al.* (1978)
Prose
   Sherlock Holmes
      Neisser and Hupcey (1974)
   Dick and Jane Primers
      Read and Barnsley (1977)
   Classic Passages
      Rubin (1977)
Advertisements
      Burtt and Dobell (1925); Blankenship and Whiteley (1941); Bucci (1973); Bekerian and Baddeley (1980); Holbrook and Lehman (1980); Wagenaar (1978)
Famous Faces
      Yarmey (1973); Marslen-Wilson and Teuber (1975); Albert *et al.* (1979); Cohen and Squire (1981).
Acquaintance Faces
      Bahrick *et al.* (1975); Baddeley (1979b)
Acquaintance Names
      Williams and Hollan (1981); Whitten and Leonard (1981)
Places
   Floorplans
      Norman and Rumelhart (1975)
   Environment
      Kozlowski and Bryant (1977), Bahrick (1979)
Common objects
      Nickerson and Adams (1979); Walker (1975)
Possessions
      Parry and Crossley (1950)
Formal knowledge
      Nelson and Narens (1980); Shimamura *et al.* (1981)

College entrance exams
  Hunt, (1978)
Spanish comprehension
  Bahrick and Karis (1982)

Episodic MQs

Salient recent life events
  Casey *et al.* (1967); Jenkins *et al.* (1979)
Salient remote life events
  Field (1981)
Personally experienced historical event
  Colgrove (1899); Brown and Kulik (1977); Yarmey and Bull (1978)
Group meeting
  Keenan *et al.* (1977); Kintsch and Bates (1977)
Past sport matches
  Baddeley and Hitch (1976)
Participation as a subject in laboratory research
  Baddeley *et al.* (1978)
Past events in general
  Miles (1893); Colgrove (1899); Henri and Henri (1897); Robinson (1976);
  Rubin (1982); Linton (1975, 1978, 1982)
Past Actions
  Voting
  Himmelweit *et al.* (1978)

---

e.g. recognition of faces of high school classmates on the basis of yearbook pictures (Bahrick *et al.*, 1975), memory for responses to a previous survey (Field, 1981), and memory for major life events (Casey *et al.*, 1967). But in other cases, there are no means to verify the accuracy of responses, e.g. recollections of past events (such as studied by Brown and Kulik, 1977; Robinson, 1976), voting (Himmelweit *et al.*, 1978), and questions about one's past, such as are asked on initial clinical interviews for patients suspected of cognitive deficits (Talland, 1968; Erickson and Scott, 1977). In these situations, records are poor or non-existent; similarly, witnesses are rarely available, and even when they are, their account of events are usually no more trustworthy than those of the subjects being studied.

When there is no external information to use in scoring episodic MQs, accuracy of recall cannot be assessed directly from a protocol. Nevertheless, accuracy may be inferred sometimes from secondary aspects of a protocol. First, professed ability to recall little or nothing from an episode may be regarded as reflecting a poorer memory for the event than professed ability to recall all of the episode (Herrmann, 1982a). However, such an inference is far from being watertight since a low level of recall may be due to a subject being cautious and a high level of recall may be due to a subject confabulating. Second, recall protocols may be checked for internal consistency. Minor inconsistency may detract less from judged accuracy of recall than major inconsistency on the principal details of the episode (Neisser, 1967). Third, recall protocols may be assessed for psycholinguistic properties (e.g. sentence length, abstract concreteness; see Neisser and Hupcey, 1974) or for attributes (e.g. time, location, social context; Herrmann, 1982a).

Interpretation of non-verifiable episodic-memory scores must, obviously, be done with caution. Nevertheless, it is clear that non-verifiable memories as assessed with episodic MQs behave in at least some respects like verifiable memories. For example, research on non-verifiable memories indicate that life events are forgotten over time (Casey et al., 1967; Colgrove, 1899; Robinson, 1976; Rubin, 1982; Waldfogel, 1948), retention of a life event is greater if it is salient (Colgrove, 1899; Brown and Kulik, 1977), recall depends on the nature of cues (Robinson, 1976), and difficulty in recalling facts about one's background (as on a clinical intake exam) indicates the presence of severe memory disorders (Erickson and Scott, 1977).

When there is external information, it is obviously easy to score and interpret an episodic MQ. These two properties (ease of scoring and of interpretation) make this kind of questionnaire well suited to investigating the determinants of memory accuracy in everyday life, and also for investigating whether laboratory findings and theories generalize to everyday uses of memory. For example, verifiable episodic MQs have in recent years provided insights into the retention of daily experience (e.g. rugby scores, Baddeley and Hitch, 1976; participation in psychological research, Baddeley et al., 1978).

IV. METAMEMORY QUESTIONNAIRES (MMQs)

In the past several years considerable interest has been given to understanding the relationship between a person's self knowledge and performance (Brown, 1978; Cavanaugh and Perlmutter, 1982; Ceci and Howe, 1982; Flavell, 1977; Herrmann, 1982b; Lieberman, 1979; Morris, 1984, Chapter 9 this volume; Nisbett and Wilson, 1977; Pryor, 1980; Smith and Miller, 1978; White, 1980). MMQs represent an extension of this interest. MMQs ask one or more of several kinds of questions about a person's memory performance. Answers to these questions, as described above, represent a person's beliefs* concerning his or her memory experiences (Herrmann, 1982b; Chaffin and Herrmann, 1983). This section will first review briefly the psychometric properties of MMQs (based on a more extensive review, Herrmann (1982b) and on research reported since that review; see also Martin and Jones, 1984, Chapter 10 this volume; and Reason and Mycielska, 1982), and then the content of MMQs will be analysed.

---

* The beliefs sampled by MMQs pertain to memory functioning, either generally or within a designated recent interval. Thus, the purpose of MMQs is to assess beliefs about memory aptitude. Beliefs about an isolated memory experience (e.g. that I believe I forgot a person's name last Thursday) are not sampled by MMQs since a belief about a particular experience cannot be expected on its own to reveal a person's memory aptitude.

A. Psychometric properties

At present, 18 MMQs have been developed, most independently of each other. The names of these instruments and the sources originally reporting them are presented in Table II. All of these questionnaires use self reports to assess one or more aspects of memory performance: how frequently the respondents forget, how clearly they remember, how their memory has changed, how easily they learn, what memory strategies they use, and how they feel about their memory performance.

Table II. Metamemory questionnaires

Questionnaire	Original Report
Cognitive Failures Questionnaire (CFQ)	Broadbent, *et al.* (1982)
Everyday Memory Questionnaire (EMQ)	Sunderland *et al.* (1983)
Everyday Memory Questionnaire (EMQ-M)	Martin (1983) cited by Martin and Jones (1983)
Head Injury Postal Questionnaire (HIPQ)	Harris and Sunderland (1980)
How Good is Your Memory Questionnaire (HGMQ)	Wright (1975)
Inventory of Learning Processes (ILP)	Schmeck *et al.* (1977)
Inventory of Memory Experiences (IME)	Herrmann and Neisser (1978)
Short Inventory of Memory Experiences (SIME)	Herrmann (1979)
Memory Change Questionnaire (MCQ)	Cronholm and Ottoson (1961)
Memory Questionnaire (MQ)—Ash	Ash (1977)
Memory Questionnaire (MQ)—Perlmutter	Perlmutter (1978)
Memory Scale (MS)	Sehulster (1981a)
Metamemory Questionnaire (MMQ)	Zelinski *et al.* (1980)
Self Assessment of Laboratory Tasks (SALT)	Herrmann *et al.* (1983)
Slips of Action Inventory (SAI)	Reason (1981)
Task/Error Questionnaire (TEQ)	Reason (1983)
Error Proneness Questionnaire (EPQ)	Reason (1981)
Subjective Memory Questionnaire (SMQ)	Bennett-Levy and Powell (1980)

Note: For a questionnaire concerning attention, see Martin's Everyday Attention Questionnaire (referred to in Chapter 10 of this volume)

MMQs generally possess comparably high reliabilities (test retest $r \doteq .8$) and, moderate to low validity (validity coefficients are usually $<.5$; see Herrmann, 1982a). For example, correlations between face recognition accuracy and self reports of face recognition performance, as given on the SIME, have been low ($r \doteq .3$; Shlechter et al., 1982) to non-existant (Ken Deffenbacher, personal communication). Two questionnaires (the SIME and the SMQ) have been found to have moderate correlations (about .4) between recall on a digit span task and self estimates of tendency to forget rote information like phone numbers and addresses (see also Martin and Jones, 1984, Chapter 10 this volume).

Validity coefficients have sometimes been larger when the criteria were not direct measures of performance. For example, a person's self reports of memory performance for various kinds of information (as assessed by the SIME and the CFQ) has been found to have low (.2) to substantial (.7) correlations with reports on the person's performance made by his or her spouse (Broadbent et al., 1982; Chaffin et al., 1980). Another study indicated that college students' reports about specific events (e.g. going to a party) were also only weakly correlated with how well the student indicated he or she remembers these events (on the SIME; Thompson, 1982).

Individual differences that one might expect to occur with MMQs often do: psychiatric patients rate their memory worse than do normals (on the MCQ, and MQ-Ash); neurologically impaired patients do likewise (on the EMQ, HIPQ, and the SMQ). However, some expected individual differences are not found. Questionnaire responses and performance on memory tasks are uncorrelated for both psychiatric patients and neurologically-impaired patients (Ash, 1977; Bennett-Levy and Powell, 1980; Cronholm and Ottoson, 1961; Sunderland et al., 1983). In addition, some elderly subjects rate their memory higher than younger subjects and other elderly subjects rate their memory lower than younger subjects (in studies using either the SIME, HIPQ, or the SMQ; for more details on these results, see Chaffin and Herrmann, 1983; Sunderland et al., 1984, Chapter 11 this volume; Zelinski et al., 1980).

The pattern of these findings shows that MMQ validity ranges from weak to moderate. The range of validity precludes use of MMQs as a substitute for measurement of actual memory performance. The lack of adequate validity for direct assessment of performance has two possible causes: inadequate design of current MMQs and/or inadequate self knowledge of people for their memory abilities. While it is likely that refinements of current MMQs will improve their validity (see Morris, 1984, Chapter 9 this volume), two recent investigations indicate that the prime reason for less-than-satisfactory validity is the poor self knowledge of memory abilities. Both of these investigations show that experience observing oneself perform enhances correspondence between self reports on MMQs and observed memory performance. Shlechter and Herrmann (1981) failed to find significant correlations between the SIME and the frequency of various kinds of forgetting recorded subsequently in a diary (kept for 10 days). However, answers to a second administration of the SIME, given after keeping the diary, correlated significantly (about .5) for five of the eight factors. Herrmann *et al.* (1983) found either no, or a weak, relationship between reported ability to perform ten laboratory memory tasks (on the SALT questionnaire; see Table II) and subsequent tests of performance on these tasks (<.42). However, answers to a second administration of the SALT, given after performance of the memory tests (with no feedback), yielded eight significant correlations (from .30 to .87) across three replications of the study. Thus, awareness of one's memory aptitude, in and out of the lab, is fostered by recent experience with the appropriate memory task and with judging the adequacy of performance in this task. Moreover, since several of the validity coefficients in these two studies were substantial (i.e. >.5) when questionnaire responses were made after the relevant experience, MMQs are seen to be capable of eliciting accurate self reports after all. Thus, MMQ design is not the major reason validities have been low to moderate in past research, but it is rather that subjects have been unaware of their performance capabilities either through inattention or lack of experience (cf. Morris, 1984, Chapter 9 this volume).

Although the low to moderate validity of MMQs precludes their use in assessment of performance, they may be useful in indicating how people process information in memory tasks because beliefs about memory ability, like other beliefs people hold, affect behaviour. First, beliefs about memory ability determine whether or not a person chooses to engage in a behaviour (Sehulster, 1981a; e.g. some people avoid parties because they believe they are poor at learning or recalling names). Second, beliefs about memory ability influence how a person goes about performing a memory task; e.g. people with poorer impressions of their memory ability report using both external memory aids, such as notepads (Zelinski *et al.*, 1980), and internal aids, such as rehearsal (Perlmutter, 1978), but check relevant information less often (Barnard *et al.*, 1982). Third, people who believe their memory is poor are more susceptible to cognitive failure under stress (Broadbent *et al.*, 1982; see Sehulster, 1981b, 1982; Martin and Jones, 1984, Chapter 10 this volume; Reason, 1984, Chapter 7 this volume).

The role of beliefs in guiding memory behaviour takes on greater importance when considered in light of MMQ validity. As has been discussed, MMQ validity indicates that the beliefs people hold about their memory aptitude are full of inaccuracies. If beliefs are often inaccurate and if beliefs influence a person's use of strategies, then people often apply the wrong strategy for the task at hand. For example, people who falsely believe they are good at learning names may pay less than complete attention during introductions.

B. MMQ content

MMQs are not all alike. Their content overlaps but not completely. Since the content of individual questionnaires has been described previously (Herrmann, 1982b), the present analysis of MMQ content will elucidate the kinds of beliefs sampled in general.

The content analysis is reported below in two sections. The first section examines the kinds of *memory phenomena* investigated with MMQs. The second section examines the types of *memory task* or *experience* respondents are asked about by MMQs. The analysis was based on those MMQs in Table II that were original, i.e. that were not derived from an earlier questionnaire.

Memory phenomena. Across MMQs, six different kinds of memory phenomena have received investigative attention (see Perlmutter, 1978). These memory phenomena include normal memory performance, memory performance under stress, memory demands (environmental pressures to use memory, e.g. a demanding job), mnemonic strategy use, changes of performance with age, and memory knowledge (of the laws and principles of memory performance). Questions about normal memory performance invariably occur in all MMQs; questions about the remaining phenomena are

Table III. Memory tasks asked about by metamemory questionnaires

Common events and tasks		Semantic information	
Routine acts	9	Facts	4
Appointments	7	Vocabulary	4
Places	7	Rote information	5
Conversations	6	Trivia	1
Recalling names	6		
Recognizing people	6		
Errands	4	*Skill memory*	
Voices	2	Mnemonic skills	1
Odours	1	Other skills	1
Shows	1		
Music	1		
Emotion	1	*Memory vulnerabilities*	
Directions	2	Performance of memory task under stress	1
		Inclination to perceptual errors	1
Specific Episodes			
Middle years	3		
Recent events	3		
Childhood	2		
Prior act	1		
Trauma	1		
Books	2		

Note: Each count represents the number of metamemory questionnaires (out of a maximum of ten) that contained at least one question dealing with the tasks listed.

much less frequent, i.e. occurring on three MMQs or less. Within each kind of phenomena the questions sometimes deal specifically with a particular stage of memory processing (acquisition, retention, or retrieval), and they may specify the type of test (e.g. *recognizing* a face or *recalling* a name).

Memory Tasks. In addition to indicating the kinds of memory phenomena, MMQs also point out the kinds of daily tasks that questionnaire compilers believe most often challenge memory. Examples of tasks reported as leading to memory failure most often are the learning of names and the keeping of appointments. Examples of less troublesome memory tasks are remembering names of products and optional chores (Herrmann and Neisser, 1978).

A systematic analysis of the kinds of tasks queried by MMQs (those starred in Table II) is presented in Table III. This analysis examined task content of MMQs at a general and specific level. At a general level, MMQs were judged to ask about five kinds of content. The first content area, common events, refers to classes of memory failures that confront us, intermittently through-out our lives. Besides performing routine memory tasks (misplacing things, remembering appointments: see Norman, 1981; Reason, 1981, 1984, Chapter 7 this volume; Reason and Mycielska, 1982), people are called upon to re-member a variety of aspects of events (what was said, who was present, a person's voice, etc.). The second content area, unique events, simply refers to the remembering of personal experience or autobiographical experience. The third content area is concerned with the retention of semantic information (regardless of events leading to acquiring the information). The second and third content areas correspond to what Tulving (1972) has called semantic and episodic memory; all three content areas correspond to the factors of Sehulster's (1981a, 1982a, 1982b) Memory Scale. The fourth and fifth content areas are concerned with aspects of task performance that transcend many kinds of memory tasks. The fourth content area pertains to remembering how one performs various skills, e.g. how well one plays tennis, how one uses memory strategies in a learning task. Finally, the fifth content area, memory vulnerability, has to do with how often failures at memory tasks are precipitated by non-memory factors, e.g. stress, perceptual difficulties.

The content analysis also found that several specific kinds of memory tasks occurred within each of the five general categories. These specific tasks are also listed in Table III. The number alongside each specific task represents the number of questionnaires (out of ten) that had one or more questions asking about the task or aspect of task performance. Many of the kinds of specific memory tasks listed in the table have been identified as separate by factor analyses of MMQs (Bennett-Levy and Powell, 1980; Herrmann and Neisser, 1978; Sehulster, 1981a, b, 1982; Schmeck *et al.*, 1977; Schmeck, 1983). Others I have isolated to make clear content differences where factor analyses have not been done or where factor analyses failed to capture otherwise apparent differences.

It might be argued that the content differences among questionnaires are not very great and, thus, not a matter for concern. For example, Broadbent *et al.* (1982) cited data of James Reason that showed that the CFQ, SIME, and SAI questionnaires correlate with each other substantially (r's≐.6). Although there is good reason to assume that MMQs reflect (in part) an overall belief about memory aptitude, these correlations among questionnaires should not be interpreted as showing that MMQs are all alike (cf. Morris, 1984, Chapter 9 this volume). Indeed, the variance common to any two of these questionnaires is no more than about 36% and when the common variance is analysed according to subscales rather than to entire questionnaires, it becomes clear that some parts of different questionnaires agree more than other parts (Bennett-Levy and Powell, 1980; Martin and Jones, 1984, Chapter 10 this volume).

V. DISCUSSION

The present review has shown that questionnaires used to study memory are not all alike. Differing in kind and content, each questionnaire requires a particular interpretation. Because each questionnaire is unique in some ways, it may be useful to discuss the utility of the questionnaire approach to memory while heeding variations in content.

The utility of MQs and that of MMQs are similar in that both may be used as an index of a person's everyday memory functioning. However, the low-to-moderate predictive validity of MMQs argues against such a use unless employed with an LMT. The MQ need not be used with an LMT but the MQ may not be as valid as LMTs. The validity of MQs, while very good, may be less adequate than that of LMTs because the conditions of acquisition and retention of relevant experience are unknown (Baddeley, 1979a). Since it is likely that these conditions will rarely, if ever, be fully determined for the information queried by MQs the implications of these questionnaires for measuring retention will usually be less clear than that of laboratory tests of retention. This latter point applies also to the validity of MMQs as measures of memory aptitude except that this validity is undermined further by the inaccuracy of a person's beliefs about one's memory performance in everyday life (see Morris, 1984, Chapter 9 this volume). Since it is likely that under normal conditions memory aptitude beliefs will always be inaccurate, the validity of current MMQs will never approach that for LMTs or for MQs either.

The memory ability beliefs reflected by MMQs offer a second kind of utility for these questionnaires. In that these beliefs may influence use of memory strategies, memory aptitude beliefs may provide useful clues as to why a person uses his or her memory system in a particular way. The utility of using MMQs to elucidate a person's memory aptitude beliefs will always be limited, however, by the degree to which self reports on these questionnaires are honestly given.

The utility of MQs and MMQs is constrained further by the content of questionnaires. Content is important because validity varies within it. Current evidence indicates that, like memory aptitude (Baddeley, 1983; Underwood *et al.*, 1981), memory ability beliefs are domain specific (Herrmann and Neisser, 1978; Schmeck *et al.*, 1977; Schmeck, 1983; Sehulster, 1981a). Because the content of MQs (Table I) and MMQs (Table III and text) ranges over so many domains, great care must be exercised in generalizing questionnaire results until the boundaries for generalization have been established.

In conclusion, what has been gained, and what is to be gained, from the use of questionnaires in memory research? What *has* been gained is, primarily, the development of a new methodology, and secondarily, a more detailed account of memory in everyday life. What *is* to be gained depends on the ingenuity of those who use the new methodology (cf. Baddeley, 1981; 1983; Neisser, 1978, 1982). Like the memory drum when it was introduced approximately 80 years ago, questionnaires about memory offer memory researchers an innovative and promising new way to investigate memory.

ACKNOWLEDGMENT

I thank Phil Barnard, John Harris, Jonathan Schooler and Alan Sunderland for very helpful advice on this chapter. I also thank Roger Chaffin, Royal Grueneich, Lori Grubs, Dick Neisser, Ted Shlechter, and Ron Sigmundi for helping me understand various facets of memory in everyday life discussed in this chapter.

REFERENCES

Albert, M. S. Butters, N. and Levin, J. (1979). Temporal gradients in the retrograde manesia of patients with alcoholic Korsakoff's disease. *Archives of Neurology*, **36**, 211–216.

Ash, R. C. (1977). Memory: Clinical assessment and behaviour measures—a short study of the Wechsler Memory Scale. Unpublished M.Phil. dissertation, University of London.

Baddeley, A. D. (1979a). The limitations of human memory: Implications for the design of retrospective surveys. *In* "The Recall Method in Social Sciences" (L. Moss and H. Goldstein eds), University of London Institute of Education series, London.

Baddeley, A. D. (1979b). Applied cognitive and cognitive applied psychology: The case of face recognition. *In* "Perspectives in Memory Research" (L. G. Nilsson, ed.), Erlbaum, Hillsdale, N.J.

Baddeley, A. D. (1981). The cognitive psychology of everyday life. *British Journal of Psychology*, **72**, 257–269.

Baddeley, A. D. (1983). Domains of recollection. *Psychological Review*, **89**, 807–729.

Baddeley, A. D. and Hitch, G. (1976). *In* "Attention and Performance II" (S. Dornic, ed.), Academic Press, New York and London.

Baddeley, A. D. Lewis, V. and Nimmo-Smith, I. (1978). When did you last . . . ? *In* "Practical Aspects of Memory" (M. Gruneberg, P. Morris, and R. Sykes, eds), Academic Press, London and New York.

Baddeley, A. D. and Wilkins, A. J. (1984). Taking memory out of the laboratory. *In* "Everyday Memory, Actions and Absent-Mindedness" (J. E. Harris and P. E. Morris, eds), Academic Press, London, Orlando and New York.

Bahrick, H. P. (1979). Maintenance of knowledge: Questions about memory we forget to ask. *Journal of Experimental Psychology: General*, 108, 296–308.

Bahrick, H. P., Bahrick, P. O. and Wittlinger, R. P. (1975). Fifty years of memory for names and faces: A cross-sectional approach. *Journal of Experimental Psychology: General*, 104, 54–75.

Bahrick, H. P. and Karis, D. (1982). Long-term ecological memory. *In* "Handbook of Research Methods in Human Memory and Cognition" (C. R. Puff, ed.), Academic Press, New York and London.

Barnard, P. J. Hammond, N. V. MacLean, A. and Morton, J. (1982). Learning and remembering interactive commands in a text-editing task. *Behaviour and Information Technology*, 1 (4), 347–358.

Bekerian, D. A. and Baddeley, A. D. (1980). Saturation advertising and the repetition effect. *Journal of Verbal Learning and Verbal Behavior*, 19, 17–25.

Bennett-Levy, J. and Powell, G. E. (1980). The Subjective Memory Questionnaire (SMQ). I: An investigation into the self-reporting of "real life" memory skills. *British Journal of Social and Clinical Psychology*, 19, 177–178.

Blankenship, A. B. and Whitely, P. L. (1941). Proactive inhibition in the recall of advertising material. *Journal of Social Psychology*, 13, 311–322.

Botwinick, J. and Storandt, M. (1974). "Memory-related functions and age", Thomas, Springfield, Ill.

Botwinick, J. and Storandt, (1980). Recall and recognition of old information in relation to age and sex. *Journal of Gerontology*, 75, 70–76.

Broadbent, D. E., Cooper, P. F., Fitzgerald, P. and Parkes, K. R. (1982). The Cognitive Failures Questionnaire (CFQ) and its correlates. *British Journal of Clinical Psychology*, 21, 1–16.

Brown, A. L. (1978). Knowing when, where, and how to remember: A problem of metacognition. *In* "Advances in Instructional Psychology" (A. R. Glaser, ed.), Erlbaum, Hillsdale, N.J.

Brown, R. and Kulik, J. (1977). Flashbulb memories. *Cognition*, 5, 73–99.

Bucci, R. P. (1973). Erroneous recall of media. *Journal of Advertising Research*, 13, 23–27.

Burtt, H. E. and Dobell, E. M. (1925). The curve of forgetting for advertising material. *Journal of Applied Psychology*, 9, 5–21.

Carroll, J. B. and Maxwell, S. E. (1979). Individual differences in cognitive abilities. *Annual Review of Psychology*, 30, 603.40.

Casey, R. L., Masuda, M. and Holmes, T. H. (1967). Quantitative study of recall of life events. *The Journal of Psychosomatic Research*, 11, 239–247.

Cavanaugh, J. C. and Perlmutter, M. (1982). Metamemory: A critical examination. *Child Development*, 53, 11–28.

Ceci, M. and Howe, M. (1982). Metamemory. *In* "Consciousness" (Jones, ed.), Academic Press, London and New York.

Chaffin, R., Deffenbacher, K. and Herrmann, D. J. (1980). Awareness and lack of awareness of memory function between spouses. Trenton State College, Trenton, N.J.

Chaffin, R. and Herrmann, D. J. (1983). Self reports of memory performance as a function of age in adulthood. *Human Learning*, 2, 17–28.

Cohen, N. J. and Squire, L. R. (1981). Retrograde-amnesia and remote memory impairment. *Neuropsychologia*, 19, 337–356.

Colgrove, F. W. (1899). Individual memories. *American Journal of Psychology*, 10, 228–225.

Cronholm, B. and Ottoson, J. O. (1961). The experience of memory function after electroconvulsive therapy. *British Journal of Psychiatry*, 109, 251–258.

Erber; J. T. (1981). Remote memory and age: A review. *Experimental Aging Research*, 7, 189–199.

Erickson, R. C. and Scott, M. L. (1977). Clinical memory testing: A review. *Psychological Bulletin*, 84, 1130–1149.

Field, D. (1981). Retrospective reports by healthy intelligent elderly people of personal events of their adult lives. *International Journal of Behavioral Development*, 4, 77–97.

Flavell, J. H. (1977). "Cognitive Development", Prentice Hll, Englewood Cliffs, N.J.

Flavell, J. H. and Wellman, H. M. (1977). Metamemory. *In* "Perspectives on the Development of Memory and Cognition" (R. V. Kail and J. W. Hagan, eds), Erlbaum, Hillsdale, N.J.

Gruneberg, M. M. and Morris, P. E. (1979). "Applied problems in memory", Academic Press, New York and London.

Harris, J. E. (1980). Memory aids people use: Two interview studies. *Memory and Cognition*, 8, 31–38.

Harris, J. E. and Sunderland, A. (1980). Head injury postal questionnaire. Presented at Trauma International Meeting, Northampton.

Harvey, M. T. and Crovitz, H. F. (1979). Television questionnaire techniques in assessing forgetting in long-term memory. *Cortex*, 15, 609–618.

Henri, V. and Henri, C. (1897). Enquete sur les premiers de l'enfance. *L'Annee Psychologique*, 3, 184–198.

Herrmann, D. J. (1979). The validity of memory questionnaires as related to a theory of memory introspection. Presented at the British Psychological Meeting, London.

Herrmann, D. J. (1982a). Remembering past experiences: theoretical perspectives past and present. Conference on Current Trends in Cognitive Science, Cortland, New York.

Herrmann, D. J. (1982b). Know thy memory: The use of questionnaires to assess and study memory. *Psychological Bulletin*, 92, 434–452.

Herrmann, D. J., Grubs, L., Sigmundi, R. and Grueneich, R. (1983). Awareness of memory aptitude as a function of memory experience. British Psychological Society, York.

Herrmann, D. and Neisser, U. (1978). An inventory of everyday memory experiences. *In* "Practical Aspects of Memory" (M. M. Gruneberg, P. E. Morris and R. N. Sykes, eds) Academic Press, New York and London.

Himmelweit, H. T., Biberian, M. J. and Stockdale, J. (1978). Memory for past vote—implications of a study of bias in recall. *British Journal of Political Science*, 8, 365–375.

Holbrook, M. B. and Lehman, D. R. (1980). Form versus content in predicting starch scores. *Journal of Advertising Research*, 20, 53–62.

Hunt, E. (1978). Mechanics of verbal ability. *Psychological Review*, **85**, 109–130.

Jenkins, C. D., Hurst, M. W. and Rose, R. M. (1979). Life changes: Do people really remember? *Archives of General Psychiatry*, **36**, 379–384.

Johnson, H. and Klingler, D. (1976). A questionnaire technique for measurement of episodic long-term memory. *Psychological Reports*, **39**, 291–298.

Johnson, H., Klingler, D. and Williams, T. A. (1977). Recognition in episodic long-term memory in schizophrenia. *Journal of Clinical Psychology*, **33**, 643–647.

Keenan, J. M., MacWhinney, B. and Mayhew, D. (1977). Pragmatics in memory: A study of natural conversation. *Journal of Verbal Learning and Verbal Behavior*, **16**, 549–560.

Kintsch, W. and Bates, E. (1977). Recognition memory for statements from a classroom lecture. *Journal of Experimental Psychology: Human Learning and Memory*, **3**, 150–159.

Kozlowski, L. T. and Bryant, K. J. (1977). Sense of direction, spatial orientation, and cognitive maps. *Journal of Experimental Psychology: Human Perception and Performance*, **3**, 590–598.

Levin, H. S., Grossman, R. G. and Kelley, P. J. (1977). Assessment for long-term memory in brain-damaged patients. *Journal of Consulting and Clinical Psychology*, **45**, 684–688.

Lieberman, D. A. (1979). Behaviorism and the mind: A (Limited) call for a return to introspection. *American Psychologist*, **34**, 319–333.

Linton, M. (1975). Memory for real-world events. In "Explorations in Cognition" (D. H. Norman and D. E. Rumelhart, eds), Freeman, San Francisco.

Linton, M. (1978). Real-world memory after six years: An *in vivo* study of very long-term memory. In "Practical Aspects of Memory" (M. Gruneberg, P. Morris and R. N. Sykes, eds), Academic Press, London and New York.

Linton, M. (1982). Transformations of memory in everyday life. In "Memory Observed" (U. Neisser, ed.) Freeman, San Francisco.

Marslen-Wilson, W. D. and Teuber, H. L. (1975). Memory for remote events in anterograde amnesia: Recognition of public figures from news-photographs. *Neuropsychologia*, **13**, 353–364.

Martin, M. and Jones, G. V. (1984). Cognitive failures in everyday life. In "Everyday Memory, Actions and Absent-Mindedness" (J. E. Harris and P. E. Morris, eds.), Academic Press, London, Orlando and New York.

Miles, C. (1893). A study of individual psychology. *American Journal of Psychology*, **6**, 534–558.

Morris, P. E. (1984). The validity of subjective reports on memory. In "Everyday Memory, Actions, and Absent-Mindedness" (J. E. Harris and P. E. Morris, eds), Academic Press, London, Orlando and New York.

Morris, P. E., Gruneberg, M., Sykes, R. N. and Merrick, A. (1981). Football knowledge and the acquisition of new results. *British Journal of Psychology*, **72**, 479–484.

Neisser, U. (1967). "Cognitive Psychology", Appleton-Century-Crofts, New York.

Neisser, U. (1978). Memory: What are the important questions? In "Practical Aspects of Memory" (M. M. Gruneberg, P. Morris and R. N. Sykes, eds), Academic Press, London and New York.

Neisser, U. (1982). "Memory Observed", W. H. Freeman, San Francisco.

Neisser, U. and Hupcey, J. A. (1974). A Sherlockian experiment. *Cognition*, **3**, 307–311.

Nelson, T. O. and Narens, L. (1980). Norms of 300 general information questions:

Accuracy of recall, latency of recall, and feeling-of-knowing ratings. *Journal of Verbal Learning and Verbal Behavior*, **19**, 338–368.

Nickerson, R. S. and Adams, M. J. (1979). Long-term memory for a common object. *Cognitive Psychology*, **11**, 287–307.

Nisbett, R. E. and Wilson, T. D. (1977). Telling more than we can know: Verbal reports on mental processes. *Psychological Review*, **84**, 231–259.

Norman, D. A. (1981). Categorization of action slips. *Psychological Review*, **88**, 1–15.

Norman, D. A. and Rumelhart, D. E. (1975). Memory and knowledge. *In* "Explorations in Cognition" (D. A. Norman and D. E. Rumelhart, eds), Freeman, San Francisco.

Parry, H. J. and Crossley, H. M. (1950). Validity of responses to survey questions. *Public Opinion Quarterly*, **14**, 61–80.

Perlmutter, M. (1978). What is memory aging the aging of? *Developmental Psychology*, **14**, 330–345.

Perlmutter, M., Metzger, R., Miller, K. and Negwolski, T. (1980). Memory of historical events. *Experimental Aging Research*, **6**, 46–60.

Poon, L. W., Fozard, J. L., Paulshock, D. R.and Thomas, J. C. (1979). A questionnaire assessment of age differences in retention of recent and remote events. *Experimental Aging Research*, **5**, 401–411.

Pryor, J. B. (1980). Self reports and behaviour. *In* "The Self in Social Psychology" (D. M. Wegner and R. R. Vallacher, eds), Oxford University Press, New York.

Read, J. D. and Barnsley, R. H. (1977). Remember Dick and Jane? Memory for elementary school readers. *Canadian Journal of Behavioral Science*, **9**, 361–370.

Reason, J. T. (1981). Lapses of attention. *In* "Varieties of Attention" (R. Parasuraman, R. Davies, and J. Beatty, eds), Academic Press, New York and London.

Reason, J. T. (1984a). Absent-mindedness and cognitive control. *In* "Everyday Memory, Actions and Absent-Mindedness" (J. E. Harris and P. E. Morris, eds), Academic Press, London, Orlando and New York.

Reason, J. T. (1983b). Task/Error questionnaire. University of Manchester.

Reason, J. T. and Mycielska, K. (1982). "Absent-minded? The Psychology of Mental Lapses and Everyday Errors", Prentice-Hall, Englewood Cliffs, N.J.

Riegel, K. F. (1973). The recall of historical events. *Behavioral Science*, **18**, 354–363.

Robinson, J. A. (1976). Sampling autobiographical memory. *Cognitive Psychology*, **8**, 578–595.

Rubin, D. C. (1977). Very long-term memory for prose and verse. *Journal of Verbal Learning and Verbal Behavior*, **16**, 611–621.

Rubin, D. C. (1982). On the retention function for autobiographical memory. *Journal of Verbal Learning and Verbal Behavior*, **21**, 21–38.

Sanders, H. I. (1972). The problems of measuring very long-term memory. *International Journal of Mental Health*, **1**, 98–102.

Schmeck, R. R. (1983). Learning styles of college students. *In* "Individual Differences in Cognition" (R. Dillon and R. R. Schmeck, eds), Academic Press, Orlando, New York and London.

Schmeck, R. R., Ribich, F. and Ramanaiah, N. (1977). Development of a self-report inventory for assessing individual differences in learning processes. *Applied Psychological Measurement*, **1**, 413–431.

Sehulster, J. R. (1981a). Structure and pragmatics of a self-theory of memory. *Memory and Cognition*, **9**, 263–276.

Sehulster, J. (1981b). Phenomenological correlates of a self theory of memory.

American Journal of Psychology, **94**, 527–537.

Sehulster, J. R. (1982). Phenomenological correlates of a self theory of memory II: Dimensions of memory experience. *American Journal of Psychology*, **9**, 442–454.

Shimamura, A. P., Landwehr, R. F. and Nelson, T. O. (1981). Fact retrieval. *Behavior Research Methods and Instrumentation*, **13**, 691–692.

Shlechter, T. M. and Herrmann, D. J. (1981). Multimethod approach for investigating everyday memory. Presented at the Eastern Psychological Association, New York.

Shlechter, T. M., Herrmann, D. J., Stronach, P., Rubenfeld, L. and Zenker, S. (1982). An investigation of people's knowledge of their everyday memory abilities. Paper presented at the meeting of the American Educational Research Association, New York.

Smith, E. R. and Miller, F. D. (1978). Limits on perception of cognitive processes: A reply to Nisbet and Wilson. *Psychological Review*, **85**, 355–362.

Squire, L. R. (1982). The neuropsychology of human memory. *Annual Review of Neuroscience*, **5**, 241–273.

Squire, L. C. and Cohen, N. (1979). Memory and amnesia. Resistance to disruption develops for years after learning. *Behavioral and Neural Biology*, **25**, 115–125.

Squire, L. R., Chace, P. M. and Slater, P. C. (1975). Assessment of memory for remote events. *Psychological Reports*, **37**, 223–234.

Squire, L. R. and Fox, M. M. (1980). Assessment of remote memory—validation of the television test by repeated testing during a 7-year period. *Behavior Research Methods and Instrumentation*, **12**, 583–585.

Squire, L. R. and Slater, P. C. (1975). Forgetting in very long-term memory as assessed by an improved questionnaire technique. *Journal of Experimental Psychology: Human Learning and Memory*, **104**, 50–54.

Squire, L. R. and Slater, P. C. (1978). Anterograde and retrograde memory impairment in chronic amnesia. *Neuropsychologia*, **16**, 313–322.

Squire, L. R., Slater, P. C. and Chace, P. M. (1975). Retrograde amnesia: Temporal gradient in very long term memory following electro-convulsive therapy. *Science*, **187**, 77–79.

Storandt, M., Grant, E. A. and Gordon, B. C. (1978). Remote memory as a function of age and sex. *Experimental Aging Research*, **4**, 365–375.

Sunderland, A., Harris, J. E. and Baddeley, A. D. (1983). Do laboratory tests predict everyday memory? A neuropsychological study. *Journal of Verbal Learning and Verbal Behavior*, **22**, 341–357.

Sunderland, A., Harris, J. E. and Baddeley, A. D. (1984). Assessing everyday memory after severe head injury. *In* "Everyday Memory, Actions and Absent-Mindedness" (J. E. Harris and P. E. Morris, eds), Academic Press, London, Orlando and New York.

Talland, G. A. (1968). "Disorders of Memory and Learning", Penguin Books, Harmondsworth.

Thompson, D. (1982). The roommate study. *Memory and Cognition*, **10**, 324–332.

Tulving, E. (1972). Episodic and semantic memory. *In* "Organization of Memory" (E. Tulving and W. Donaldson, eds), Academic Press, New York and London.

Underwood, B. J., Baruch, R. F. and Malmi, R. A. (1978). Composition of episodic memory. *Journal of Experimental Psychology: General*, **107**, 393–419.

Wagenaar, W. A. (1978). Recalling messages broadcast to the general public. *In* "Practical Aspects of Memory" (M. M. Gruneberg, P. E. Morris, and R. N. Sykes, eds), Academic Press, London and New York.

Waldfogel, S. (1948). The frequency and affective character of childhood memories.

Psychological Monographs, **62** (4), Whole No. 291.

Walker, J. H. (1975). Real-world variability, reasonableness judgments, and memory representation for concepts. *Journal of Verbal Learning and Verbal Behavior*, **14**, 241–252.

Warrington, E. K. and Sanders, H. I. (1971). The fate of old memories. *Quarterly Journal of Experimental Psychology*, **23**, 432–442.

Warrington, E. K. and Silberstein, M. (1970). A questionnaire technique for investigating long-term memory. *Quarterly Journal of Experimental Psychology*, **22**, 508–512.

Wechsler, D. (1945). A standardized memory scale for clinical use. *Journal of Psychology*, **19**, 87–95.

White, P. (1980). Limitations on verbal reports of internal events: A refutation of Nisbett and Wilson and of Bem. *Psychological Review*, **87**, 105–112.

Whitten, W. B. and Leonard, J. M. (1981). Directed search through autobiographical memory. *Memory and Cognition*, **9**, 546–579.

Williams, M. D. and Hollan, J. D. (1981). The process of retrieval from very long-term memory. *Cognitive Science*, **5**, 87–119.

Wright, N. (ed.) (1975). "Understanding Human Behavior", B.P.C. Publishing Limited, New York.

Wu, S., Schenkenberg, T., Wing, S. D. and Osborn, A. G. (1981). Cognitive correlates of diffuse cerebral atrophy determined by computed tomography. *Neurology*, **31**, 1180–1184.

Yarmey, A. D. (1973). I recognize your face but I can't remember your name: Further evidence of the tip-of-the-tongue phenomenon. *Memory and Cognition*, **I**, 287–290.

Yarmey, A. D. and Bull, M. P. III (1978). Where were you when President Kennedy was assassinated? *Bulletin of the Psychonomic Society*, **11**, 133–135.

Zelinski, E. M., Gilewski, M. J. and Thompson, L. W. (1980). Do laboratory tests relate to self assessment of memory ability in the young and old? *In* "New Directions in memory and aging" (L. W. Poon, J. L. Fozard, L. S. Cemak, D. Arenberg and L. W. Thompson, eds), Erlbaum, Hillsdale, N.J.

9

The Validity of
Subjective Reports on Memory

P. E. Morris

I. REASONS FOR THE USE OF SUBJECTIVE REPORTS ON MEMORY

Some topics in psychology are regarded with sceptisism, if not derision by the general public, but one attraction of studying everyday memory problems is that it is immediately recognized as worthwhile subject for research by non-psychologists. Almost everyone can remember some occasion when their memory let them down, and many people suspect that their memories are less efficient than they would like, and might be improved. Set against a background of academic research, which for decades was concerned with no more than the memorizing of lists of words, the temptation to try to investigate memory in everyday life is enormous. However, once the decision to take on real world remembering is made, the psychologist tends to reel back in the face of the problems that sent Ebbinghaus, who was well aware of the interest and variety of memory phenomena, in search of the nonsense syllable.

In the laboratory it is possible to have at least partial control over some of the variables and to have confidence in the measure of memory performance. Numbers of words, latency of response, even idea units or propositions from prose, are quantifiable without too much difficulty. There is no need to suspect under normal circumstances that the people being tested are producing misleading responses. The material to be memorized is well specified, and to some extent the past experience of the participant with it can be controlled. However, if one decides to study those things that the man in the street wants to know about memory, i.e. those that occur in everyday life, then the task is immediately daunting. The types and forms of such remembering are not yet classified and adequately described, let alone understood. There is an enormous variety in the opportunity for memory errors between jobs and life-styles, while skills, motivations, interests and experience all vary in unquantified but no doubt vital ways. One important factor is that while memory failures may be common, those that seem important to the non-psychologist are relatively rare. In the ideal laboratory memory experiment, the average number of errors is around 50%. In the real world, life would come to an almost immediate stop if such an error rate occurred regularly without corrections which prevent the errors having long-term consequences. Instead, we all arrange ways of avoiding all but the occasional embarrassing error by using memory aids, such as notes and diaries, and by organizing our lives to use references (e.g. books, indexes) that remove a dependence on memory.

Given these problems, it is not surprising that many researchers have looked to reports by people of their memory failures as a good first step towards understanding everyday memory. In Chapter 8 of this volume, Herrmann (1984) lists 18 subjective memory questionnaires, all developed in the hope of quantifying some aspects of everyday memory problems, and in Chapter 4 Reason and Lucas (1984) provide two examples of diary studies, in which volunteers keep records of their memory failures. The use of such questionnaires and diaries has been a main growth area in the study of everyday memory during the last few years. This research has not been as successful as one might have hoped. As Herrmann (1984) comments in Chapter 8, the correlations that have been found between questionnaire scores and the various objective tests of memory have generally been less than 0.5. I shall describe a few examples of such studies here, and further examples will be found in the chapters by Sunderland et al. (1984; Chapter 11) and by Martin and Jones (1984; Chapter 10) while Herrmann (1982) provides a fuller review.

Harris and Wilkins (1982) found "some suggestion" of a relationship between performance on the Cognitive Failures Questionnaire (CFQ) and the number of times subjects were late when monitoring a clock while watching a film. However, Wilkins and Baddeley (1978) report no relationship between the CFQ and remembering to press a button in an experiment stimulating pill taking. Broadbent et al. (1982) report finding no significant correlations between the CFQ and immediate memory span, longer-term recall of categorized material or delayed recall. Shlechter and Herrmann (in press) found no significant correlations between the Short Inventory of Memory Experiences (SIME) and frequency of memory errors, subsequently reported in diary studies. On the memory questionnaire designed by Perlmutter (1978), scores for self knowledge correlated 0.3 with recall of a word list and memory strategy scores 0.3 with recall for a list of facts. Rabbitt (1982) found no correlation between the Everyday Memory Questionnaire (EMQ) developed by Harris and Sunderland (1981; see also Chapter 11) and recall on a range of tests. However, when his subjects rated their relative change in memory as they had aged, these ratings correlated better than 0.4 (Spearman r_s) with both free recall and cumulative learning of word lists. In a recent, unpublished study, I found no relationship between either the CFQ or the Harris and Sunderland Questionnaire and the recall of details from a video film. The two questionnaires correlated 0.02 and −0.04 respectively with the performance of 48 subjects who answered 37 questions about the film.

The reason for the low correlations between subjective questionnaires and objective measures may be that subjective measures of this sort do not accurately assess memory failure. Alternatively, or additionally, the fault may lie with the objective tests or the assumption that the subjective and objective measures used should intercorrelate. I shall discuss all these possibilities, but shall begin by critically considering the validity of subjective estimates of memory ability.

II. PROBLEMS WITH SUBJECTIVE QUESTIONNAIRES AND DIARIES

The fundamental problem with memory questionnaires and diaries is their reliance upon the participant for the answers. Questionnaires normally ask "How often do you . . . ?", "How often have you . . . ?", "Rate how often you forget to . . . ?" etc. Diaries involve the recording of such instances. For both diaries and questionnaires there are five stages that the participant must complete successfully. He or she must (1) Have an appropriate memory failure, (2) classify it as a failure, (3) remember the failure later when the time comes to report it, (4) judge the failure to be reportable, (5) classify or describe it accurately. At each of these stages a failure can occur that undermines the accuracy of the measure, so each will be separately examined below.

A. Having an appropriate memory failure

The following are examples taken from the questions in the SIME (Herrmann and Neisser, 1978) which illustrate the type of question asked in many memory failure questionnaires.

(1) "Think of times when you have made a long-distance call with the area code and number written down on a piece of paper in front of you . . ."

(2) "How often do you find that just when you want to introduce someone you know to someone else you cannot think of their name?"

(3) "When you are in a restaurant and want to speak to your waiter or waitress, how often do you forget what he or she looks like?"

(4) "If you go to a supermarket to buy four or five things (without a written shopping list), how often do you forget at least one of them?"

Any rating should be based upon a pool of instances that is large enough to provide a reasonable sample. If you are someone that rarely makes long-distance phone calls, does not frequently have to introduce people, tends to eat in self-service cafés rather than restaurants and does all your shopping in one big weekly session, then the pool of instances for these questions will be small. These are not carefully chosen examples from one specific test; they relate to a fundamental problem for all such questionnaires. The need is to specify questions closely enough for them to cue retrieval of instances so that a judgement can be made, while still capturing enough instances and being applicable to a wide section of the population. A comparison of elderly people living in an old people's home with young active subjects may well involve the participants making their judgements upon quite different pools of instances, or even no such instances at all. The whole event of eating out, introducing people or telephoning long distance may be quite different for someone that does them very infrequently compared to a busy businessman.

The alternative to specific questions is a general one such as "How often do you misplace things?" (Perlmutter, 1978). Here the pool of opportunities is certainly large, but it is so imprecise that it is unclear what should be included. More importantly, because specific memory cues are better than general ones (e.g. Harris, 1979), and because recall often depends on the availability of appropriate retrieval cues, the question may fail to trigger a good sample of instances from memory. This is shown by, for example, the research on encoding specificity and context dependent memory (e.g. Tulving and Thomson, 1973; Godden and Baddeley, 1975). This relates to the issue of the basis of subjective judgements, to which I shall turn later. Notice, however, that even general questions on memory failure allow an enormous range of variation in the opportunities for such failures. So, for the example given above, the more you own and the more open your life is to interruptions, the more likely you are to misplace something.

B. Classifying as a failure

I take it for granted that I have to look up many telephone numbers, especially those of people I have rung only once or twice before. I do not normally classify this as a memory failure since it seems obviously beyond my ability to remember every telephone number that I use. On the other hand, if I fail to remember the telephone number of a close friend or relative, I complain to myself on the poverty of my memory. The point is that subjects base their judgements upon what they expect to be able to remember, and that expectation is itself moulded by their memory efficiency. If, for example, I *could* usually remember a telephone number after one encounter, in the way that I normally expect to recognize faces, then I might rate as poor my memory for telephone numbers if I remembered half a dozen failures—while everyone else might envy my extraordinary recall!

Failures to remember are brought home more obviously in some circumstances than others. People who continually suffer because of the consequences of their memory failures are made acutely aware of their inability. However, often we are blithely unaware that information was potentially available in memory but was not actually retrieved. Every minute of the day there are probably past experiences that might be valuable if recalled. There is no chance that one can estimate such memory failures for oneself. This might not matter if the situation were the same for everyone, but some people will be more aware of such failures than others as they need to make greater use of their memories, or have more opportunities to be reminded of their failures.

Expectations about memory efficiency derive both from one's own experience and from other sources: other people, TV, stories and so on. I hardly classify my inability to remember a telephone number that I have used once as a memory failure not only because I know that I never do remember such numbers, but also because I frequently have my assessment that this is normal confirmed when I watch others in real life or in TV programmes reaching for the telephone directory. It is quite possible that people expect memory failures in some situations (names, shopping, appointments), but whole classes of memory failures are not recognized as such at all. Such expectations will influence responses to memory questionnaires or diary entries. The expectations of the elderly may be influenced by the common belief that memory declines with age. They may find support for this in the memory of a few vivid memory failures, or counter evidence in their friends' abilities to recount endless anecdotes from childhood.

C. Remembering the memory failure: subjective judgements of probability

There is an obvious paradox that Herrmann (1979) has called "the Memory Introspection Paradox", the fact that those people most likely to make memory errors are also those most likely to forget that such an error took place. Beyond this general paradox, however, there are other problems related to remembering memory failures.

It might be the case that some system exists within people that monitors memory failures and keeps an up to date count. Unfortunately, this is unlikely. There are, no doubt, many cognitive counting and evaluating systems, but these are acquired because of the demands of the world in which we live. As I shall argue later in this section, most memory failures do not have important consequences, so there is no reason to keep a mental record of these memory errors. People who fill in memory failure questionnaires are unlikely to have been monitoring their memory efficiency during the period about which they are questioned. In the absence of such records, they probably make their judgements in the same way that people make other judgements about probability: that is, by using heuristics, "rules of thumb", based upon what they can recall of their memory failures.

There has been considerable research in recent years on the way in which the layman and experienced statisticians and psychologists base their decisions about probabilities. Much of the research has been initiated by Kahneman and Tversky (e.g. Kahneman and Tversky, 1971, 1973; Tversky and Kahneman, 1971, 1973, 1974) and has been developed by social psychologists (see, e.g. Nisbett and Ross, 1980).

Tversky and Kahneman (1973) argued that when people make judgements about the probability of events such as the frequency of memory failures, they do so by using heuristics which may often allow approximations to the probability to be calculated, but which may be influenced by the properties of our memories, or other psychological influences. Life-long experience, they assert, has taught us that instances of large categories are recalled faster and better than those of small categories and that likely events are easier to imagine than unlikely ones. So we may estimate the frequency and probability of our memory failures by judging how easy examples are to recall, how many examples are recalled and how easily we can imagine such failures. Errors occur in the use of these heuristics because other factors influence the ease of recall or imagining beyond sheer frequency. Such errors are, I shall argue, especially likely when judging the frequency of memory failures.

Tversky and Kahneman provide several demonstrations of the biasing of judgements through the influence of other factors on memory. For example, when asked whether a letter from the set K, L, N, R, V was more frequent as the first or third letter of a word, they found that subjects estimated that the letters were twice as frequent as first letters as they were as third letters in a word. Actually, they are all more common as the third letter. The mistake seems to occur because it is easier to generate words beginning with the given letter than it is to think of those in which the letter is in the third place.

In another experiment in which the names of 19 very famous women and 20 less famous men (and vice versa) were read to subjects who had to judge whether they had heard more male or female names, over 80% of the subjects wrongly judged that there had been more of the famous name group. This appeared to be because when thinking about the lists of names, more of the famous names could be recalled. Tversky and Kahneman found that over 50% more of the very famous names were recalled in a recall test.

Tversky and Kahneman did show that their subjects could sometimes accurately predict frequencies. So, for example, there was a correlation of 0.93 between the number of words that one group of subjects predicted could be recalled from given categories in two minutes and the number actually recalled.

People are not necessarily bad at estimating their past or future performance. Errors occur if the recall of the data on which the judgement is based is distorted in some way. If we assume that when making judgements about their memory failures people use the same heuristics as they appear to do in Tversky and Kahneman's research, then they will base their judgements upon the ease with which some instances of memory failure can be retrieved. If several are easily recalled, the subject will conclude that his or her set of memory failures is large and that they frequently occur. Failure to recall many instances will imply, for them, a reasonably efficient memory.

For most of us, memory failures probably occur frequently, perhaps every few minutes. We have problems thinking of the right words to say, we forget to ask a question to someone we meet, we leave letters unposted, and so on. Most of such errors are trivial. Our lives are organized to survive them with the least inconvenience. If they do not intrude upon the smooth running of our day, they are unlikely to be remembered subsequently. They are not a part of the plan we are following, they do not occupy our attention, they are commonplace and not the subject of cognitive processing which might produce an elaborate or distinctive memory. Like the names of people to whom we have been introduced, unless for some reason we attend to them and do something with them, they are rapidly forgotten. Such errors will not be recalled when evaluating memory failures. However, a small number of memory failures have important consequences. They disrupt the smooth running of life, and often cause embarrassment. So, a missed appointment, a forgotten name, the need for an extra trip to town because some shopping was forgotten—all these kinds of errors cause annoyance, lower our image of ourselves and require modifications in our plans. Consequently, such memory failures are likely to be highly memorable. Given a suitable cue, such as a specific question on say the SIME, one or two instances may come vividly to mind, along with the memory of all their subsequent disruptions or frustrations.

So, rare memory failures may be reported as occurring more frequently than they actually do. What is more, insofar as they are distinctive, and that increases with their rareness as well as their embarrassment, they are easily recalled. I would expect more such recall by people who lead lives where more opportunities for such errors occur, by those for whom the error is likely to be valued as important, and by individuals whose personalities are such that emotional events have a marked effect upon them. This suggests some potentially interesting research on the perception of memory ability as a function of personality and life-style. However, the use of memory aids complicates matters.

Those people who have discovered that the costs of memory failures outweigh the inconvenience of making lists, keeping diaries and so on will then make fewer embarrassing memory errors. Memory aids reduce, or at least obscure memory failures by converting a major error into a trivial one which is soon overcome by consulting the diary or shopping list. The end result is that judgements about memory failures are based upon memories of the few failures that had consequences for our everyday life. The opportunities for such failures vary with life-style, and those with the greatest opportunity to make important errors may not actually do so since they can compensate by adopting memory aids.

D. Questionnaire responses with ageing

An example of the problems in the sampling of memories of memory errors is provided by one of the most popular applications of memory questionnaires in comparing young and elderly individuals. It is generally assumed that memory ability declines with age, but this is not reflected in the results of questionnaire studies.

When comparing old and young respondents, Perlmutter (1978) and Zelinski et al. (1980) found elderly subjects reporting poorer memories, but in two studies, Harris and Sunderland (1981; see Sunderland *et al.*, 1984, Chapter 11) found significantly better ratings of memory ability by their older subjects. A study by Bennett-Levy and Powell (1980), produced similar results, while Chaffin and Herrmann (1983) described a variable pattern of results, with essentially little difference between old (e.g. mean age 69 or 82) and young (ages 18 and 25 years) subjects, and with one of three studies showing older subjects rating their memories as better than the younger participants.

As Miller (1979) comments when reviewing memory and ageing:

> in general terms it is true to say that almost every investigator who has given the same memory task to both older subjects and younger adults has found that the older sample perform less well. (p. 128)

Even though Miller goes on to discuss the problems with much of this research, it remains, as he says ". . . reasonably certain that an individual's memory at, say, 80 years is not what it was as a young adult" (p. 130–1). So why is this not reflected in the questionnaire scores? One possibility is that older people have less active lives with fewer variations in their routine and hence less opportunities for memory failures. Another is that they may have had more time and reason to develop strategies for avoiding failure and may use more memory aids. Perhaps they are less perturbed by the consequences of memory errors? All these factors tend to reduce the pool of memory failures that they might recall, as well as making the failures themselves less memorable.

E. Classifying or describing the memory failure accurately

There is the obvious selection that occurs in diary studies, where errors that are very personal or embarrassing for the individual will probably be omitted. The extent to which this biases the findings will depend on the purpose of the research. It would, for example, make it difficult to test the plausible hypothesis that people are less likely to forget things that are very important to them. However, it may not markedly bias most studies (see also Reason and Lucas, 1984; Chapter 4 of this volume).

I have already discussed many factors that contribute to an inaccurate describing of memory failures. However, I want to go beyond those already mentioned to note some further distortions that may occur at the final stage of rating the errors. These relate to the weighting of the available evidence and the response category that the subject chooses. I have argued that memory failures are often very important to the individual. Nisbett and Ross (1980) have reviewed evidence, both experimental and anecdotal, suggesting that when subjects attempt to summarize their experience, and make decisions, then vivid individual case histories and experiences often outweigh far more reliable, but less emotive data such as statistics on probability. So, for example, the mastectomies performed on Mrs Ford and Mrs Rockefeller in

1974 produced a flood of visits to cancer-detection clinics, vastly exceeding the impact of many years of the advertising of statistics on the probability of breast cancer. Taylor and Thompson (1982), while questioning whether vividness is a general factor influencing decisions, conclude, in their review, that individual case histories are usually more influential on decision-making than are descriptive statistics. If individual instances are weighed far beyond their true value in decision-making, it is likely that remembered instances of memory failure that have had marked consequences for the individual will excessively influence the evaluation of memory failures.

There are many demonstrations in the research literature of the difficulty that people have in thinking about probabilities such as those that are the basis of memory questionnaire responses (see Anderson, 1981, for an introductory review). So, for example, Kahneman and Tversky (1973) found that if subjects were asked the probability of either an engineer or a lawyer being drawn from a set of 70 lawyers and 30 engineers, they could reply correctly; however, if they were also given a description of a man who had, supposedly, been drawn from the group, and which contained no information relating to a possible profession, they gave a .50 probability of his being a lawyer. The description eliminated the subjects' ability to use prior probabilities, that is, their knowledge of the proportions of lawyers and engineers, in making their judgment. For present purposes, the point is that since we know so little about the processes underlying the use of estimates of memory errors when completing the questionnaires, we must not be too confident that, even if the probabilities can at some stage be correctly estimated by the subject, that estimation will be properly used in making the response. Ideally we should look for validation of questionnaires, perhaps by comparing them to the frequency of errors reported in diary studies. However, when Shlechter and Herrmann (in press) did compare the frequency of subjects' diary entries for various types of memory failures with the subjects' ratings on the SIME made before the diaries were begun, no correlation exceeded .15 (Pearson r). Only the total SIME score correlated significantly with total frequency of errors reported, and then by only .32. The correlations improved dramatically when diary reports were compared to SIME ratings *after* the diary study. Then, when the subjects had been attuned to be aware of memory failures, two of the correlations exceeded .7. It seems that, for the reasons that are discussed in this chapter, people are not good at accurately assessing the probability with which they make memory failures, unless they are practised in recording the failures.

When asked to make a response on a rating scale, the subject will review the range of options that are open. Poulton (1975, 1979) has discussed the biases that are associated with the use of subjective rating scales. Among these are a tendency for subjects to spread their responses over the full range of the given set of scale points, defining the end-points by the strongest and weakest stimuli in the given sample, while preferring to use the middle points of the scale, and to average around the middle point. There are many complex biases that Poulton (1979) reviews, but some of these are important only if the researcher hopes to obtain an absolute value from the ratings. Comparisons within subjects during one set of ratings are less problematic, but even then there is a danger that what the subject remembers from earlier responses may influence later answers (Poulton, 1975).

Harris (1979) noticed a range effect when asking students how frequently they used various memory aids. Apparently they used the response categories "never", "rarely", "sometimes" and "often" differently with external aids (such as diaries, for which once a week may seem rare when compared to people who use them several times a day), and with internal aids (such as first-letter mnemonics, for which once a week may seem very frequent). The range effect was eliminated, or at least substantially reduced in subsequent studies (reported in full in Harris, 1980) in which a more objective scale was used. On the basis of this, Harris (1979) suggested a version of the objective scale that is easier for the subject to use. It is considered more objective in that more precise alternatives (e.g. "about once a week") are offered than vague terms such as "sometimes" or "often", which are open to subjective interpretation. Harris and Sunderland (1981) used the new scale successfully with a postal questionnaire, and Reason has also adopted it for a number of his questionnaires. However, most memory questionnaires still use the more subjective terms.

For several of the memory questionnaires, the usable set of scale points is small for anyone without a pathological memory problem. On the SIME, for instance, the scales measuring forgetting have seven points, but the end two are labelled "always" and "never", while the intermediate steps are marked as "once in a while, now and then, about half the time", and "very often". Probably no one *never* makes a memory error of the types investigated by the SIME, and since errors at the rate of one per two opportunities would rapidly reduce the individual to helplessness (imagine forgetting the ending of every second joke or the name of every other person you introduced), only the "once in a while" and "now and then" points will usually apply! While this may seem like a criticism of the SIME (and it is!), at least the relatively clear specification of some of the points on the scales will help to control range effects.

F. Validation of memory questionnaires

There are lessons to be learned from the psychometric tradition on the construction and validation of questionnaires. One common problem for self report psychometric tests is the confounding of acquiescence and social desirability factors with the responses.

Styles of responding vary between individuals independently of their actual belief about their memories. Some people are more likely to be influenced by the positive wording of the questions, acquiescing to the suggestion that their memories may be faulty. The common memory failure questionnaires all consist of positive questions and are open to affirmation biases. In addition, the wish to make a good impression on the scorer of the questionnaire may lead some subjects to make what they consider to be the most socially desirable response, while others may be more honest. Even widely used diagnostic tests can be flawed in these ways. Jackson and Messick (1967a) found that when they factor analysed the Minnesota Multiphasic Personality Inventory (MMPI) approximately three quarters of the common variance was interpretable in terms of response styles of acquiescence and desirability. A similar confounding of social desirability has been shown by Di Vesta *et al.* (1971) for questionnaires that try to assess subjective experience of vividness and control of mental imagery.

Broadbent *et al.* (1982) attempted to measure the influence of social desirability on their CFQ by using the Lie Scale from the Eysenck Personality Questionnaire (EPQ). The correlations found were small, though statistically significant. However, the Lie Scale questions on the EPQ are transparent, and Broadbent *et al.* omitted them from later versions of the CFQ as respondents found them "objectionable" (p. 4). Such obvious catch questions are not likely to trap many seekers after a socially desirable image. Broadbent *et al.* also acknowledge the possibility of affirmation biases in the CFQ. They reject mixed wordings of positive and negative questions because it might introduce the possibility of misreading. While they assert that "the proper check against . . . affirmation bias is to examine the correlation with other measures of that bias" (p. 3), they do not do so.

The intercorrelation of memory failure questionnaires is sometimes cited as further evidence of validity (see Broadbent *et al.*, 1982; and Martin and Jones, 1984, Chapter 10 of this volume). However, since the questionnaires are so similar in form, they should be expected to measure the same *opinions* about memory, which may bear no relationship to actual ability. Moreover, since the questionnaires run the same risks of acquiescence and social desirability bias, it is possible that some of their shared variance reflects the response styles of the respondents rather than an underlying memory flaw. As I described at the beginning of the chapter, efforts have been made to show correlations between memory questionnaire responses and actual instances of forgetting. These appear, however, to be the only first steps towards establishing the construct validity of the tests (see e.g. Jackson and Messick, 1967b).

G. General and specific memory skills

One weakness of most memory failure questionnaires is their attempted generality. They try to capture memory failure of many types: jokes, faces, plots, dreams, smells etc., in one test applicable to the whole general public and to special subsets of people who may have marked memory problems. This may be in the tradition of grand tests of intelligence and personality, but it introduces so much variance and so many issues over comparisons that more specialized tests may prove better. If there are really worthwhile questions to be asked about memory difficulties, then tests designed to assess specifically those problems are more likely to produce interpretable results.

Perhaps the major problem facing the study of everyday memory is in knowing what questions to ask. What will prove to be the dimensions on which memory varies? The answers are likely to be quite specific to the skills, interests and backgrounds of the individuals involved, and gross efforts to assess memory skills may miss the important variations as our naked-eye view of the moon misses the dramatic variations in the moon's surface. There are several hints in the literature from reports of comparisons between different memory tasks that there may not be one, or a few general memory abilities, but rather specific memory skills which are brought into operation under particular conditions. Battig (1979) reports research by Masson who found that the median intercorrelation between performance on 30 difficult memory tasks was 0.17. Underwood et al. (1978) examined intercorrelations of the performance of 200 students on 31 laboratory memory tasks. In their factor analysis, separate factors emerged for free recall, paired associate learning, memory span and verbal discrimination. The free recall and paired-associate measures loaded about .2–.3 on the other's factor, while the other variables appeared to be virtually independent of one another. Measures of spelling ability and vocabulary, which Underwood et al. regarded as indexes of semantic memory were also unrelated to the other tests, as were scores on the Scholastic Aptitude Test. It would seem, therefore, that even laboratory tasks draw upon a range of skills that vary between individuals. In the real world, a greater variety of experience and skills are probably employed, and it is not surprising that Wilkins and Baddeley (1978) found a negative relationship between subjects' free recall scores and their probability of remembering to respond in a simulated pill-taking task.

The specific nature of memory skills is illustrated in a recent experiment that I conducted (Morris and Gruneberg, 1982) in which subjects heard and then tried to recall either new real soccer scores or scores that simulated real results as closely as possible. With real scores, there was a very high correlation (0.82) between performance on a soccer knowledge questionnaire and the number of scores correctly recalled. However, when the subjects were aware that they were hearing simulated scores, the correlation between soccer knowledge and recall dropped to 0.36. While with real soccer scores there was no significant correlation between free recall performance with a list of common words (0.32), this correlation was highly significant for simulated results (0.67). The pattern of results indicates that even though superficially the recall of real and simulated scores may seem similar tasks, the underlying skills that are activated are different, one drawing on factors relating to knowledge and interest in soccer, the other on free recall skills.

In a study of eyewitness testimony that Valerie Morris and I have recently carried out, we found that the recall by subjects when giving a narrative report on a film they have seen correlated only approximately 0.2 with the amount and accuracy of recall by the same subjects when answering a set of specific questions. Here, even though the recall was, presumably, based upon the same information stored in memory, its retrieval and reporting varied so much with the style of testing that it is not possible to say that an observer had a good or bad memory for the film without the qualification of how the memory was tested.

My argument is that in everyday life, where enormous variations in knowledge, experience, interest and emotion are possible, it may be necessary to think of remembering as involving a very large number of skills specific to facets of the individual's life and not capturable in gross scores on memory failure questionnaires. Perhaps, when the whole cognitive system has suffered major damage, with head injury or senile decay, then many of these special skills may decline together, but for normal people there is no reason to expect such a correlated change in memory skills.

II. IN DEFENCE OF SUBJECTIVE REPORTS OF MEMORY FAILURES

So far I have been critical of self report studies of memory failure. Now I want to turn to arguments in their favour. In particular, I want to concentrate upon countering some criticisms of self reports as data.

A. On what can we report?

There is a long history of criticisms of subjective reports in psychology. I have dealt more fully with these in Chapter 2 of Morris and Hampson (1983) and in Morris (1981a,b).

There are, essentially, three types of criticisms of self reports. One is that of philosophers such as Ryle, Wittgenstein and their disciples, who have tried to show that we cannot report upon our conscious experiences either because we have made a logical error in our conceptualization of such experiences, or because of the necessary consequences of the private nature of these experiences. The second argument is that self reports are a form of introspection, and that introspection was shown in the early years of this century to be unreliable, a view that has been strengthened by some recent studies of self reports. The third argument is that introspections are unnecessary because to be acceptable they require external criteria to validate them, but if such criteria exist introspections are unnecessary.

Since this is not a philosophy text, I shall consider the philosophical arguments only briefly here, and refer the reader to Morris and Hampson (1983) for a fuller discussion. Ryle (1949) argued that talk about the mind was not referring to some "occult episodes", but to "overt acts and utterances themselves". Yet, however successful his attempt to interpret concepts like "intelligent" in terms of dispositions to behave in certain ways, there remain references to conscious experiences, memories, images and so on which cannot be satisfactorily dealt with in this way. His criticisms of our descriptions of our experience of, for example, mental images are all flawed and fail to discredit introspection. Wittgenstein (1953) appeared to doubt the possibility of introspective reports on mental events because only one person could be aware of his or her own mental images etc., and any reference to these would involve a private language which would not have publicly checkable rules. It is, however, arguable whether a language needs publicly checkable rules, as well as whether descriptions of our conscious experiences are not publicly checkable. In themselves, these philosophical arguments are not compelling enough to justify abandoning self reports.

The second argument against self reports asserts that they are a form of introspection. This can be disputed, in the case of memory failure questionnaires since what is being reported appears to be observable behaviour, that is, instances of forgetting that someone other than the person completing the questionnaire could also have observed. However, it is more accurate to say that the reports are based upon the memories and impressions of the respondant, and that these memories and impressions themselves are not open to observation by others. It is, therefore, probably correct to regard the responses on memory failure questionnaires as depending upon introspections. However, they have the attraction of being introspections that can often be checked for their accuracy.

The argument that introspections are unreliable draws upon the disputes about introspective data that accompanied early research in the structuralist tradition (Titchener, 1909) including the Imageless Thought Controversy (e.g. Humphrey, 1951). However, while these disputes revealed that not all psychological processes could be examined through introspection, they did not show that all introspections were irrelevant. Subsequent disputes in other areas of psychology should have helped to show that disagreement over introspective data is not simply a function of the data being subjective. Nor was subjective data abandoned. In the study of perception its use continued largely unaffected (Woodworth and Sheenan, 1964). Much of the initial dissatisfaction with introspection can be traced to the invalidity of the theoretical basis of structuralism rather than the inadequacy of subjective reports. Many criticisms of introspections, such as the danger that the imposition of the second task of introspecting may drastically change the one under study have not been supported by evidence.

The argument that introspections are unreliable can be refined into two separate criticisms. One is that because the person who is introspecting is the only one that has access to the experience, the report must always be open to doubt. The other is that introspections appear to be applicable to only some cognitive tasks, and that there is no clear means of saying independently which tasks, nor of identifying whether reports that subjects offer are real introspections or merely rationalizations to explain processes that are not consciously accessible. The first argument establishes only the need for caution and perhaps a permanent reservation of some doubt over introspective reports. There are many well established and well researched phenomena in psychology including the common visual illusions, that rely on the fact that the same physical conditions do lead to similar subjective experiences for most people. This ability to reproduce the mental experiences removes doubts. It is also possible to check the honesty and reliability of introspecting subjects and to confirm that they share with the experimenter the meanings of the words used. Predictions and theories can be devised that incorporate interpretations of the processing revealed by the introspections, and insofar as they are supported by further data, the introspections themselves receive indirect support. In summary, there is no good reason for the complete rejection of introspective data, even if objective data is preferable where it can be obtained.

Nisbett and Wilson (1977) and Evans (1980a,b) have argued that subjects frequently are unaware of the causes of their behaviour but offer "explanations" that the experimental manipulations show to be incorrect. Elsewhere (Morris, 1981a,b) I have disputed some of their conclusions, as well as some of the evidence on which they are based. I argued that it is necessary to separate speculation about the causes of behaviour that subjects may offer if pressed, which I called self-hypotheses, from reports of conscious experiences. While agreeing that people have few useful introspections to offer on many cognitive processes, in Morris (1981a) I argued that there is no good evidence to show that introspections about the reasons for intentional behaviour are usually misleading. I claimed that the cognitive system is hierarchically organized in its control structure, and that consciousness is associated with the information that is supplied to the part of the system in overall control which I have labelled BOSS. BOSS selects and directs actions but leaves their control to lower level EMPLOYEE systems. Information on those memory failures that require major changes in the individual's plans will certainly be fed to BOSS. Within the general BOSS-consciousness model, therefore, there is every reason to believe that some memory failures will be consciously recognized if they are associated with the dislocation and modification of intentional behaviour, and introspections on the experiences should be possible. However, those memory failures that are rapidly corrected through flexible adjustments in the processing of the EMPLOYEE systems may not be consciously recognized since they require no modification in the current plan of action. The questions that are asked in subjective memory questionnaires, whatever their faults, are not likely to be interpreted as requests for self hypotheses. While they are influenced by the expectations of the subjects, they should not be merely a function of the subject's beliefs about memory.

The third objection to introspection that I introduced earlier was that introspections require external criteria to validate them, and so they are redundant. One version of this argument derives from Wittgenstein (1953) and Skinner (1953), and points out that there must be observable indicators that are associated with a particular mental event before a name for that event can be taught. So, for example, children must be seen to fall, cut themselves, cry etc., before their parents can describe what they are feeling as "hurting" and "pain". This is an important argument for localizing what mental events can be named, but it does not show that there is always external evidence that a particular mental experience is taking place. It is only necessary that external evidence exists on some of the occasions when the mental experience occurs, and once the name has been learned it can be used whenever the experience occurs, which may be independent of any obvious external evidence.

B. The reliability and validity of objective tests of memory failure

One strength of subjective memory questionnaires is their reliability, which, as Herrmann notes in Chapter 8, is usually around 0.8 on test–retest measures. Objective memory tests usually inspire such confidence in their face objectivity that their reliability is rarely questioned. Yet some memory tests have a low reliability. For example, Christian et al. (1978) tested the free recall of 900 words by four sets of 80 subjects. The intercorrelations between the four sets of subjects for the number of times each word was recalled was averaged and the Spearman-Brown measure of reliability calculated. The result was a value of 0.57, which implies that the average intercorrelation of the four replications was only 0.4. The correlation between the recall of the control subjects used by Morris and Reid (1970), who had a paired-associate task of recalling concrete nouns to the number 1–10 as stimuli, was 0.47 between the first and second trials on an A-Br paradigm. Even for the successive trials on free recall of the same material, where there should be carry-over in recall, the correlation between performance on trials 1 and 2 of Morris and Reid (1971) for the recall of adjective-noun pairs was only 0.62. Underwood et al. (1978) noted the reliability of their memory tasks as a major problem, and took measures, such as the combining of data from several long lists, and practice lists to minimize variability. Even so, the median reliability for their memory tasks is 0.68, markedly lower than that usually found for everyday memory questionnaires.

Reliability increases with the number of items in the test, and, given the nature of the tasks that are used to assess memory, especially everyday memory, the common levels of reliability are not embarrassing, but they do limit the extent to which any two measures can be expected to intercorrelate. The maximum correlation that can be expected between two variables equals the square root of the product of their respective reliabilities. If, for example, an attempt is made to validate a memory questionnaire that has a reliability of 0.8 against an objective test of memory with a reliability of only 0.5, even a perfect relationship between the two will lead to a correlation of only 0.63. Some ingenious measures of absentmindedness, such as Herrmann's (1979) coat-hook test where subjects recall on which peg they hung their coats before entering the laboratory, are based on few test items, and probably have a low reliability. It would be misleading to conclude from low intercorrelations with such tests that a given subjective memory questionnaire was invalid.

It is always possible, given accurate estimates of the reliability of two measures to correct their correlation for attenuation by dividing it by the square root of the product of the reliabilities (Ghiselli, 1964). It could be wrong, however, to regard the relatively low reliabilities of objective memory tests as merely the result of limitations in the measurement of reliability. Low reliability may reflect the flexibility and variability of memory processes; an interaction between subjects and the different items they memorize. As I argued earlier, gross measures of memory, either subjective or objective, may overlook the specific variations in prior knowledge, interest and encoding activity which determine how individual entries are encoded into memory.

CONCLUSIONS

There are many points at which inaccuracy can enter to distort responses to subjective memory questionnaires. Comparisons with objective data suggest that these distortions do undermine the credibility of such studies as sources of information about real world remembering, although they may, as Herrmann argues in Chapter 8 provide valuable guides to opinions about memory failures. Diary studies are less open to subjective errors, but they are still susceptible. Unfortunately, objective tests that could replace memory questionnaires have yet to be developed, and it may prove difficult to select valid objective tests that really measure everyday memory abilities. Self reports may make valuable contributions to the study of everyday memory but they are not a substitute for the observation and preferably the manipulations of actual acts of remembering. They have not provided a short cut on what still seems to be a very daunting journey towards an understanding of the processes of memory in everyday life.

REFERENCES

Anderson, J. R. (1981). "Cognitive Psychology and its Implications", Freeman, San Franciso.

Battig, W. F. (1979). The flexibility of memory. In "Levels of Processing in Human Memory" (L. S. Cermak and F. I. M. Craik, eds), Erlbaum, Hillsdale, N.J.

Bennett-Levy, J. and Powell, G. F. (1980). Subjective memory questionnaire (SMQ). I: An investigation into the self-reporting of "real life" memory skills. British Journal of Social and Clinical Psychology, 19, 177–188.

Broadbent, D. E., Cooper, P. F., Fitzgerald, P. and Parkes, K. R. (1982). The Cognitive Failures Questionnaire and its correlates. British Journal of Clinical Psychology, 21, 1–16.

Chaffin, R. and Herrmann, D. J. (1983). Self reports of memory abilities by old and young adults. Human Learning, 2, 17–28.

Christian, J., Bickley, W., Tarka, M. and Clayton, K. (1978). Measures of free recall of 900 English nouns: Correlations with imagery, concreteness, meaningfulness, and frequency. *Memory and Cognition*, 6, 379–390.

Di Vesta, F. J., Ingersoll, G. and Sunshine, P. (1971). A factor analysis of imagery tests. *Journal of Verbal Learning and Verbal Behavior*, 10, 471–479.

Evans, J. St. B. T. (1980a). Thinking: Experimental and information processing approaches. *In* "Cognitive Psychology: New Directions" (G. Claxton, ed.), Routledge and Kegan Paul, London.

Evans, J. St. B. T. (1980b). Current issues in the psychology of reasoning. *British Journal of Psychology*, 71, 227–239.

Ghiselli, E. E. (1964). "Theory of Psychological Measurement", McGraw-Hill, New York.

Godden, D. R. and Baddeley, A. D. (1975). Content-dependent memory in two natural environments: on land and underwater. *British Journal of Psychology*, 66, 325–332.

Hamill, R., Wilson, T. D. and Nisbett, R. E. (1979). Ignoring sample bias: Inferences about collectivities from atypical cases. Reported in R. Nisbett and L. Ross (1980). "Human Inference: Strategies and Shortcomings of Social Judgment", Prentice Hall, Englecliffs, NJ.

Harris, J. E. (1978). External memory aids. *In* "Practical Aspects of Memory" (M. M. Gruneberg, P. E. Morris and R. N. Sykes, eds), Academic Press, London and New York.

Harris, J. E. (1980). Memory aids people use: Two interview studies. *Memory and Cognition*, 8, 31–38.

Harris, J. E. (1979). Everyday cognitive functioning: The need for assessment and some basic methodological issues. Paper presented to the London Conference of the British Psychological Society. Abstracted in *Bulletin of the British Psychological Society*, 33, 26.

Harris, J. E. and Sunderland, A. (1981). Effects of age and instructions on an everyday memory questionnaire. Paper presented to Memory Conference of the Cognitive Psychology Section of the British Psychological Society in Plymouth. Abstracted in *Bulletin of the British Psychological Society*, 35, 212.

Harris, J. E. and Wilkins, A. J. (1982). Remembering to do things: a theoretical framework and an illustrative experiment. *Human Learning*, 1, 123–136.

Harris, P. (1978). Developmental aspects of children's memory. *In* "Aspects of Memory" (M. M. Gruneberg and P. Morris, eds), Methuen, London.

Herrmann, D. J. (1979). The validity of memory questionnaire as related to theory of memory introspection. Paper presented to the London Conference of the British Psychological Society. Abstracted in *Bulletin of the British Psychological Society*, 33, 26.

Herrmann, D. J. (1982). Know thy memory: The use of questionnaires to assess and study memory. *Psychological Bulletin*, 92, 434–452.

Herrmann, D. J. (1984). Cognitive Questionnaires. *In* "Everyday memory, actions and absentmindedness" (J. E. Harris and P. E. Morris, eds), Academic Press, London, Orlando and New York.

Herrmann, D. J. and Neisser, U. (1978). An inventory of everyday memory experiences. *In* "Practical Aspects of Memory" (M. M. Gruneberg, P. E. Morris and R. N. Sykes, eds), Academic Press, London and New York.

Howe, M. J. A. and Ceci, S. J. (1979). Educational implications of memory research. *In* "Applied Problems in Memory" (M. M. Gruneberg and P. E. Morris, eds),

Academic Press, London and New York.

Humphrey, G. (1951). "Thinking", Methuen, London.

Jackson, D. N. and Messick, S. (1967a). "Problems in Human Assessment", McGraw Hill, New York.

Jackson, D. N. and Messick, S. (1967b). Response styles and the assessment of psychopathology. In "Problems in Human Assessment", (D. N. Jackson and S. Messick, eds), McGraw Hill, New York.

Kahneman, D. and Tversky, A. (1971). Subjective probability: A judgment of representativeness. Cognitive Psychology, 3, 430–454.

Kahneman, D. and Tversky, A. (1973). On the psychology of prediction. Psychological Review, 80, 237–251.

Martin, M. and Jones, G. V. (1984). Cognitive failures in everyday life. In "Everyday memory: actions and absentmindedness" (J. E. Harris and P. E. Morris, eds), Academic Press, London, Orlando and New York.

Miller, E. (1979). Memory and aging. In "Applied Problems in Memory" (M. M. Gruneberg and P. E. Morris, eds), Academic Press, London and New York.

Morris, P. E. (1981a). The cognitive psychology of self reports. In "The Psychology of Ordinary Explanations of Social Behaviour" (C. Antaki, ed.), Academic Press, London and New York.

Morris, P. E. (1981b). Why Evans is wrong in criticising introspective reports of subject strategies. British Journal of Psychology, 72, 465–468.

Morris, P. E. and Gruneberg, M. M. (1982). Knowledge, interest and the recall of real and simulated football scores. Paper presented to the British Psychological Society. Abstracted in Bulletin of the British Psychological Society, 35, 214.

Morris, P. E. and Hampson, P. J. (1983). "Imagery and Consciousness", Academic Press, London, Orlando and New York.

Morris, P. E. and Reid, R. L. (1970). Repeated use of mnemonic imagery. Psychonomic Science, 20, 337–338.

Morris, P. E. and Reid, R. L. (1971). Imagery and the compatability of pairing in the free recall of adjective-noun pairs. Quarterly Journal of Experimental Psychology, 23, 393–398.

Nisbett, R. and Ross, L. (1980). "Human Inference: Strategies and Shortcomings of Social Judgment", Prentice-Hall, Englewood Cliffs, NJ.

Nisbett, R. and Wilson, T. D. (1977). Telling more than we can know: Verbal reports of mental processes. Psychological Review, 84, 231–259.

Perlmutter, M. (1978). What is memory aging the aging of? Developmental Psychology, 14, 330–345.

Poulton, E. C. (1975). Range effects in experiments on people. American Journal of Psychology, 88, 3–32.

Poulton, E. C. (1979). Models for biases in judging sensory magnitude. Psychological Bulletin, 86, 777–803.

Rabbitt, P. M. A. (1982). How good do you think you are? Paper presented to the Experimental Psychological Society, London.

Reason, J. and Lucas, D. (1984). Using cognitive diaries to investigate naturally occurring memory blocks. In "Everyday memory, actions and absentmindedness" (J. E. Harris and P. E. Morris, eds), Academic Press, London, Orlando and New York.

Ryle, G. (1949). "The concept of mind". London: Hutchinson.

Shlechter, T. M. and Herrmann, D. J. (in press). An ecological investigation of self knowledge of memory performance as assessed by memory questionnaires. *Memory and Cognition*.

Sehulster, J. R. (1981). Structure and pragmatics of a self-theory of memory. *Memory and Cognition*, **9**, 263–276.

Skinner, B. F. (1953). "Science and Human Behaviour", Macmillan, New York.

Sunderland, A., Harris, J. E. and Baddeley, A. D. (1984). Assessing everyday memory for severe head injury. *In* "Everyday memory, actions and absent-mindedness" (J. E. Harris and P. E. Morris, eds), Academic Press, London, Orlando and New York.

Taylor, S. E. and Thompson, S. C. (1982). Stalking the elusive 'vividness' effect. *Psychological Review*, **89**, 155–181.

Titchener, E. B. (1909). "Lectures on the Experimental Psychology of the Thought Processes", Macmillan, New York.

Tulving, E. and Thomson, D. M. (1973). Encoding specificity and retrieval processes in episodic memory. *Psychological Review*, **80**, 352–373.

Tversky, A. and Kahneman, D. (1971). Belief in the law of small numbers. *Psychological Bulletin*, **77**, 105–110.

Tversky, A. and Kahneman, D. (1973). Availability: A heuristic for judging frequency and probability. *Cognitive Psychology*, **5**, 207–232.

Tversky, A. and Kahneman, D. (1974). Judgment under uncertainty: Heuristics and biases. *Science*, **185**, 1124–1131.

Underwood, B. J., Boruch, R. F. and Malmi, R. (1978). Composition of episodic memory. *Journal of Experimental Psychology: General*, **107**, 393–419.

Wilkins, A. J. and Baddeley, A. D. (1978). An approach to absentmindedness. *In* "Practical Aspects of Memory" (M. M. Gruneberg, P. E. Morris and R. N. Sykes, eds), Academic Press, London and New York.

Wittgenstein, L. (1953). "Philosophical Investigations", Blackwell, Oxford.

Woodworth, R. S. and Sheenan, M. R. (1964). "Contemporary Schools of Psychology", Methuen, London.

Yarmey, D. A. (1979). "The Psychology of Eyewitness Testimony", Free Press, New York.

Zelinski, E. M., Gilewski, M. J. and Thompson, L. W. (1980). Do laboratory tests relate to self assessment of memory ability in the young and old? *In* "New Directions in Memory and Aging" (L. W. Poon, J. L. Fozard, L. S. Cermak, D. Arenberg and L. W. Thompson, eds), Erlbaum, Hillsdale, NJ.

10

Cognitive Failures in Everyday Life

M. Martin and G. V. Jones

A cognitive failure is defined here, using a phrase normally associated with the game of tennis, as an "unforced error" of cognitive origin. That is, it is a cognitive error that occurs during the performance of a task that is normally well within the ability of the person carrying it out. An example is the action of the shop assistant who recently, while giving directions to another customer, offered one of the authors the change from £5, instead of from the £1 that had actually been tendered. The consequences of such a cognitive failure are often not too important. If the task is a potentially dangerous one, such as driving, flying or parachuting, however, the consequences may be very serious indeed. Furthermore, even if the consequences themselves of the cognitive failures are not important, it is possible that cognitive failures may still be important for what they reveal about the person who commits them.

Perhaps the most celebrated work to deal with the implications of everyday errors is the early "Psychopathology of Everyday Life" of Freud (1901). In this, Freud elaborated upon the role that the *Fehlleistung* or "faulty function" (to translate it into English, the single word "parapraxis" has been coined) could play in illuminating unconscious processes. He suggested psycho-dynamic interpretations of phenomena that included the forgetting of proper names, foreign words, impressions and resolutions, and mistakes in speech, reading, and writing. The similarity of some of Freud's concepts to modern ideas in cognitive psychology has been remarked upon by Norman (1981). However, it is probably true to say that the majority of the small number of recent investigations of cognitive failure can be located more readily within the conceptual framework articulated by William James (1890), which has been well described by Reason (in press).

The position at which the present chapter arrives can be related most closely to neither Freud nor James, but instead to the relatively neglected William McDougall, Oxford scholar and at Harvard, a successor to James. In a striking passage that it is worth citing at some length, McDougall proposed that cognitive failures result from difficulties in distributing attention.

We all have in various degrees the power of distributing our attention and of carrying on two or more tasks concurrently. If I am writing an easy straight-forward letter, I can, without interrupting my writing, overhear and understand conversation going on in the same room, and may even intervene in it . . . In writing, one's pen flows on, producing the appropriate words, while one thinks perhaps of the sentence or phrase that must come next. And sometimes the fact is brought vividly home to one by an error or slip, which consists in writing some word thought of but rejected, or belonging to a phrase next in order to that which the hand is writing. Or at table one thinks momentarily of taking salt and continues the conversation, while one's hand carries out the purpose thus momentarily formed; and again an error, such as seizing the pepper-pot instead of the salt-cellar, may make one realise how we commonly rely upon this subconscious execution of purposes consciously formed . . . Our attention oscillates between the two tasks, and, in the intervals in which it is directed to the one, our executive organs continue to carry out the movements appropriate to the other. Individuals differ widely in respect of their capacity for distributing their attention in this way. (McDougall, 1923, pp. 281–283).

As with Freud and James, McDougall's theorizing was intuitive to a considerable degree, but it will transpire here that some recent empirical research concurs in implicating the efficiency with which attention is distributed as a determinant of individual differences in the frequency with which cognitive failures are experienced.

In studying cognitive failures, one may distinguish three major methods of obtaining data on their occurrence. These can be referred to briefly as the *observation*, *experimental simulation*, and *questionnaire* methods.

A. Observation

This method is simple in principle. A collection is formed of as many as possible naturally occurring examples of the specified range of errors, a process that may be facilitated by the use of systematic aids to observation (including self-observation) such as special report forms or diaries. Many collections of this sort have concentrated on verbal errors (see Fromkin, 1973, 1980), with one of the earliest corpora, that of Meringer, containing an estimated 8 800 errors of speaking and reading (Meringer, 1908; Meringer and Mayer, 1895). More recently, some notable collections of errors of action have been formed (e.g. Norman, 1981; Reason, 1977, 1979; see also Chapter 4 this volume, Reason and Lucas, 1984).

The advantage of corpora of cognitive failures is that they place taxonomic constraints on the nature of theories that might be proposed to account for such failures. It should be possible to allocate each item to membership of one of the limited number of categories of the particular taxonomy allowed by the theory under consideration. As an example, on the basis of a theory representing action sequences as involving a range of schemas and sub-schemas, Norman (1981) was able to categorize action slips into three different major categories, as relating to either the incorrect selection, activation, or triggering of schemas.

B. Experimental simulation

In this method, cognitive failures are induced and studied experimentally. The best-known cognitive failure to be studied in this way is the tip-of-the-tongue phenomenon, in which a person is temporarily unable to retrieve a name or other word that subsequently returns to them. It has been shown by Brown and McNeill and others that the phenomenon can be simulated experimentally by asking people to identify rare words on the basis of their dictionary definitions (Brown and McNeill, 1966; Koriat and Lieblich, 1974; Rubin, 1975).

The advantage of experimental simulation as a method of studying cognitive failures is that it brings the phenomenon into the laboratory and allows the gathering of systematic data. In the case of the tip-of-the-tongue phenomenon, for example, it has been shown by Koriat and Lieblich that, for words that are ultimately identified correctly, the final letter, initial letter, and number of syllables are estimated correctly on 53%, 79%, and 92% of occasions, respectively, showing that the phenomenon can only rarely if ever be the consequence of a complete failure of activation.

C. Questionnaires

This method resembles the observation method in that it concerns itself with naturally occurring cognitive failures, but differs in that it is generic rather than specific. That is, it produces overall indices of individuals' susceptibilities to cognitive failure, rather than detailed descriptions of particular occasions on which this was manifested. It may be used to provide systematic evidence about performance even when (as is the case for most types of cognitive failure) no relevant experimental simulations have been devised.

Like the data yielded by the two preceding types of method, questionnaire data can be examined in isolation in order to elucidate the operation of cognitive systems. For example, Herrmann and Neisser (1978) concluded on the basis of a questionnaire study that approximately eight different factors could be distinguished in everyday forgetting. More often, however, this method employs some further manipulation, by administering a questionnaire both before and after a relevant event, or by examining its relation to a second questionnaire. Perhaps the most informative of strategies is to investigate how individuals' questionnaire scores relate to their performances on experimental tasks. The discovery of systematic associations between the two types of measure would suggest areas of common mechanism that could significantly increase our understanding of the generation of cognitive failures in everyday life. One of the purposes of this chapter is to review recent results which suggest that theoretical progress of this kind may in fact be possible. Knowledge of specific associations between questionnaire scores and experimental performance is beneficial in other ways as well. In applied contexts particularly, it may be useful to be able to supplement questionnaires' self-report information by objective performance data.

This chapter focusses upon a particular questionnaire, the Cognitive Failures Questionnaire of Broadbent and his colleagues (Broadbent et al., 1982). Its relation to some other cognitive questionnaires is considered first, followed by consideration of its relation to experimental measures of performance, and finally by consideration of the relation between cognitive failures and certain aspects of personality in general.

I. QUESTIONNAIRES FOR COGNITIVE PERFORMANCE

It is not intended to attempt here a comprehensive review of questionnaires that are relevant to the topic of cognitive failure (for wide-ranging accounts of memory questionnaires see Herrmann, 1982, 1984, Chapter 8 this volume). Instead, the first two parts of this section are intended to give the flavour of several specific measures for which empirical results will be discussed. As indicated previously, these results centre upon the Cognitive Failures Questionnaire of Broadbent and his colleagues, one of the most widely explored instruments for the subjective assessment of everyday slips and errors. In addition, the scales of Herrmann and Neisser, Reason, and Martin will be described, and in the third and final part of the section the empirical relations of their results to those of the Cognitive Failures Questionnaire will be reviewed.

A. The cognitive failures questionnaire

The Cognitive Failures Questionnaire (CFQ) described by Broadbent et al. (1982) contains 25 items that cover a variety of possible cognitive lapses. Examples of items probing for failures of everyday perception, memory and action are "Do you fail to notice signposts on the road?", "Do you find you forget whether you've turned off a light or a fire or locked the door?", and "Do you bump into people?", respectively. Respondents indicate for each question the frequency with which the relevant event has occurred to them within the last six months on a five-point ordinal scale ranging from "never" to "very often".

Responses to each of the individual items correlate positively with the overall score, with all but one Pearson $r(96)$ values being greater than 0.2. Performance is fairly stable over time, the value of the test-retest correlation over a period of 16 months, $r(71) = .54$, being at about the same level as those of several well-established trait measures.

B. Other cognitive questionnaires

Several further questionnaires for assessing cognitive performance have been employed by a variety of investigators, and will be briefly described in turn.

(1) *The inventory of memory experiences*

The Inventory of Memory Experiences (IME) of Herrmann, Neisser, and Gottlieb (see Herrmann and Neisser, 1978), together with its close relative, the Short Inventory of Memory Experiences (SIME), consists of two parts. One scale, Part F, consists of 48 questions about everyday forgetting, and produces eight different factors concerning forgetting of different types. Factors F1 to F8 correspond to rote memory, absent-mindedness, names, people, conversations, errands, retrieval and places, respectively. The other scale, Part R, consists of eight questions from each of three sections. The first and third sections, R-1 and R-3, concern early childhood and conversations, respectively. The second differs from the other questions in the inventory by relating to both recent and remote events, and hence Herrmann and Neisser state that importance cannot be attached to simple average scores from it. Example questions from Part F and Part R are "How often do you find, at the end of a conversation, that you forgot to bring up some point or some question that you had intended to mention" (seven-point response scale from "never" to "always") and "Do you remember any time that you were sick or hurt as a young child? Think of whatever time you remember best. How well do you remember it?" (seven-point response scale from "not at all" to "perfectly"), respectively.

(2) *The slips of action questionnaire*

Reason has developed a number of questionnaires designed to investigate the occurrence of unplanned actions. The Slips of Action Questionnaire (SAQ) consists of 30 items that diary studies suggested were representative of such actions. For each item a response is assigned using a seven-point scale from "never" to "nearly all the time". An example of an SAQ item is "I selected two different items of cutlery from the drawer. Then I decided I didn't need one of them, but instead of replacing that one, I put the item I did want back into the drawer". For each item, respondents are asked to judge how often this *kind* of thing happens to them.

(3) *The everyday attention and everyday memory questionnaires*

The Everyday Attention Questionnaire (EAQ) and Everyday Memory Questionnaire (EMQ) have been devised by one of us (Martin) in order to provide comparable but explicitly differentiated measures of two basic components of cognitive activity.

The EAQ consists of 18 probes designed to assess how easy people find it to pay attention in different everyday activities: responses are made on a five-point scale. An example probe is "Imagine that you are carrying out some task you find easy (perhaps something at work; or peeling potatoes; or knitting). What is the effect of humming or whistling to yourself on your ability to do this sort of task?" (response scale from "very distracting" to "very helpful".)

The EMQ consists of 37 relatively simple probes all of which "ask you to judge how good you are at remembering different types of things, relative to most other people". The five-point response scale is from "very poor" to "very good", and an example probe is "The words of songs or poems". It is the uniform simplicity of the probes that makes it practicable to seek judgements that are not absolute, but instead explicitly require the respondent to locate himself or herself relative to the remainder of the population.

C. Relation of CFQ to other cognitive questionnaires

The CFQ's empirical relation with the SIME of Herrmann and Neisser and with the EAQ and EMQ has been investigated by Martin (1983). The matrix of correlations between the CFQ and each of the ten subcomponents of the SIME, and the EAQ and EMQ, are shown in Table 1. For this sample of twenty members of the Oxford Subject Panel, it can be seen that the CFQ scores correlate highly with seven of the eight factors of the SIME's Forgetting scale, but do not correlate significantly with either of the Remembering scale's subcomponents. The CFQ scores also have a considerable correlation with the EMQ scores (negative in sign, since deficiencies in cognitive performance attract high ratings in the CFQ and SIME, but low ratings in the EMQ), but not with the EAQ scores. In addition, it can be seen

Table I. Correlations between CFQ, EMQ, EAQ and SIME (F Factors and R Sections) Scores

	CFQ	EMQ	EAQ
EMQ	−.64[b]	—	—
EAQ	.05	.08	—
F1	.68[b]	−.49[b]	−.17
F2	.47[a]	−.47[b]	−.06
F3	.44[a]	−.08	−.14
F4	.55[a]	−.27	−.32
F5	.51[a]	−.29	−.18
F6	.16	.00	−.18
F7	.55[a]	−.54[a]	−.22
F8	.63[b]	−.52[a]	−.04
F Total	.74[b]	−.50[a]	−.20
R-1	.23	−.18	.37
R-3	−.35	.15	−.47[a]

Note: a = $p < .05$, b = $p < .01$.

that the EMQ correlates significantly with four of the Forgetting scale subcomponents, while the EAQ on the other hand correlates only with one of the Remembering scale subcomponents, with a non-significant correlation between EMQ and EAQ scores. This evidence suggests, therefore, that the SIME and the EMQ are closely related to the CFQ, but that the EAQ assesses an aspect of cognitive performance that is either weakly or not at all related. The dissociation provides evidence against the possibility that the test results are subject to a general confounding by a factor such as desirability.

Further evidence indicating the close relation of the SIME to the CFQ has been provided by Reason (cited by Broadbent *et al.*, 1982), who found a significant correlation of .59 between CFQ and SIME Forgetting scale scores for a sample of 94 psychology undergraduates. In addition, Reason found correlations of similar magnitude between the CFQ and his inventories of slips of action and of absent-mindedness.

It thus appears that the CFQ provides the user with information that agrees quite well with that provided by several other ostensibly related measures, while at present the only cognitive questionnaire for which empirical data suggest a lack of overlap with the CFQ is the EAQ.

II. QUESTIONNAIRE AND EXPERIMENTAL MEASURES

The positive relations between the CFQ and some (but not all) questionnaire measures of everyday cognitive performance provide support for the validity of the CFQ as an assessment tool. More direct evidence may in principle be obtained, however, by investigating relations between questionnaire performance and objective performance in behavioural experiments. Among the advantages of this procedure are, firstly, that the qualitative dissimilarity between the two measures under examination means that they are relatively unlikely to be merely covarying with some third, unsuspected factor; and, secondly, that by investigating performance in experiments that isolate specific cognitive mechanisms some steps may be taken towards identifying those processes that are being tapped by the questionnaire.

Using this approach, it has already proven possible to discount several objective measures of cognitive processes potentially important in determining CFQ performance. Broadbent *et al.* (1982) found no significant correlations between CFQ and immediate memory for nine-item lists, for longer-term memory for categorized material, for performance on the Williams delayed recall test, or between CFQ and the size of suffix and articulatory suppression effects, and efficiency of blurred word identification. Further, Martin has found no significant correlation between CFQ and mental arithmetic performance.

Having excluded several objective aspects of performance as predictors of a person's assessment of the incidence of cognitive failures, we consider next two further areas of objective performance that recent research has on the other hand implicated as being of some importance. These are the areas of attention and of memory for serial order.

A. Cognitive failures and attention

In this part, empirical evidence that bears upon the conjecture of McDougall cited earlier is considered. That is, it is investigated whether individual differences in reported susceptibility to cognitive failure are related to those in the objective ability to distribute attention. For this purpose, it is useful to distinguish two different types of cognitive task. In a *distributed attention* task, a person attempts to perform successfully each of two or more concurrent tasks. In a *focussed attention* task, on the other hand, a person is instructed to attend to only one of two or more concurrent streams of information.

(1) *Distributed attention*

Several lines of research have indicated that the efficiency with which a person can distribute attention is linked with the occurrence of cognitive failures.

In one of a series of experiments carried out with Oxford Subject Panel members (Martin and Jones, 1983), 20 subjects had to perform detection and reading tasks concurrently, using a paradigm similar to that of Martin (1977). The first task was to respond by button-pressing as quickly as possible to the occurrences of a particular sound (/n/, /s/, /t/, /ɪ/, or /aʊ/) in a list of words presented over headphones. The second task was to read printed passages of text aloud as fast as possible. The speed of performance of each task was analysed both for each task in isolation and for simultaneous performance of the two tasks. In addition, error rates in the detection task were examined (there were too few errors in the reading task for analysis). All these measures were compared with previously obtained CFQ scores. Detection accuracy did not correlate significantly ($p > .05$) with CFQ score either in isolated or concurrent performance ($r = .03$ and $-.32$, respectively). But there were significant correlations between CFQ scores and both the temporal measures when the tasks were performed concurrently, with correlations of .64 and $-.46$ for target detection latencies and reading speeds, respectively. On the other hand, neither of the corresponding correlations between CFQ scores and the objective measures, though of the same polarities, reached significance when each task was performed in isolation ($r = .27$ and $-.43$, respectively). Thus the study provides evidence of a significant relation between CFQ scores and performance in an objective test of the ability to distribute attention.

Evidence consistent with the above finding has been reported also in a "Young Scientist of the Year" project by Wakeford *et al.* (1980). It was found that children who reported many cognitive failures in a diary-based study were also less good at concurrently counting backwards and mirror-drawing, though their performance of the tasks in isolation did not differ significantly from those with few cognitive failures. Broadbent *et al.* have failed to replicate this finding in two studies using the CFQ with adults, but suggest that this may be due to the less homogeneous nature of their subject samples.

Further evidence in support of the divided attention hypothesis comes from a study by Harris and Wilkins (1982). In this, subjects had to keep check of a digital clock in order to signal at particular times. They did this while concurrently watching a film of which their recall was to be tested. It was found that high CFQ scores were significantly associated with the number of times subjects signalled late.

There thus appears to be a growing, if not yet conclusive, body of evidence that associates a reported susceptibility to the commission of cognitive failures with relatively poor objective performance in a task that makes strong demands on the ability to distribute attention. The critical factor here does not appear to be one of overall limitations in general processing capacity (e.g. Kahneman, 1973), however. The latter should produce associations between cognitive failures and performance on a wide range of tasks. Rather, the limitation appears to be of a type proposed by Allport (1980): that of maintaining correctly the goals appropriate to several different independently active tasks (cf. Reason's, 1984, "Intention System" in Chapter 7 of this volume).

(2) Focussed Attention
The defining characteristic of a focussed-attention task is that it involves the selection of one source of information to be responded to, and the simultaneous rejection of other, often confusingly related, sources of information. Though superficially one might expect a similar relation with CFQ performance for distributed and focussed-attention, it can be seen that this is not necessarily the case. The distributed-attention task assesses the ability to do *more than* one thing at a time. The focussed-attention task assesses a very different ability: that of being able to do *only* one thing at a time (cf. Johnston and Dark, 1982). Consequently it is perhaps not surprising that the research to be reviewed here has failed to find strong links between cognitive failures and ability to focus attention.

Perhaps the best-established focussed-attention method is that of Stroop (1935). In this, people are required to sort cards on the basis of ink colour. If the ink forms the name of a different colour then, owing to an inability to focus attention completely on the ink colour, it is generally found that performance is worse than in a control condition in which the ink forms only a neutral set of letters. In a study with 32 subjects, Martin (1983) found no significant relation between CFQ scores and the size of the Stroop effect (defined as the difference between the experimental and control times divided by the control time), or between CFQ scores and experimental or control times in isolation. This result was examined further in two studies in which the Stroop task was performed either silently or else while continuously counting aloud. It was found that the results were consistent in that for both conditions in both experiments there was no significant correlation between overall CFQ scores and the magnitudes of either the Stroop effect or the experimental or control times in isolation. The first experiment did produce a significant correlation between the Stroop effect and one of the products of an early factor analysis of the CFQ, Factor B, but this result was not repeated in the second experiment. Finally, similar negative results were obtained in a reverse Stroop task in which sorting is by name rather than by colour. There were no significant correlations between CFQ scores and the magnitudes of either the reverse Stroop effect or the experimental or control times in isolation, for performance that was either silent or with continuous irrelevant articulation.

A second method for investigating ability to focus attention is via the Embedded Figures Test of Witkin *et al.* (1971). The subject's task on each trial is to attempt to locate a simple visual figure that is hidden within a larger, complex visual figure. In keeping with the results of the Stroop experiments, however, an experiment with 20 subjects (Martin, 1983) found no significant correlation between CFQ scores and speed of performance on the Embedded Figures Test.

Finally, ability to focus attention was also examined using a particular version of the dichotic listening paradigm. An experiment similar to one reported by Martin (1978b) was carried out, in which twenty people were presented successively with four pairs of words, one word of each concurrent pair being presented to each ear. The subjects were instructed to concentrate their attention on the words of only one side. Subsequently, they attempted to recall either the attended words followed by the unattended ones, or vice versa. Again in keeping with the previous results, there were found to be no significant correlations between CFQ scores and the levels of recall of attended or unattended words. Similarly, the experimental measures did not correlate significantly with Herrmann and Neisser's SIME or Martin's EMQ. In contrast, however, there were significant correlations between scores on Martin's Everyday Attention Questionnaire and levels of recall of attended words, whether recalled first or second, with $r(18) = -.46$ and $-.83$, respectively; for unattended words, the correlations were not significant. The negative nature of the correlations suggests that the EAQ may be assessing the degree to which people prefer to divide their attention, and that this is negatively related to their objective ability to focus attention.

The relation of the EAQ to focussed-attention performance may be contrasted with the lack of evidence for an association with distributed-attention performance. As noted earlier, there is a significant correlation between distributed-attention performance and CFQ scores, but not between the latter and EAQ scores. This pattern of results is unexpected, but perhaps indicates that the degree to which people prefer concurrent inputs in everyday life relates only to the degree of difficulty experienced in focussing attention on a single input, and does not depend upon actual levels of dual-task performance.

B. Cognitive failures and seriation

Despite the classic paper of Lashley (1951), the central importance to the study of behaviour of the problem of seriation has continued to be underestimated. For example, consider the Method of Loci, the technique for facilitating memory that has been in use since its origins in classical rhetoric (Yates, 1966). Many recent accounts have stressed only the role of visual imagery in facilitating the recall of information concerning the identity of the "objects" placed along the route that is mentally traversed. The method is at least equally important, however, in facilitating seriation (Roediger, 1980): the well-learned sequence of loci that is used ensures that the orator recalls not only the identities of the topics that have been encoded, but recalls them also in the correct order.

The Method of Loci provides one instance of the general rule that it may be useful to distinguish between the processing of identity information and that of sequential information (cf. Jones, 1976; Sperling and Melchner, 1976). In the present context, this approach suggests that an important factor in the causation of cognitive failures may be the forgetting not of actions themselves but rather of the order in which they are to be performed. This possibility may be examined by comparing CFQ scores with an experimental measure of seriation in recall. Martin (1978a) has provided evidence that forward digit span is primarily a measure of an individual's recall of seriation rather than identity information; backward span, on the other hand, emphasizes the operation of reversal rather than the maintenance of seriation itself. Thus it may be hypothesized that CFQ scores should be related to experimental measures similar to that of forward digit span.

The above hypothesis has been examined by the present authors in an experiment with twenty subjects. The forward measure adopted was the number of items of the correct identity recalled in the correct serial position, for forward recall of 13-digit lists. The backward measure derived similarly from the backward recall of 10-digit lists (overall performance was approximately the same in the two cases). It was found that there was indeed a significant correlation (of $-.41$) between CFQ scores and the size of the forward measure, whereas the correlation of CFQ and the backward measure was not significant.

III. COGNITIVE FAILURES AND PERSONALITY

This section examines personality-related factors that are associated with the reporting of cognitive failures. It is divided into three parts. First, the relations between cognitive failures and a variety of specific measures of personality are examined. Second, the association between cognitive failures and psychiatric symptoms is reviewed. Third, it is questioned whether the frequency of reporting cognitive failures is related in any degree to a general preparedness to admit to imperfection.

A. Personality measures

(1) *Anxiety*

It might be anticipated that one group of people who are likely to commit an above average number of cognitive failures are the highly anxious. People who are anxious have a tendency to attend to their internal states rather then task-relevant cues (Wine, 1980a, 1980b), and thus their ability to distribute attention over different tasks may be expected to be impaired. Support for this hypothesis comes from two studies that employed the Eysenck Personality Questionnaire. Broadbent *et al.* (1982) reported that, in a large-scale study testing 221 student nurses (Parkes, 1982), there was a significant correlation of .28 between scores on the CFQ and the relevant N scale of the EPQ; similarly in a study of twenty undergraduate and postgraduate students, the present authors found a significant correlation of .50 between the same variables. In neither study, on the other hand, was there a significant correlation between CFQ scores and scores on the E or P scales of the EPQ, relating to extraversion and psychoticism rather than neuroticism. In addition to the EPQ, Parkes and Martin administered two further different sets of tests. Consistent with the EPQ result, Parkes found a significant correlation of .31 between CFQ and the Trait-Anxiety measure of Spielberger *et al.* (1970), while Martin found a significant correlation of .51 with the Anxiety scale of Paisey (1980).

In view of the consistency of the relation between CFQ and anxiety, it might be wondered whether the correlation between CFQ scores and objective cognitive performance referred to earlier was in fact mediated by this personality variable, especially since an effect upon cognitive performance has previously been demonstrated (Young and Martin, 1981). This is not the case, however. As already described, it was found that concurrent performance in a detection/reading task correlated significantly with CFQ score. But further analysis of that experiment's results shows that although CFQ score correlated significantly with N score, there was not a significant correlation between distributed-attention performance and N score. Furthermore, the partial correlations (with N held constant) between CFQ and both target detection latencies and reading speeds remained significant, $r(17) = .54$ and $-.48$, respectively.

(2) *Other variables*

The studies referred to in the preceding part of this section have also provided some evidence of the relation of CFQ scores to some further personality variables.

It can be hypothesized that those who are prone to make cognitive errors may view such events as evidence that the outcome of events is often dictated by factors outside their control rather than by their own efforts. In accordance with this hypothesis, CFQ scores have been found, in the study of nurses previously referred to, to have a significant correlation of .35 with the

Externality of Control measure of Rotter (1966).

In the study referred to earlier, the present authors examined the relationships of students' CFQ scores to a number of stable personality scales derived by Paisey (1980), and in particular to strength of excitation (see Mangan, 1982; Paisey and Mangan, 1982). The CFQ was found to have a significant correlation of −.41 with the Strength of Excitation scale derived from the Temperament Inventory of Strelau (1972), but a non-significant correlation with the Strength of Inhibition scale derived from the same source. The negative correlation between CFQ and strength of excitation perhaps resulted from a positive relation between CFQ and reactivity or sensitivity since it has been proposed (e.g. Nebylitsyn, 1972) that the latter are negatively related to strength of excitation.

There was in addition a significant correlation of .56 between the CFQ and the Schizophrenism scale derived from that of Nielsen and Petersen (1976), and a significant correlation of .55 between the CFQ and the Distractability scale. It is possible that both results have an attentional basis. Distractability is clearly linked with attentional difficulty, while it has been proposed (Hemsley, 1975, 1977; Ottmanns, 1978) that the symptomatology of schizophrenia can in part also be usefully viewed as a disorder of attention. Hence the relations of both these variables to cognitive failure may be mediated via difficulties in the distribution of attention.

B. Psychiatric symptoms

In several studies, Broadbent et al. (1982) have observed consistently high correlations between the CFQ and a modified version of the Middlesex Hospital Questionnaire, or MHQ (Crisp et al., 1978; Crown and Crisp, 1966). The MHQ is a measure of state rather than trait that is concerned with the occurrence of a range of mild psychiatric symptoms. The CFQ was found to correlate reliably not only with overall MHQ score but also with individual scales of Anxiety, Somatic, Depression and Obsessional symptoms.

Informative data on the development of such symptomatology has been provided by Parkes (1980, 1982). She administered the CFQ to 53 nurses before they went on to relatively low-stress wards, and to 48 nurses who went on to relatively high-stress wards. She found that in the former case subsequent MHQ scores were unrelated to the CFQ scores, but that in the latter case there was a highly significant tau of .46 for the relation of CFQ and subsequent MFQ scores. On the other hand, CFQ scores themselves were not changed by going on either type of ward. Broadbent et al. (1982) deduced therefore that the CFQ provides an index of vulnerability to the effects of stress, rather than a direct index of stress itself.

C. Self-criticalness

A noteworthy feature of the CFQ and similar questionnaires is that their accurate completion may be viewed as requiring that a person should be able to be self-critical in admitting to cognitive imperfections. To what extent, if any, does reluctance to engage in self-criticism impair the accuracy of CFQ scores? Two sets of results that have already been described provide evidence that such an effect, if any, must be relatively small in magnitude. First, it could not have been large enough to destroy the significant relationships observed between CFQ scores and performance on objective distributed-attention and seriation tasks. Secondly, and conversely, though such an effect would presumably be common to both the CFQ and Martin's EAQ, it could not have been large enough to generate a significant correlation between the two measures. Some further evidence to be described points in a similar direction.

Comparison may be made between scores on the CFQ and on the L scale of the EPQ, which assesses willingness to admit to social rather than cognitive imperfections. In the large-scale study of nurses and the smaller-scale study of students referred to earlier, the correlation between the two measures was significant at $-.18$, and non-significant at $-.11$, respectively. Thus the effect of any general factor of self-criticalness in producing high CFQ and low L-scale scores can account for only a few percent of the variance in these responses. A rather larger significant correlation of $-.25$ among nurses was found between the CFQ and the Defensiveness scale of the Adjective Checklist of Gough and Heilbrun (1965).

It may be concluded therefore that CFQ scores are subject to some modulation as a function of the individual's level of self-criticalness. The evidence is, however, that the effects of such modulation are limited in their scope. Nevertheless, it should be borne in mind that the results discussed here were obtained in research contexts, in which respondents had no specific reason to inhibit self-criticalness. It is possible that such a factor might become operative in some applied contexts, and in these the use of objective tests of performance might prove advantageous in spite of the greater costs in terms of equipment and personnel usually associated with such procedures.

IV. CONCLUSIONS

Although the modern revival of interest in cognitive failures is still at a relatively early stage, it appears that progress has been achieved in understanding the cognitive and other factors involved in their production.

The work considered in the preceding three sections has used as its principal measure the Cognitive Failures Questionnaire (CFQ) of Broadbent et al. (1982). The appropriateness of this scale is suggested by the consistency of its results with those of kindred questionnaires. Furthermore, CFQ scores have been found to be predictive of objective experimental data.

The empirical evidence that has been reviewed suggests that inefficiency in the distribution of attention between two or more concurrent tasks is a significant cause of cognitive failure, as hypothesized by McDougall more than half a century ago. Perhaps surprisingly, however, there appears to be no evidence that the generation of cognitive failures in everyday life is related to inefficient performance in laboratory tasks that require the focussing of attention upon a single channel of information (as opposed to its distribution over more than one channel). These results imply that cognitive failures are likely to be the consequence not of fluctuations in an otherwise satisfactory level of performance of individual tasks, but rather the consequence of attempting to perform adequately two or more tasks whose joint require-ments (e.g. in terms of goal maintenance) may interact to exceed temporarily the resources available. In addition, the results of one study suggest that cognitive failures are related to poor levels of seriation performance. This result is complementary to the distributed-attention hypothesis in implic-ating, as causes of cognitive failures, limitations not only in the magnitude of processing resources but also in the accuracy of their temporal deployment.

Certain personality types appear more likely than others to be susceptible to cognitive failures. There is considerable evidence that the occurrence of the latter is associated with a relatively high level of anxiety or neuroticism. This result also is highly consistent with the explanation of cognitive failure advanced here as the consequence of excessive distributed-attention demands. As concluded in a recent review (Eysenck, 1982, p. 99),

> the task-irrelevant information involved in worry and cognitive self-concern competes with task-relevant information for space in the processing system. As a consequence, highly anxious subjects are in effect in a dual-task or divided attention situation, in contrast to non-anxious subjects who primarily process task-relevant information.

In addition, there is some evidence that cognitive failure is associated with the factors of belief in the externality of control, strength of excitation, schizophrenism, and distractability. Self-reported levels of cognitive failure are also associated with a general disposition to be self-critical; this factor, though important, nevertheless accounts for only a small proportion of the variance in self-report data.

Finally, there is some evidence to associate the experience of cognitive failures with mild psychiatric symptoms. Of particular interest is the finding that measuring levels of cognitive failure may help to identify those people who are relatively likely to develop mild psychiatric symptoms on exposure to raised levels of stress. If reliable, this result suggests that susceptibility to cognitive failures may provide useful information in appropriate circum-stances.

ACKNOWLEDGEMENT

Acknowledgements are due to Donald Broadbent, David Clark, John Harris and Peter Morris for their helpful comments on a draft of this chapter, and to the MRC and SERC for their support of the first author's research.

REFERENCES

Allport, D. A. (1980). Attention and performance. *In* "Cognitive Psychology: New Directions" (G. Claxton, ed.), Routledge & Kegan Paul, London.

Broadbent, D. E., Cooper, P. E., Fitzgerald, P. and Parkes, K. R. (1982). Cognitive Failures Questionnaire (CFQ) and its correlates. *British Journal of Clinical Psychology*, 21, 1–16.

Brown, R. and McNeill, D. (1966). The "tip of the tongue" phenomenon. *Journal of Verbal Learning and Verbal Behavior*, 5, 325–337.

Crisp, A. H., Gaynor-Jones, M. and Slater, P. (1978). The Middlesex Hospital Questionnaire: A validity study. *British Journal of Medical Psychology*, 51, 269–280.

Crown, S. and Crisp, A. H. (1966). A short clinical diagnostic self-rating scale for psycho-neurotic patients. *British Journal of Psychiatry*, 112, 917–923.

Eysenck, M. W. (1982). "Attention and Arousal", Springer-Verlag, Berlin.

Freud, S. (1901). Zur Psychopathologie des Alltagsleben. *Monatsschrift für Psychiatrie und Neurologie*, 10, 1–32 and 95–143. Translated by A. Tyson (1960) as "The Psychopathology of Everyday Life", Vol. 6 of J. Strachey (ed.), "The Standard Edition of the Complete Psychological Works of Sigmund Freud", Hogarth Press, London.

Fromkin, V. A. (1973). "Speech Errors as Linguistic Evidence". Mouton, The Hague.

Fromkin, V. A. (1980). "Errors in Linguistic Performance: Slips of the Tongue, Ear, Pen and Hand", Academic Press, New York and London.

Gough, H. G. and Heilbrun, A. B. (1965). "The Adjective Checklist Manual", Consulting Psychologists Press, Palo Alto, California.

Harris, J. E. and Wilkins, A. J. (1982). Remembering to do things: A theoretical framework and an illustrative experiment. *Human Learning*, 1, 123–136.

Hemsley, D. R. (1975). A two-stage model of attention in schizophrenic research. *British Journal of Social and Clinical Psychology*, 14, 81–89.

Hemsley, D. R. (1977). What have cognitive deficits to do with schizophrenic symptoms? *British Journal of Psychology*, 130, 167–173.

Herrmann, D. J. (1982). Know thy memory: The use of questionnaires to assess and study memory. *Psychological Bulletin*, 92, 434–452.

Herrmann, D. J. (1984). Questionnaires about memory. *In* "Everyday Memory, Actions and Absent-Mindedness" (J. E. Harris and P. E. Morris, eds), Academic Press, London, Orlando and New York.

Herrmann, D. J. and Neisser, U. (1978). An inventory of everyday memory experiences. *In* "Practical Aspects of Memory" (M. M. Gruneberg, P. E. Morris and R. N. Sykes, eds), Academic Press, London and New York.

James, W. (1890). "The Principles of Psychology", Holt, New York.

Johnston, W. A. and Dark, V. J. (1982). In defense of intraperceptual theories of attention. *Journal of Experimental Psychology: Human Perception and Performance*, 8, 407–421.

Jones, G. V. (1976). A fragmentation hypothesis of memory: Cued recall of pictures and of sequential position. *Journal of Experimental Psychology: General*, 105, 277–293.

Kahneman, D. (1973). "Attention and Effort", Prentice-Hall, Englewood Cliffs, NJ.

Koriat, A. and Lieblich, I. (1974). What does a person in a "TOT" state know that a person in a "don't know" state doesn't know. *Memory & Cognition*, 2, 647–655.

Lashley, K. S. (1951). The problem of serial order in behavior. *In* (L. A. Jeffress, ed.), "Cerebral Mechanisms in Behavior". Wiley, New York.

Mangan, G. L. (1982). "The Biology of Human Conduct". Pergamon, Oxford.

Martin, M. (1977). Reading while listening: A linear model of selective attention. *Journal of Verbal Learning and Verbal Behavior*, **16**, 453–463.

Martin, M. (1978a). Assessment of individual variation in memory ability. *In* "Practical Aspects of Memory" (M. M. Gruneberg, P. E. Morris and R. N. Sykes, eds), Academic Press, London and New York.

Martin, M. (1978b). Retention of attended and unattended auditorily and visually presented material. *Quarterly Journal of Experimental Psychology*, **30**, 187–200.

Martin, M. (1983). Cognitive failure: Everyday and laboratory performance. *Bulletin of the Psychonomic Society*, **21**, 97–100.

Martin, M. and Jones, G. V. (1983). Distribution of attention in cognitive failure. *Human Learning*, **2**, 221–226.

McDougall, W. (1923). "An Outline of Psychology", Methuen, London. C. Scribner's Sons, New York.

Meringer, R. (1908). "Aus dem Leben der Sprache: Versprechen. Kindersprache. Nachahmungstrieb". B. Behr's Verlag, Berlin.

Meringer, R. and Mayer, K. (1895). "Versprechen und Verlesen: Eine Psychologish-linguistische Studie". G. J. Goschen'sche Verlagshandlung, Stuttgart.

Nebylitsin, V. D. (1972). "Fundamental Properties of the Human Nervous System", Plenum Press, New York.

Nielsen, T. C. and Petersen, K. E. (1976). Electrodermal correlates of extraversion, trait anxiety and schizophrenism. *Scandinavian Journal of Psychology*, **17**, 73–80.

Norman, D. A. (1981). Categorization of action slips. *Psychological Review*, **88**, 1–15.

Ottmanns, T. (1978). Selective attention in schizophrenia and manic psychoses: The effects of distraction on information processing. *Journal of Abnormal Psychology*, **87**, 212–225.

Paisey, T. J. H. (1980). *Individual differences in psycho-physiological response*. Doctoral thesis, University of Oxford.

Paisey, T. J. H. and Mangan, G. L. (1982). Neo-Pavlovian temperament theory and the biological bases of personality. *Personality and Individual Differences*, **3**, 189–203.

Parkes, K. R. (1980). Occupational stress among student nurses—1: A comparison of medical and surgical wards. *Nursing Times*, **76**, 113–116; Occasional Paper No. 25.

Parkes, K. R. (1982). Occupational stress among student nurses: A natural experiment. *Journal of Applied Psychology*, **67**, 784–796.

Reason, J. T. (1977). Skill and error in everyday life. *In* "Adult Learning" (M. J. A. Howe, ed.), Wiley, London.

Reason, J. T. (1979). Actions not as planned: The price of automatization. *In* "Aspects of Consciousness, Vol. 1" (G. Underwood and R. Stevens, eds.), Academic Press, London and New York.

Reason, J. T. (in press). Lapses of attention. *In* "Varieties of Attention" (R. Parasuraman, R. Davies and J. Beatty, eds), Academic Press, New York and London.

Reason, J. T. (1984). Absent-mindedness and cognitive control. *In* "Everyday Memory, Actions and Absent-Mindedness" (J. E. Harris and P. E. Morris, eds), Academic Press, London, Orlando and New York.

Reason, J. T. and Lucas, D. (1984). Using cognitive diaries to investigate naturally occurring memory blocks. *In* "Everyday Memory, Actions and Absent-Mindedness" (J. E. Harris and P. E. Morris, eds), Academic Press, London, Orlando and New York.

Roediger, H. L., III (1980). The effectiveness of four mnemonics in ordering recall. *Journal of Experimental Psychology: Human Learning and Memory*, **6**, 558–567.

Rotter, J. B. (1966). Generalized expectancies for internal versus external control of reinforcement. *Psychological Monographs*, **80** (1, Whole No. 609).

Rubin, D. C. (1975). Within word structure in the tip-of-the-tongue phenomenon. *Journal of Verbal Learning and Verbal Behavior*, **14**, 392–397.

Sperling, G. and Melchner, M. (1976). Estimating item and order information. *Journal of Mathematical Psychology*, **13**, 192–213.

Spielberger, C. D., Gorsuch, R. L. and Lushene, R. E. (1970). "Manual for the State-Trait Anxiety Inventory", Consulting Psychologists Press, Palo Alto, California.

Strelau, J. (1972). A diagnosis of temperament by non-experimental techniques. *Polish Psychological Bulletin*, **3**, 97–105.

Stroop, J. R. (1935). Studies of interference in serial verbal reactions. *Journal of Experimental Psychology*, **18**, 643–661.

Wakeford, F., Clements, K., Viner, J. and Whay, J. (1980). "An investigation into the incidences and causes of absent-minded behaviour", British Broadcasting Corporation "Young Scientist of the Year" report.

Wine, J. D. (1980a). Cognitive-attentional theory of test anxiety. *In* "Test Anxiety: Theory, Research, and Application" (I. G. Sarason, ed.), Erlbaum, Hillsdale, NJ.

Wine, J. D. (1980b). Evaluative anxiety: A cognitive attentional construct. *In* "Achievement, Stress, and Anxiety" (H. W. Krohne and L. C. Laux, eds), Hemisphere, Washington, D.C.

Witkin, H. A., Oltman, P. K., Raskin, E. and Karp, S. A. (1971). "A Manual for the Embedded Figures Test", Consulting Psychologists Press, Palo Alto, California.

Yates, F. A. (1966). "The Art of Memory", Routledge and Kegan Paul, London.

Young, G. C. D. and Martin, M. (1981). Processing of information about self by neurotics. *British Journal of Clinical Psychology*, **20**, 205–212.

11

Assessing Everyday Memory after Severe Head Injury

A. Sunderland, J. E. Harris and A. D. Baddeley

In recent years clinical psychologists have become increasingly involved in the treatment of memory disorders following brain injury (Lewinsohn et al., 1977; Crovitz, 1979; Gianutsos and Gianutsos, 1979; Harris and Sunderland, 1981a). The evaluation of the effectiveness of treatment has generally relied on patients' performance on memory tests such as free recall of word lists or paired associate learning. Clearly, the ultimate goal of memory assessment in this context is not to discover the patients' ability to perform memory tests but to predict, from their test performance, whether memory in everyday situations will be significantly impaired. The accuracy of such predictions is likely to be limited for two reasons.

First, memory tasks like paired associate learning of words are very far removed from the sorts of memory task commonly encountered in everyday life; so cognitive skills that are crucial in everyday situations may not be assessed by tests such as these. Second, the frequency of memory failures suffered by individuals is only in part determined by their cognitive abilities and must to some extent depend on the demands placed on memory by their environment and life-style. People with very limited memory capabilities will suffer few memory failures if they lead a sheltered life and make frequent use of memory aids. On both these grounds, the clinician who is trying to assess the frequency with which a patient may suffer memory failure in everyday life should not rely solely on the patient's performance on memory tests borrowed from the psychological laboratory. There is clearly a need to develop methods of directly assessing everyday memory. Such assessment techniques would be useful clinical instruments in their own right as well as allowing various forms of memory test to be validated as predictors of everyday performance.

This chapter describes the development and evaluation of methods of measuring everyday memory after severe head injury. Head injury is the most common cause of brain damage in young adults, in the order of 7500 severe injuries occurring in Britain each year (Lewin, 1970), mostly as a result of road traffic accidents. Typically, the severely head-injured patient has suffered diffuse brain damage at a microscopic level as well as focal injuries to vulnerable brain areas (Strich, 1969; Hooper, 1969). The psychological consequences are a global cognitive deficit but with a marked difficulty on episodic memory tests. Brooks (1972, 1975) showed that patients several months after a severe injury were significantly impaired in the free recall or paired associate learning of word lists, in the recall of short stories and in the recall or recognition of pictorial material. This memory deficit is also apparent in everyday life. For example, Oddy *et al.* (1978) interviewed 50 severely head-injured patients six months after their accidents by which time they had all returned home. The patients and also relatives living with them were asked whether the patient was suffering from any of a list of symptoms including irritability, rapid fatigue and "trouble in remembering things". All of these symptoms occurred more frequently among the head-injured patients than in a control group, and forgetfulness was found to be the symptom most often reported by patients and relatives. However, there was no attempt in this or in previous studies to measure systematically the type and frequency of memory failures suffered by such patients. The initial step in our research was to decide on what forms of measurement might be useful here.

I. MEASURING EVERYDAY MEMORY

Memory failures in everyday life can only rarely be directly observed by the experimenter or clinician. One approach to measurement has therefore been to ask subjects to attempt tests that are close analogues of everyday activities such as remembering to take pills (Wilkins and Baddeley, 1978) or route-finding (Wilson, 1982). However, there is a limit on the range of everyday tasks that can be easily simulated in this fashion, and there may be doubts over whether subjects' behaviour in an analogue test is a true reflection of their behaviour in normal life. The alternative approaches are to ask subjects to report on their own memory failures in everyday situations or to rely on the observations of someone in daily contact with them. Such information can be gathered either by using questionnaires that ask about the typical frequency of different forms of memory error (see Chapter 8 in this volume by Herrmann, 1984, and Chapter 10 by Martin and Jones, 1984) or else by using diaries (see Chapter 4 by Reason and Lucas, 1984) or checklists to record the incidence of errors over a restricted period. The major problem here is that of validity: can questionnaires, diaries or checklists provide an accurate account of the actual incidence of memory failures? Morris (1984, Chapter 9) has given a number of reasons for being cautious in the interpretation of such subjective data.

   The assessment of brain-injured patients by these methods has to contend with additional difficulties. Patients who are cognitively impaired may find it particularly difficult to give accurate reports of their own memory lapses. Furthermore, both the patients and those caring for them may be unwilling to admit that frequent memory failures occur as this may be taken as a sign of mental incapacity. Despite these difficulties, questionnaires and checklists do have considerable advantages in that they are easy to administer and most forms of memory failure can be considered. These methods were therefore selected to investigate memory after head injury, but it was acknowledged that a primary goal of this research had to be to establish whether they had any validity.

In the absence of any means of directly observing all memory failures, there is no way in which the accuracy of questionnaires and checklists can be wholly determined; but if these methods do have any validity then they must necessarily show two features. First, if two or more measures are used to assess one aspect of the everyday memory of a subject, then there should be agreement between them, otherwise at least one of the measures must be invalid. Second, if it is known that a certain subject group, such as head-injured patients, suffer from an increased frequency of memory failures, then valid measures must indicate this increased frequency. Therefore, in evaluating the validity of subjective measures, we can look for the presence of these two features. Also, if a systematic relationship is found between the reported frequency of memory failures and performance on some memory test, then this lends greater credibility to the everyday memory measures. However, for reasons stated earlier, such a relationship is by no means a logical necessity.

All of these validity checks were carried out in an interview study of the after-effects of head injury (Sunderland et al., 1983). A list of 35 different forms of cognitive failure was drawn up. These were all difficulties that even patients leading restricted lives might suffer and that could have arisen from memory failure (some examples appear in Tables IV and V). This list formed the basis of four different kinds of subjective assessment of the patients (who were all male). It was initially presented during an interview with the patient, and he rated each item for frequency of occurrence in the recent past, using a 5-point scale ranging from "never" to "several times each day". After the interview, he was given a booklet that contained the same 35 items in checklist form. He was asked to keep this checklist for 7 days, indicating on each day which of the failures had occurred. A relative or friend in daily contact with the patient gave independent assessments of the patient's everyday memory using identical questionnaire and checklist methods. A group of 32 severely head-injured patients were assessed in this way, between two and eight years after their injury. They were compared with a group of 37 orthopaedic patients who had suffered recent accidents but no head injuries.

In the first validity check, the extent of agreement between the four subjective measures was investigated. Obviously, perfect agreement between patients and relatives was not to be expected as the relatives would only have been able to observe some of the patients' memory failures. Even so, inconsistencies were apparent in that relatives in both subject groups commonly reported observing failures that the patients did not record. Perhaps it was unrealistic to expect that these subjective measures might give accurate information on individual memory failures. A more reasonable goal was that they might indicate, in more general terms, what forms of memory failure occurred most frequently, and which patients showed the poorest everyday memory performance. There was evidence to suggest that at least some of the subjective measures were successful in both these roles.

There was good agreement within and between subject groups on what forms of memory failure were relatively common and which were rare. For example, "losing things around the home" was reported to occur frequently by all methods, whereas "failing to recognize a friend or relative by sight" hardly ever appeared. While this did show some consistency in the way in which subjects responded during the assessments, this could have arisen due to their prior beliefs about the nature of everyday memory (cf. Herrmann, 1979; Morris, 1984, Chapter 9) rather than from a common dependence of these measures on the patient's actual behaviour. The most convincing support for some validity came from the correlations between total scores for the four measures (see Table I). These total scores were regarded as indicators of the overall level of everyday memory impairment (see below). The correlations among these totals indicated that there was agreement between the four measures on which subjects had good and which poor everyday memory. (The correlations were somewhat lower for the control group than for the head-injured patients as would be expected for a group where the range of performance was much smaller.) The one glaring exception was the very low correlation between the patients' questionnaire and relatives' question-naire in the control group. As the lowest correlation in the head-injured group also involved the patients' questionnaire, there was a suggestion that this measure was showing greater independence than the other three. One

Table I. Correlations between the totals for the subjective measures (Spearman's Rho).

	Head-injured group (N=32)			Control group (N=37)		
	PQ[a]	PC[b]	RQ[c]	PQ	PC	RQ
PC	.54**			.53**		
RQ	.58**	.65**		.09	.39*	
RC[d]	.38*	.61**	.81**	.45**	.60**	.49**

[a]PQ = patients' questionnaire
[b]PC = patients' checklist
[c]RQ = relatives' questionnaire
[d]RC = relatives' checklist
*$p<.05$, one tail
**$p<.01$, one tail

interpretation of this was that this questionnaire might be an inaccurate measure of everyday performance.

Support for this view came from the differences in the reported frequency of memory failures in the two subject groups. There were very strong expectations that memory failures should be more frequent for the head-injured patients than for the controls. This was what was found for both of the relatives' measures and the patients' checklist where total scores were significantly higher for the head-injured group. However, the difference between the head-injured and control groups did not reach significance for the totals of the patients' questionnaire (see Table II).

Table II. Group differences in total scores for the subjective measures.

| Subjective measure | Mean Scores[a] | | One—tailed |
	Head-injured group	Control group	t-test
Patients' questionnaire	27	23	p = .09
Relatives' questionnaire	22	15	p = .01
Patients' checklist	23	14	p = .05
Relatives' checklist	18	8	p = .03

Note: The maximum possible scores (indicating that each form of memory failure happened several times each day) are 140 for the questionnaires and 490 for the checklists.
[a]All of the subjective measures discussed in this chapter produced total scores with positively skewed distributions. The square root of these scores was therefore used in all statistical procedures, including the calculation of means. The equivalent untransformed scores are shown in all the tables.

The final confirmatory piece of evidence on the low validity of the patients' questionnaire came from correlations with performance on memory tests. After completing the subjective assessments, the patients attempted a battery of tests, including five tests of episodic memory. These were paired associate learning of words, forced-choice word recognition, short story recall and tests of face and pattern recognition (see Sunderland *et al.*, 1983). Significant correlations were found between test scores and some of the subjective measures. The strongest correlations were seen with performance on the short story recall test in which the subject was read two short newspaper stories. Recall was tested immediately after each and then again after a period of 10–15 min during which a vocabulary test was performed. The correlations between immediate recall and the totals for the subjective measures are shown in Table III. In both subject groups, the patients' questionnaire showed the least association between low test scores and reports of frequent memory failure. A similar pattern was apparent among the weaker correlations with other episodic memory tests.

Table III. Correlations[a] between the totals for the subjective measures and immediate recall of prose (Spearman's Rho).

Subjective Measure	Head-Injured Group	Control Group
Patients' questionnaire	.36*	−.25
Patients' checklist	.50**	−.02
Relatives' questionnaire	.72**	.41**
Relatives' checklist	.58**	.22

[a]The sign of these correlations has been adjusted so that a positive correlation indicates an association between poorer test scores and more frequent reported memory failures.
*p < .05, one tail
**p < .01, one tail

So, a coherent picture emerged from all three validity checks. The degree of consistency between the subjective measures, the differences between the subject groups in reported frequency of memory failures and the correlations with objective tests, all suggested that the patients' questionnaire was a poor measure of everyday memory. This appeared to be true both for the control and the head-injured groups and in both cases the relatives' questionnaire emerged as the strongest measure. It appeared to have some validity, at least as an index of the general level of everyday memory performance.

II. IMPROVING THE QUESTIONNAIRE

Information from the interview study was used in an attempt to produce a new questionnaire that would show greater sensitivity to the memory deficit after severe head injury. In the interview study, the total for the patients' questionnaire was not significantly higher for the head-injured patients than for the controls, but they did give significantly higher frequency ratings than the controls for 8 of the 35 questionnaire items (see Table IV). As it was possible that these eight items described difficulties of which head-injured patients in general were particularly aware, they were included in the new questionnaire. Similarly, eight items were selected on the basis of high frequency ratings by relatives (see Table V).

Six "floor" items were added which described difficulties that all subjects in the interview study had said occurred only very rarely, e.g. "Failing to recognise a friend or relative by sight". These items were included as a check on whether some subjects might be responding with uniformly high frequency ratings, irrespective of item content. They are therefore analogous to "lie" items in personality questionnaires (cf. Broadbent et al., 1982; Martin

Table IV. Questionnaire items that were given significantly higher frequency ratings by head-injured patients.[a]

(4)	Unable to cope with a change in your daily routine. Following your old routine by mistake.
(5)	Having to go around checking whether you have done everything you meant to do.
(8)	Forgetting something you were told yesterday or a few days ago.
(16)	Forgetting what you have just said. Maybe saying "What was I talking about?"
(17)	Unable to follow the thread of a newspaper story. Lose track of what it is about.
(18)	Forgetting to tell somebody something important. Perhaps forgetting to pass on a message or remind someone of something.
(25B)	Getting lost on a journey or walk which you've only been on once or twice before.
(27)	Repeating something you have just said or asking the same question several times.

[a]Mann Whitney U tests were used to compare ratings given by the first 30 head-injured subjects to enter the study with the first 30 controls. These items all showed significant differences at $p < .05$, one tail.

Table V. Questionnaire items given significantly higher frequency ratings by the relatives of head-injured patients.

(1)	Forgetting where he has put something. Losing things around the house.
(2)	Failing to recognize places that he has often been to before.
(10)	Letting himself ramble on to talk about unimportant or irrelevant things.
(12)	Unable to pick up a new skill such as a game or working some new gadget after he has practised once or twice.
(13)	Finding that a word is "on the tip of his tongue".
(15)	Forgetting what he did yesterday or getting the details of what happened mixed up and confused.
(20)	Getting the details of what someone has told him, mixed up and confused.
(21)	Repeating a story or joke that he has already told.

Note: Items 5, 8 and 25B (already shown in Table IV) were also given significantly higher ratings.

and Jones, 1984—Chapter 10). Finally, six new items were devised following descriptions by head-injured patients or their relatives of difficulties that were not included in the original list of 35 items, e.g. "Forgetting when something happened; for example whether it was yesterday or last week".

In the interview study, subjects had used a five-point rating scale to give estimates of the absolute frequency of memory failures (e.g. "about once each day") rather than comparative judgements such as "sometimes" or "often". While little accuracy was expected from these absolute frequency judgements, this seems a more satisfactory method than asking for comparative ratings. Comparative rating scales have been used in other memory questionnaires (e.g. Broadbent *et al.*, 1982; Herrmann and Neisser, 1978; Bennett-Levy and Powell, 1980), but scales of this type are ambiguous in that a rating of "often" could mean that the subject thinks that the memory failure in question happens frequently compared to other types of failure, or that he suffers that difficulty more frequently than other people. If the second sort of comparison is being made then the subject's ratings say nothing about the relative frequency of different forms of memory failure; in fact an item given a rating of "often" might occur less frequently than one given a rating of "very rarely" if one is seen as unusual for people in general and the other is regarded as commonplace (see Harris, 1979, 1980). In view of these problems with comparative rating scales, an absolute frequency scale was retained for use with the new questionnaire, with 8 points ranging from "not at all in the past three months" to "more than once a day" (Harris, 1979).

The questionnaire was produced in both a patients' and a relatives' version and in a format that allowed self-administration. This meant that large numbers of head-injured patients could be assessed after they had been discharged from hospital by sending the questionnaires to them through the post.

The new questionnaire was first used to investigate some aspects of self-assessment in a study with normal subjects (Harris and Sunderland, 1981b). In the earlier interview study, the orthopaedic patients and their relatives had been informed that they were acting as a control group in a study of the effects of severe head injury. This is common practice in neuropsychological studies where patients with no history of brain injury have to be given a reasonable explanation to induce them to attempt mental tests. It seemed possible that the responses given by the subjects in the orthopaedic control group may have been influenced by the knowledge that they were being compared to a brain injured group. The effect of such information was investigated in a study of 64 members of the Applied Psychology Unit subject panel. Half of them were informed that they were acting as controls for head-injured patients while the rest were told that they were taking part in a study of normal everyday memory. The effects of age and sex on self-assessment were also of interest, so half the subjects comprised a young group (aged between 20 and 36 years), while the others were all aged over 68 years (69 to 80-years-old) with equal numbers of each sex in both groups.

Age produced the only significant main effect in this study but not in the expected direction. The young subjects reported significantly *more frequent* memory failures than the elderly subjects. One possible explanation was that the older subjects might have been leading less active lives with fewer opportunities for memory failure. The study was therefore repeated with a second young group and an older group who had not reached retirement age (age range, 50 to 60 years). Despite this attempt to control for the activity level of the subject groups, the same effect re-emerged (see Table VI).

Table VI. The effect of age on the frequency of memory failures reported by normal subjects.

	Mean questionnaire score[a]	Main effect of age
Study 1		
Young group (N = 32)	45	$F(1,56)=6.68$, $p=.01$
Old group (N = 32)	32	
Study 2		
Young group (N = 47)	52	$F(1,87)=26.62$, $p<.001$
Pre-retirement group (N = 48)	33	

[a]The maximum possible score here was 224 which would indicate that all 28 forms of memory failure occurred more than once each day. See note [a] in Table II regarding data transformation.

This effect could still be explained in terms of differences in life-style between the young and old groups with the older subjects perhaps making greater use of memory aids and therefore suffering fewer memory failures. This argument is weakened by the study by Rabbitt (1982) using the same questionnaire. He found that elderly subjects were virtually unanimous in saying that the difficulties listed in the questionnaire happened more frequently to them now than when they were young. Unless cultural changes have produced a much more forgetful young generation, it is hard to avoid the conclusion that, as in the interview study, self-assessment with this questionnaire has little validity.

In the first study of young and old subjects, the effect of instructional changes appeared to be complex. We had predicted that if subjects were informed that their responses were being compared to those of head-injured patients then they might report fewer memory failures. In this context, memory failures might be viewed as symptoms of mental impairment, and subjects would therefore be reluctant to admit that frequent failures occurred. In fact, these instructions produced a sex-dependent effect. Male subjects showed a shift in the expected direction, but female subjects who were given head-injury control instructions tended, if anything, to report more memory failures. The study with the second group of young subjects and the pre-retirement group failed to reproduce this interaction, and no significant effects of sex or instruction were observed. A third study was concerned with the effect of these instructional changes on a relatives' version of the questionnaire. Sixty-four spouses of panel members rated their partners on the questionnaire items but no effects of sex or instruction were found.

So, no clear overall conclusion emerged from these studies of the effect of telling subjects that they were being compared to a brain-injured group. The significant interaction found in the first study suggested that this could bias responses in some circumstances and it seemed possible that this might have occurred in the interview study. The reports of lower frequencies for some forms of memory failure in the control group than in the head-injured group could conceivably have arisen because the orthopaedic patients or their relatives were unwilling to admit that frequent memory failures occurred. In order to evaluate this possibility, the new questionnaire was used to compare patients with severe head injury with others who had suffered only very mild injuries (Sunderland *et al.*, in press). This had the advantage that all subjects could simply be informed that they were taking part in a study of the after-effects of head injury, and no reference was made to any comparison of severe with mild cases. Clearly, this did not avoid the problem that the subjects in either group may have been influenced by their evaluation of how acceptable it was to admit that memory failures occurred. However, such effects should be more balanced in these two subject groups than when normal subjects were informed that they are being compared to an abnormal group.

Questionnaires were completed by 50 severely head-injured patients and their responses were compared with those of 33 mildly injured patients. The results were similar to those for the interview study. The total for the patients' questionnaire showed no significant effects of severe head injury but a large effect was apparent for the relatives' questionnaire (see Table VII).

Table VII. Frequency of memory failures reported after mild and severe head injury.

Patients' questionnaire	Mean Questionnaire Score	Main Effect of Severity
Mild group (N = 33)	36	
Severe group (N = 50)	44	$F(1,79)=1.29$, p=.25
Relatives' Questionnaire		
Mild group (N = 30)	21	
Severe group (N = 49)	38	$F(1,75)=4.77$, p=.03

[a]See note [a] in Table II regarding data transformation.

It seems that while attitudinal effects may well influence the questionnaire responses given by patients or their relatives, any such effects are not so strong as to undermine the sensitivity of the relatives' questionnaire to memory impairment after head injury.

III. FORGETFULNESS AND METAMEMORY

The study of the effects of head injury with the new questionnaire confirmed the low validity of self-assessment by questionnaire. This low validity probably stems from a tendency for forgetful patients to forget their own memory lapses. Two pieces of evidence support this view. First, in the interview study, the patients' checklist appeared to have greater validity than their questionnaire. It produced higher correlations with memory tests and showed greater sensitivity to the higher rate of memory failures in the head-injured group. This may have been because this assessment method made smaller demands on the patient's memory than the questionnaire. The questionnaire required the subject to recall memory failures that had happened over the past few weeks whereas the checklist was concerned only with failures in the previous 24 hours. The shorter retention interval and the possibility of retracing the day's events to provide retrieval cues would mean that forgetful patients would be able to give a more accurate account of their memory failures when using a checklist.

The second piece of evidence concerns the difference between the frequency of memory failures reported by the patients and observed by their relatives. In all of the subject groups studied, the mean score for the relatives' questionnaire is lower than that for the patients' questionnaire. This is to be expected if these measures have any validity in that relatives can only observe some of the patients' memory lapses. However, in the study of severely head-injured patients with the new questionnaire, this difference between the relatives' and the patients' measures decreased as the overall level of memory complaints increased. Patients who were said by both themselves and their relatives to be suffering frequent memory failures often produced lower questionnaire scores than their relatives. The correlation between the sum of the total scores and their difference was therefore negative ($r_s(N=49) = -.26$, p<.05). This may indicate that the more memory impaired a patient is, the greater the proportion of his memory failures he forgets.*

This relationship between metamemory and forgetfulness may not be restricted to subjects with severe memory impairment but might also apply within the normal range of memory. The mildly head-injured patients were unlikely to have suffered any significant memory impairment due to their injury and all but a few of them gave a higher questionnaire total score than their relative. However, as in the severely injured group, there was a negative correlation between the sum of the patients' questionnaire and relatives' questionnaire and their difference ($r_s(N=30) = -.39$, p = .01), suggesting that the most forgetful normal subjects may also report a smaller proportion of their errors. There was some support for this hypothesis from the results for the normal subjects in the other studies, although the evidence was not

* This interaction between subjective measures is open to alternative interpretations. The crossover in the scores excludes the possibility of an effect simply due to the scale of measurement chosen, but an alternative psychological interpretation was put forward by Peter Morris in his comments on a first draft of this chapter. He pointed out that when the frequency of memory failures rises above a certain level, the relative may come to believe that the patient has a memory defect and may start seeking confirming evidence. The interaction may therefore arise from an upturn in the relatives' total scores at this level rather than lower than expected patients' totals.

clear cut. In the interview study, the patients' questionnaire in the control group showed no significant correlations with test performance. In fact, the highest correlations were negative. This could be taken as indicating that any potential positive relationships were masked by forgetful subjects reporting fewer memory failures. On the other hand, the patients' checklist showed little improvement in the correlations produced despite the supposed advantages of this measure in allowing forgetful subjects to recall their memory failures.

Turning to the studies on the effects of age, the lower frequency of memory failures reported by the older groups could have occurred due to the elderly forgetting their memory failures. However, other studies on the effects of age on self-assessment of memory have produced conflicting results. Perlmutter (1978) found increased memory complaints with age while Bennett-Levy and Powell (1980) found the reverse, and Chaffin and Herrmann (1983) reported findings in both directions.

In summary, there is quite strong evidence to suggest that forgetfulness leads to underestimation in the frequency of memory failures reported by head-injured patients, but it is less clear whether this is a significant effect in self-report by young or elderly normal subjects. However, for any subject group, a complex relationship must exist between forgetfulness and meta-memory, and this will to some extent reduce the validity of self-assessment.

IV. IMPLICATIONS FOR ASSESSMENT

From the results reported in this chapter, it might seem tempting to conclude that self-assessment by questionnaire for normal or memory-impaired subjects should be avoided in favour of the use of checklists or relatives ratings. This conclusion is probably too negative. Self-assessment has the obvious advantage over relatives' observations that both overt and covert memory failures can be reported and the questionnaire method may give information about types of failure that occur too infrequently to make practicable their investigation using checklists. Although self-assessment by questionnaire appears to offer a poor quantitative measure of such memory failures, it may well provide invaluable qualitative evidence. In both experimental and clinical contexts it can be useful to know that certain forms of failure do occur without any need to determine their true frequency.

An important point to consider in terms of the clinical application of this method of assessment is that the validity checks used in our studies were concerned with the responses of groups of subjects rather than individuals. There may be large individual differences in the accuracy of self-report which would determine the usefulness of this method with any given patient. There is evidence to suggest that such individual differences are important in the evaluation of self-report by normal subjects. Herrmann (1979) reported a study of college students using the "Shortened Inventory of Memory

Experiences" (Herrmann and Neisser, 1978). This questionnaire was completed on two occasions two months apart, allowing each subject to be classified as consistent or inconsistent on the basis of his test, re-test reliability. The correlations between questionnaire scores and performance on memory tests were highest when the inconsistent subjects were excluded from the analysis, suggesting that the consistent subjects had given more accurate self-reports. In the assessment of patients with severe head injury, it might be possible to gauge the accuracy of their self-reports by similar means. We have not attempted this, but we would predict that the most forgetful patients would be the least consistent. Perhaps a goal of future work should be to determine what degree of memory impairment can be present yet still allow some accuracy in self-assessment by questionnaire.

V. PATTERNS OF MEMORY FAILURE

Ratings for individual items on the new questionnaire were very highly intercorrelated, and principal components analyses showed that the first principal component accounted for up to 60% of the variance. This suggested that the questionnaire should be largely viewed as a measure of some general factor underlying reports of everyday memory. However, there was also clear evidence from the relatives' questionnaires of a characteristic pattern of reported memory failures associated with severe head injury. Comparisons between the interview study and the study of mild vs severe injuries, indicated agreement for the relatives questionnaires on what forms of memory failure were particularly salient in the severe groups. Twenty-one of the 28 items in the new questionnaire were also used in the interview study. If these items are ranked in terms of the extent to which they were given higher frequency ratings by the relatives of patients with severe head injury, then a significant correlation is observed between these rankings in the two studies (r_s (N=21) = .39, p<.05). Of the eleven items that had been given significantly higher frequency ratings by the relatives of head-injured patients in the interview study, seven re-emerged as significant discriminators in the study of mild vs severe injury (items 1, 5, 8, 10, 15, 20 and 21 in Tables IV and V). No such regularity between the two studies was apparent for the patients' questionnaires and of the eight items that had been significant discriminators in the interview study, only two re-emerged in the later study (items 5 and 8). This provides yet further evidence of the low validity of the patients' questionnaires.

The pattern of memory failures consistently reported by the relatives appears to emphasize deficits in aspects of verbal behaviour. Of the seven items that appeared as consistent discriminators, four deal with the recall, repetition or structuring of verbal messages (items 8, 10, 20, and 21). In view of the generalized deficit on tests of memory for both verbal and non-verbal material shown by patients with severe head injury, it seems unlikely that they would show selective deficits in the more verbal aspects of everyday memory. A more plausible interpretation is that the pattern of deficits reported by the relatives is primarily determined by the ease with which they can observe different classes of memory failure. For example, a failure in face recognition will only be apparent to the relative if the patient comments on it or if he behaves inappropriately when he meets someone whom he should recognize. In contrast, difficulties in verbal tasks such as the repetition of a story or joke will be immediately obvious to the relative during conversations with the patient.

If ease of observation does determine the pattern of memory failures reported by relatives, then the relatives' questionnaire is not an unbiased measure of everyday memory. This would not completely undermine its usefulness in clinical assessment, provided that the clinician is aware that a patient might be suffering from some forms of memory failure that would not be apparent with this assessment method. This questionnaire would still give useful information on the incidence of at least those memory failures that tended to occur overtly during social interactions.

VI. CONCLUSION

The central issue in our research has been the question of whether it is possible to obtain a valid measure of the failures of memory in everyday life experienced by patients with severe head injury. It appears that a questionnaire completed by the patient himself does not, in general, provide such a measure, but a questionnaire completed on behalf of the patient by someone in daily contact with him can indicate the incidence of certain classes of memory failure. However, the pattern of reported failures of memory may say more about the difficulties of observation than about any characteristic patterns of everyday memory deficit shown by these patients. A checklist completed by the patient may also have some validity and should not be effected by such observational bias. Further development and evaluation of assessment by this method seems appropriate.

Our results suggest that these conclusions on the validity of questionnaires may apply in the assessment of normal as well as head-injured subjects. This implies that in studies of everyday memory and absent-mindedness in normal subjects, subjective data of greater accuracy might be collected if self-assessment by questionnaire were avoided in favour of other methods. However, the validity problems that have been apparent throughout the studies discussed in this chapter reinforce the conclusion drawn by several contributors to this volume: that no subjective method is likely to provide wholly accurate information on the type and frequency of cognitive failures.

As far as clinical use is concerned, perhaps the most fruitful application of subjective methods will be as a source of primarily qualitative information on what forms of memory failure tend to occur as a result of memory disorders due to brain damage. Test procedures could then be devised to simulate the everyday tasks that lead to these failures. Such analogue tests may prove the best means of assessing the ability of patients with impaired memory to avoid memory failures in everyday life.

REFERENCES

Bennett-Levy, J. and Powell, G. E. (1980). The subjective memory questionnaire (SMQ). An investigation into the self-reporting of "real-life" memory skills. *British Journal of Social and Clinical Psychology*, **19**, 177–188.

Broadbent, D. E., Cooper, P. F., FitzGerald, P. and Parkes, K. R. (1982). The cognitive failures questionnaire (CFQ) and its correlates. *British Journal of Clinical Psychology*, **21**, 1–16.

Brooks, D. N. (1972). Memory and head injury. *Journal of Nervous and Mental Diseases*, **159**, 350–355.

Brooks, D. N. (1975). Long and short-term memory in head-injured patients. *Cortex*, **11**, 329–340.

Chaffin, R. and Herrmann, D. J. (1983). Self reports of memory performance as a function of age in adulthood. *Human Learning*, **2**, 17–28.

Crovitz, H. F. (1979). Memory retraining in brain-damaged patients: the airplane list. *Cortex*, **15**, 131–134.

Gianutsos, R. and Gianutsos, J. (1979). Rehabilitating the verbal recall of brain-injured patients by mnemonic training: An experimental demonstration using single case methodology. *Journal of Clinical Neuropsychology*, **1**, 117–135.

Harris, J. E. (1979). Everyday cognitive functioning: the need for assessment and some basic methodological issues. Paper presented to the British Psychological Society meeting, London, December.

Harris, J. E. (1980). Memory aids people use: Two interview studies. *Memory and Cognition*, **8**, 31–38.

Harris, J. E. and Sunderland, A. (1981a). A brief survey of the management of memory disorders in rehabilitation units in Britain. *International Rehabilitation Medicine*, **3**, 206–209.

Harris, J. E. and Sunderland, A. (1981b). Effects of age and instruction on an everyday memory questionnaire. Paper presented to the British Psychological Society, Cognitive Section Conference on Memory, Plymouth.

Herrmann, D. J. (1979). The validity of memory questionnaires as related to a theory of memory introspection. Paper presented to British Psychological Society meeting, London, December.

Herrmann, D. J. (1984). Questionnaires about memory. *In* "Everyday Memory, Actions and Absent-Mindedness" (J. E. Harris and P. E. Morris, eds), Academic Press, London, Orlando and New York.

Herrmann, D. J. and Neisser, U. (1978). An inventory of memory experiences. *In* "Practical Aspects of Memory" (M. M. Gruneberg, P. E. Morris and R. N. Sykes, eds), Academic Press, London and New York.

Hooper, R. (1969). "Patterns of Acute Head Injury", Edward Arnold Publishers Ltd, London.

Lewin, W. (1970). Rehabilitation needs of the brain-injured patient. *Proceedings of the Royal Society of Medicine*, **63**, 28–32.

Lewinsohn, P. M., Danaher, B. G. and Kikel, S. (1977). Visual imagery as a mnemonic aid for brain-injured persons. *Journal of Consulting and Clinical Psychology*, **95**, 717–723.

Martin, M. and Jones, G. V. (1984). Cognitive failures in everyday life. *In* "Everyday Memory, Actions and Absent-Mindedness" (J. E. Harris and P. E. Morris, eds), Academic Press, London, Orlando and New York.

Morris, P. E. (1983). The validity of subjective reports on memory. *In* "Everyday Memory, Actions and Absent-Mindedness" (J. E. Harris and P. E. Morris, eds), Academic Press, London, Orlando and New York.

Oddy, M., Humphrey, M. and Uttley, D. (1978). Subjective impairment and social recovery after closed head injury. *Journal of Neurology, Neurosurgery and Psychiatry*, **41**, 611–616.

Perlmutter, M. (1978). What is memory aging the aging of? *Developmental Psychology*, **14**, 330–345.

Rabbitt, P. M. A. (1982). How good do you think you are? Paper presented to the Experimental Psychology Society meeting, London.

Reason, J. T. and Lucas, D. (1983). Using cognitive diaries to investigate naturally occurring memory blocks. *In* "Everyday Memory, Actions and Absent-Mindedness" (J. E. Harris and P. E. Morris, eds), Academic Press, London, Orlando and New York.

Strich, S. J. (1969). The pathology of brain damage due to blunt head injuries. *In* "The Late Effects of Head Injury" (E. Walker, W. Caveness and M. Critchley, eds), Charles C. Thomas, Springfield, Illinois.

Sunderland, A., Harris, J. E. and Baddeley, A. D. (1983). Do laboratory tests predict everyday memory? A neuropsychological study. *Journal of Verbal Learning and Verbal Behavior*, **22**, 341–357.

Sunderland, A., Harris, J. E. and Gleave, J. Memory failures in everyday life following severe head injury. *Journal of Clinical Neuropsychology*, (in press).

Wilkins, A. J. and Baddeley, A. D. (1978). Remembering to recall in everyday life: an approach to absent-mindedness. *In* "Practical Aspects of Memory" (M. M. Gruneberg, P. E. Morris and R. N. Sykes, eds), Academic Press, London and New York.

Wilson, B. (1982). Success and failure in memory training following a cerebral vascular accident. *Cortex*, **18**, 581–594.

12

Rehabilitation of Memory for Everyday Life

B. Wilson and N. Moffat

I. INTRODUCTION

In the rehabilitation of patients suffering from memory deficits, our concern is to minimize the disruption to their everyday lives. The approach we follow tries to alleviate the problems caused by memory impairment rather than trying to restore function, an approach that we feel is unlikely to achieve much in organically impaired adults (cf. Harris and Sunderland, 1981; Miller, 1978). There are many possible approaches, including training and the use of aids. The choice will depend on the type and extent of the deficit as well as what the patient needs to be able to do and whether intact functions and modalities can be substituted for impaired ones.

In this chapter we describe some of the methods that can be used to help people whose memory deficits result from brain damage sustained during adulthood. These methods have been drawn from various psychological fields, including experimental psychology, behaviour therapy, cognitive therapy, neuropsychology and work with clinical populations. We also discuss the best time to begin memory training, how to find the most suitable strategy for a particular patient, and the importance of evaluating individual treatments.

A. Neurological impairment and memory deficit

Memory is very sensitive to brain damage (see Lishman, 1978). This can be viewed from two levels. At the psychological level, memory is dependent on such a wide range of interacting processes (from sensory and attentional to semantic and retrieval), that even limited brain damage may affect a fraction of them. At the physical level many brain structures seem to be involved in memory processes, including the hippocampus, the hypothalamus, the thalamus and the temporal lobes. Damage to any one of these structures can result in impaired memory.

Everyday Memory

Most people with organic amnesia will have experienced one or more of the following conditions: head injury, cerebral vascular accident (resulting from intracerebral haemorrhage, thrombosis, embolism or subarachnoid haemorrhage), progressive degenerative disease (senile or pre-senile dementia), cerebral tumour, anoxia, endocrine or metabolic disorder, intracranial infection, toxic disorder, brain surgery, nutritional disorder. Lishman (1978) described these conditions in detail.

B. How memory deficits affect the neurologically impaired

Memory deficits may represent a life-long handicap for brain-damaged people and their families (Moffat, 1978). Despite the importance of memory for adequate everyday functioning, it is only recently that systematic assessment of everyday memory problems has been undertaken (e.g. Sunderland et al., 1981, 1983, 1984). This research, together with direct complaints from amnesics and their families, reveals the burden placed on families.

People with impaired memories are likely to be faced by one or more of the following:
(a) Increased annoyance of those around them. Their frequent repetition of a story or repeated failure to remember to do something may well prove exasperating to relatives, friends or staff.
(b) A reduction in the level of social interaction. Topics of conversation may be limited and conversation itself may be trivial and superficial.
(c) Increased personal danger. A gas cooker may be switched on and forgotten or a cigarette left to burn.
(d) Reduced ability to benefit from help available. They may forget therapeutic exercises, for example, or suggested solutions to cognitive impairment.

II. TREATMENT APPROACHES

A. Published attempts to alleviate the memory problems of the brain-damaged

Harris (1980a) considered three main strategies for improving memory performance: physical treatments, internal aids and external aids. Physical treatments for improving memory are usually drug treatments and are beyond the scope of this chapter. Internal aids include mnemonics, rehearsal strategies or anything a person does inside his or her head to the material which is to be remembered. External aids include diaries, notebooks and alarm clocks, as well as electronic gadgets and microcomputers. Few accounts have been published of attempts to improve memory deficits in the neurologically impaired. Of those that have most would come under the heading of "internal aids". Table I summarizes some of the recently published accounts. It does not include investigative studies of amnesics nor work with normals. All studies in the table have employed strategies to improve the performance of people with organic deficit.

The vast majority of these studies do not deal with real-life, practical

Table I. Recent accounts of attempts to improve memory functioning.

Author(s) + year	Internal	External
Warrington and Weiskrantz, 1971	Chunking	
Patten, 1972	Visual-Peg	
Fowler *et al.* 1972		Timer and printed schedule
Baddeley and Warrington, 1973	Chunking	
Barnes, 1974	Reality Orientation Therapy	
Jones, 1974	Imagery	
Brook *et al.*, 1975	Reality Orientation Therapy	
Cermak, 1975	Imagery and Verbal Meditation	
Harris and Ivory, 1976	Reality Orientation Therapy	
Lewinsohn *et al.*, 1977	Imagery	
Glasgow *et al.*, 1977	PQRST Imagery	
Woods, 1979	Reality orientation Therapy	
Crovitz, 1979	Elaborate encoding	
Crovitz *et al.*, 1979	Imagery	
Gianutsos and Gianutsos, 1979	Mnemonic Training	
Greene, *et al.*, 1979	Reality Orientation Therapy	
Wilson, 1981 a	Imagery	
Wilson, 1982 a	Imagery, Rehearsal and First letter cueing	

problems faced by their amnesic subjects. The exceptions are Fowler *et al.* (1972), Glasgow *et al.* (1977) and Wilson (1981a, 1982a). The remainder concentrate on teaching lists of words, paired associates or reality orientation therapy. Although there may be a place for seeing whether or not memory impaired people can learn experimental material, it is not the main object in memory rehabilitation. Perhaps some authors believe that amnesic patients are capable of generalizing from a procedure learned in the laboratory or clinic to everyday problems. Such generalization is by no means certain, however, and does not appear to have been convincingly established (see discussion in Harris and Sunderland, 1981).

B. Environmental changes

Altering the environment to change maladaptive behaviour is a well-recognized strategy in some fields of clinical psychology. For certain problems, particularly when general intellectual deterioration has occurred, it may be the only hope of ameliorating the situation. The procedure is not unknown for those of us without organic amnesia! In some general hospitals, for example, patients follow painted lines on the ground to find their way around. Similar procedures can be used in rehabilitation centres where it is sometimes necessary to chalk a line on the floor or the wall to remind patients how to get from physiotherapy to occupational therapy or from the canteen to the lavatory. In the case of visually impaired adults a rope or cord may solve the problem. Other examples of environmental change may be found in the provision of extra discriminative cues. Harris (1980a) described a geriatric unit where the rate of incontinence decreased when all the lavatory doors were painted a different colour from all the other doors.

C. External memory aids

External memory aids are frequently used by those with normal memory (Harris, 1980b; see Table II). However, their potential application with the amnesic patient has not been rigorously investigated. Evidence collected so far suggests that external aids can be effective in assisting problem-solving (Eimas, 1970; Hulicka and Grossman, 1967) or returning a postcard (Meacham and Singer, 1977) or making a telephone call at a predetermined date (Moscovitch and Minde, described by Harris, 1984 in Chapter 5 of this volume).

While some amnesics may make considerable use of external aids in order to function more independently, others may reject them because they fail to recognize their application to their problems. Thus, the attitude towards the aids is an important issue, and in some cases counselling may be required before aids will be accepted. When we have encouraged the use of external aids as part of individual and group memory training we have noticed that those aids the clients or group devise for themselves (e.g. placing a note under

Table II. Aids people use.

External Aids	Harris (1980b) (Students N=30)		Moffat (Head injured patients) N=10	
	Ever Used %	Used more than once a week %	Ever used %	Used more than once a week (%)
Memos to self	97	43	70	20
Putting something in special place	100	40	90	50
Diary	93	43	30	0
Asking someone to remind you	97	37	60	40
Shopping List	93	13	40	10
Writing on hand	53	20	40	0
Timer for cooking	53	7	0	0
Ringing or writing on calendar	40	10	60	10
Internal Aids				
Mental retracing of events	97	23	65	20
Alphabetic searching	80	3	60	10
First letter mnemonics	73	3	30	0
Rhymes	57	0	40	0
Loci method	13	7	10	0
Story Method	23	0	0	0
Face-Name Association	13	3	40	0
Peg Method	7	0	0	0

the watch strap to provide a detailed and specific reminder) tend to be adopted more readily and put into practice more than those that are provided by the therapist. The use of such aids can be encouraged by the setting of homework tasks and can be maintained by reinforcement. Another use of external aids is in the provision of instructions for carrying out a task. A head-injured patient who had repeatedly failed to learn an assembly task was given a card with the necessary steps or instructions written out simply and clearly. This enabled him to cope with minimal supervision on the task, with less outbursts of frustration and temper. The detailed instructions were then gradually phased out from the prompt card.

With the recent development of electronic aids and the increased use of digital alarm watches it is worth looking at such cueing devices in more detail. Certain kinds of timers and electronic aids are regularly used by normal people to remind them to do something. It is possible for memory-impaired people to use alarm clocks and watches to overcome some of their problems. Fowler *et al.* (1972) described a head-injured man who was given a small portable timer which he set to remind himself to look at his list of daily activities. Whenever the timer sounded he looked at his list and went to the next appointment. The timer was removed after several weeks, by which time the patient remembered to look at his list without the auditory signal.

Harris (1978, 1980a) described various electronic aids on the market which can be used by those with memory problems. Jones and Adam (1979) discussed potential prosthetic memory aids that use computer technology. They suggested a small tape recorder to provide instructions via an earpiece. Also included would be a panic button to remind the users where they were and what they were supposed to be doing. If pressed repeatedly, the panic button would respond with an instruction to seek help from another person. As far as the present authors know, such a machine has not yet been manufactured. However, it is possible that tape recorders alone have a part to play in memory rehabilitation. Small dictaphones would appear to be particularly useful because of their size, though we do not know of any attempt to evaluate their effectiveness. There are other microcomputer aids available that, although not designed for amnesic patients, can be used by them. The Casio PW-80, for example, is a small calculator that can be programmed to emit a sound at regular intervals from 2 seconds to 24 hours. It has been used to remind people to lift themselves from their wheelchairs to prevent pressure sores (Klein and Fowler, 1981), and by one of us (B.W.) to remind dysarthric patients to swallow saliva regularly. However, like a knot in a handkerchief, it tells you to remember something but not what to remember (Baddeley, 1976).

Electronic aids that overcome this problem have been produced by several companies (e.g. the Sharp EL 6200, and the Toshiba Memo-Note 2 and Memo-Note 60). The Memo-Note 60 is a portable but not pocket-sized calculator that accepts up to 62 messages. If the message is accompanied by a time, an alarm sounds for 16 seconds when that time is reached. The appropriate message can then be viewed on the display screen. This has obvious advantages: (i) many messages can be stored at any one time (ii) the auditory signal is accompanied by specific information about *what* is to be done and (iii) the messages will, if necessary, be repeated day after day until the batteries run out (after about a year), or until it is reprogrammed. However, there are serious disadvantages too. Firstly, the cost (about £70 in 1981) is prohibitive for many memory-impaired people, and losing such an aid would be more serious than losing a notebook. Secondly, although not immensely difficult to programme, such an aid requires an adequate memory.

Most people would need to remember their previous mistakes when learning to programme one of these aids. Memory-impared people, of course, are less able to do this. It is, therefore, necessary to teach a relative or therapist to "write in" the messages. Thirdly, even if it is programmed by somebody else, the person with the memory problem needs to remember certain steps: for example, how to clear the screen and how to scan the stored messages. It is almost impossible for severe amnesics to remember how to do this.

One of us (B.W.) has used a Toshiba Memo-Note 60 with a global amnesic patient who had a very high I.Q. He was unable to remember (a) that when reading the date on the machine the month preceded the day (in Britain most people write the day before the month), (b) how to read the previously stored messages, (c) how to clear the screen, (d) that he was *not* to switch off the alarm when it sounded, and (e) not to switch the machine on to "lock" as this meant most functions were suspended or locked. It was possible to overcome these problems by placing small sticky labels at various points on the machine such as "DO NOT SWITCH OFF ALARM, IT STOPS ITSELF AFTER 16 SECONDS". While the aid told the man what to do and where to go at various times during the day it did not provide information about his past. He wanted to know *what* had happened to him, *why* he was at a rehabilitation centre, *when* he was next going home, *how* his business was doing and so forth. The aid, unlike his notebook, could not provide sufficient detail to satisfy him.

It may be that electronic aids are more useful for amnesics with frontal lobe involvement than with temporal lobe damage. No data appear to exist on whether or not temporal patients are more likely to use notebooks and diaries than frontal patients, but our observations suggest that this hypothesis is worth testing formally. The global amnesic described above was never without his book and referred to it constantly. He had suffered a bilateral stroke affecting both temporal lobes. Another very intelligent man, with frontal lobe damage, was never seen to use his notebook either to record or to seek information unless he was asked to do so by someone else. He too used an electronic aid and, at least, read the message when the alarm sounded.

In summary, the currently available electronic aids are probably of limited use for improving the lives of memory-impaired people. A digital alarm watch used together with a notebook will be no more expensive and perhaps of more use.

D. Internal aids

(1) *Visual imagery*
In the context of rehabilitation visual imagery can be regarded as remembering by pictures. The pictures may be mental ones or they may be drawn by or for the memory-impaired person. Wilson (1982b) demonstrated that some memory-impaired people found difficulty using imagery in any form. Others

found difficulty using mental imagery but benefited from images drawn for them. A third group was able to use both kinds of imagery.

There are various visual imagery techniques. Sometimes words or sentences are read and the subjects are asked to make a mental image. If the following four words are to be remembered: *boy, jump, clock, shout*, they may be asked to see an image of a boy jumping on a clock which is shouting. For paired associates, a picture linking the two words is drawn for the subjects or they are asked to imagine the objects depicted by two words interacting in some way. Other procedures include linking the first word with the second word, the second with the third and so forth. Wilson's method, like that of Lorayne (1975), involves drawing or asking her patients to imagine a "picture" of the name to be remembered. Mary Thorne becomes a drawing of a *merry thorn*, and Julian is a jewel on a *lion*. This has proved effective for several people with left temporal damage, including aphasic patients. Figure 1 shows how a 43-year-old man seen by one of us (BW) with anomic aphasia resulting from a left temporal stroke was able to learn the names of six people in two weeks using imagery.

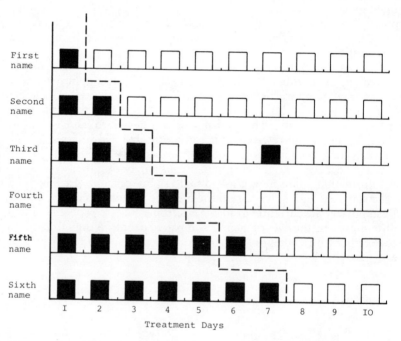

Fig. 1. Teaching a man with anomic aphasia to remember peoples' names by means of visual imagery.

■ = name not recalled, □ = name recalled, - - - - = image introduced.

Another procedure involving visual imagery is the face-name association method, used with a brain-damaged student by Glasgow *et al.* (1977) and with normal subjects by McCarty (1980). In this procedure, when you want to remember somebody's name you first choose a distinctive feature of the person's face. The second step is to transform the name itself into one or two common nouns (Campbell then would be *camp + bell* and Tony would be *toe + knee*). The final step is to link the distinctive feature with the transformed name. If the distinctive feature of Tony's face is his mouth, the image might be of a toe and knee entering Tony's mouth. McCarty found normal subjects were helped most by using all the elements of the procedure. If the distinctive feature alone or the name transformation alone were used, recall was poorer. Glasgow *et al.*, however, found face-name associations impractical with their patient, and Wilson's (1981a) patient found the procedure impaired his performance. He could not learn the separate steps involved although he could learn single images to remember names.

Recently, Carr and Wilson (1982) have investigated the ability of a mildly aphasic man to benefit from the face-name procedure. Preliminary results do not demonstrate any difference in recall of names learned by this method and those for which rehearsal time only was given. However, this appeared to be due to the man's spontaneous use of imagery for recall of those names for which no image was explicitly presented. His overall performance, therefore, was much superior to that on a pre-test before the procedure had been introduced. This would suggest he did benefit from the method. In short, the method may be suitable for some patients, particularly those with mild memory deficits.

Yet another visual imagery procedure is the visual-peg method. This has been in use since ancient times and has been described by Patten (1972) and Lorayne and Lucas (1974). The numbers one to ten are associated with words. One of the best known peg-lists starts one-bun, two-shoe. The items to be remembered are placed on the pegs. For example, if the first thing one has to do in the morning is hand in some typing, the image could be a typist sitting on top of a bun. The second task might be to go to the bank and the image could be driving to the bank in an enormous shoe. Patten found a peg method helped 4 of 7 patients. Visual-peg procedures have a place in helping people to remember shopping lists or tasks to perform. Disadvantages are encountered by some left brain-damaged people who are unable to remember the peg rhymes. Wilson's (1981a) patient, and the anomic man reported above to have benefited from drawings, were both unable to remember the pegs accurately after five presentations. They could remember the images they had used when the therapist/experimenter reminded them of the rhymes. Wilson's (1982a) patient, however, was the reverse: he remembered the rhymes with no trouble but could not recall the images he paired with them. For patients with memory deficits resulting from unilateral brain damage the visual peg method may be unsuitable as it requires remembering two distinct stages: one involving left hemisphere skills and the other right. This method is not invariably a failure, however. Our clinical experience has led us to believe that some head-injured patients with a mild memory deficit do sometimes benefit in an experimental situation.

The penultimate imagery procedure to be discussed is the Method of Loci, remembering by imagining items in different locations. Again this was a method used by the ancient Greeks. Yates (1966) described how Simonides of Thessaly was able to recall the names of many people crushed at a banquet by remembering where each guest had been seated. Luria's famous mnemonist "S" also used this method (Luria, 1968). He mentally deposited the items he was asked to remember in various places along a route. The method has been used with normal subjects (Ross and Lawrence, 1968; Groninger, 1971) as well as elderly subjects (Robertson-Tchabo, Hausman and Arenberg, 1976). Familiar campus locations or rooms were used as the loci. Other familiar loci may be used including parts of the body.

The advantages of this method are that:
(a) It has proved successful with the limited range of subjects and materials tried so far.
(b) The use of familiar loci as the links with the to-be-remembered material requires less learning than some other methods such as the peg or hook systems.
(c) The loci method uses visual imagery, which has proved successful in other areas.
(d) The elderly did not show pro-active interference effects when learning three different lists on consecutive days (Robertson-Tchabo et al., 1976).

The main disadvantages are that:
(a) The elderly did not employ this technique on a later test when not specifically instructed to use the method (Robertson-Tchabo et al., 1976).
(b) It has yet to be properly evaluated with the neurologically impaired.

Wilson carried out some investigations with patients recalling lists of words using no special strategy, and then using four mnemonic strategies (first letter cueing, visual imagery, telling a story and Method of Loci). The Loci strategy used was to ask each person to imagine their own home and place each item in a specified place, e.g. matches by the front door and tomatoes in the bathroom. Results suggested that for some people the Method of Loci is superior to other strategies, particularly in the delayed condition. However, there were considerable individual variations and preferences.

The final procedure to be described in this subsection is mental retracing of events. It is rather different from the others and may not always involve imagery. This strategy has been defined as "Mentally retracing a sequence of past events or actions in order to aid memory of something that happened, or to remember when you last had something you might now have lost, and where you might have left it" (Harris, 1980b). The need for this strategy can be inferred from the frequent reports of "Storage Failures" by normal subjects (Reason, 1977); and subjective complaints by head-injured subjects that they forget recent events. However, no study of the efficacy of the mental retracing of events could be found, despite reports that this is the most frequently used internal strategy by housewives and students (Harris, 1980b). Therefore, it can only be presumed that mental retracing could help to date recent or remote events by successive comparisons with appropriate known dates (e.g. "Have I been to the cinema since Christmas?") in the way that the use of "Anchor Points", has been applied in making perceptual judgements (Diller and Weinberg, 1977). Also, the method of retracing an event may help to relocate an object in the home by thinking when and where it was last used. So if the information to be recalled has not been dealt with by other methods, mental retracing may be particularly useful.

Previous research on the ability of amnesic people to benefit from imagery has been conflicting. Baddeley and Warrington (1973) found that normal subjects benefited greatly from using imagery to remember groups of words but amnesic subjects showed no such improvement. Jones (1974) demonstrated that patients who had undergone left temporal lobectomies were able to use imagery to improve recall of paired associates. Two global amnesics, however, were not helped at all by the procedure. Cermak (1975) found Korsakoff patients performed better under imagery than non-imagery conditions. Wilson (1981a, 1982a) found her patients were able to learn names after they had been given a visual image but not before. These differences in the findings are likely to be due to several factors including:

(i) The nature of the task. Baddeley and Warrington, for example, used groups of four words, Jones and Cermak both used paired-associates and Wilson used one word (a person's name).

(ii) The subjects themselves. Baddeley and Warrington's were subjects who had a diagnosed amnesia but no other intellectual impairment. Jones' subjects were people who had undergone surgery for the relief of epilepsy and two had bilateral, hippocampal damage. Cermak worked with Korsakoff patients and Wilson treated one man who had had a tumour and one who had had a stroke that resulted in bilateral temporal damage. It is possible that different aetiologies or syndromes respond differently to imagery. Also different results may be caused by differences in the severity of the memory impairment. Such a hypothesis received support when Wilson (1982b) found severity of deficit on a delayed verbal recall task correlated with ability to use imagery, i.e. those with severe impairment were less able to benefit from imagery.

(iii) The importance of the task. Wilson used imagery to teach something practically useful and something her patients wanted to learn. The patients of Baddeley and Warrington et al. did not, presumably, find the tasks useful in reducing their everyday memory problems. Motivational aspects and the content of the material to be learned may play important roles.

(2) Verbal strategies
(a) Alphabetical searching and first letter cueing. An occurrence of the tip-of-the-tongue phenomenon is a relatively common everyday experience among

normal and memory-impaired people. It can also be generated in experimental tasks. It is often the result of attempts to recall a particular word or name. While in a strong feeling-of-knowing (FOK) state, subjects have been able to provide partial knowledge of the to-be-recalled word such as the number of syllables and/or the first letter. Furthermore, subjects may be able to search the alphabet themselves, select the appropriate first letter and subsequently find the correct word (Gruneberg and Monks, 1976). The provision of the correct first letter for a word not recalled may act as a sufficient prompt to enable correct recall, particularly if there is a strong FOK in the first place (Gruneberg and Monks, 1974). Thus, first letter cueing can be of value in assisting recall by acting as a retrieval strategy. It may also be used as a combined encoding and retrieval system in the form of mnemonics that may be superior to either encoding or retrieval alone (Jaffe and Katz, 1975). The method may be effective for a variety of reasons:

(i) "Chunking" of information whereby the clue to the items is contained in the mnemonic. For example, *food* could be used to remember to buy Flour, Oranges, Oxtail and Dog Biscuits.

(ii) It narrows down the potential search.

(iii) It increases the time people are prepared to spend searching before giving up.

An advantage of first letter cueing is that it is easy to apply as a technique since the alphabet is usually well known. It can, of course, be written down if necessary. A disadvantage is that it focusses attention on a phonological level of information processing rather than a deeper, semantic level. This may be less effective for both memory and comprehension.

Let us now consider how first letter cueing can be used in memory training. The strategy is commonly used for remembering sequences. For example, many people have used this method to remember sequences of musical notes. The notes on stave lines may be recalled as Every Good Boy Deserves Fruit and the notes in the spaces spell out the word FACE. An example of this method used in memory rehabilitation was given by Wilson (1982a). The man described was unable to learn ten items of a shopping list until told that the initial letters of each item could be re-arranged to spell the words GO SHOPPING (Grapes, Olives, Sugar, Pears, Paper, Ink, Nails and Grass Seed). Following this explanation he rapidly learned all ten items. Furthermore, it was possible to use the procedure to enable him to master other tasks which he had failed to learn after weeks of practice. He had a particularly poor spatial memory and could not learn the positions of four pegs in a non-verbal learning task, (see Williams, 1968, for a description of the task). He was, however, helped to some extent by writing down the positions of the pegs in each board thus:

*T*op *C*entre, *T*op *L*eft, *D*ead *C*entre and *B*ottom *L*eft. He then made a sentence from the initial letters, returned to the task, and solved it correctly. The sentence was long and complicated "Try cautiously and think long but don't come with a bad lady". To most people this would be far more difficult to remember than the positions of the pegs, but a spatial solution was unavailable to this particular man. Although remembering pegs on a board is not, in itself, a useful task to learn, it is possible that the first letter procedure could help some people with severe topographical or spatial difficulties. Newcombe and Ratcliffe (1979), for example, described a young head-injured woman who was unable to learn an apparently simple task of placing five cosmetic items in a box. She could not remember the correct positions of the items although she was able to learn what was considered a more difficult task of manipulating a machine. The latter presumably depended upon a less-impaired motor memory system. In cases similar to this, first letter cueing may have a role to play.

(b) Study techniques. Amnesics often complain of difficulties remembering written prose (e.g. newspaper articles) and following stories (e.g. TV programmes). Improvements in the understanding and recall of prose have been demonstrated with normal subjects by using "advanced organizers" (Ausubel, 1960). These have consisted of a title or picture to clarify content (Bransford and McCarrell, 1975), or questions about the passage after it has been read, particularly questions that required the integration of the material in formulating an answer (Watts and Anderson, 1971). A further finding is that items higher in the hierarchical structure of a passage are more likely to be recalled than subordinate propositions (Kintsch, 1974).

Such findings lend support to the study techniques suggested by Rowntree (1970); namely the acronyms S.Q.3R and PQRST, which involve the following steps:

S.Q.3R	P.Q.R.S.T.
SURVEY	PREVIEW
QUESTION	QUESTION
READ	READ
RECALL	STATE
REVIEW	TEST

Glasgow *et al.* (1977) applied a slightly modified version of this study method to the verbal memory disorder of a 22-year-old undergraduate who had suffered a road traffic accident 3½ years previously.

The first stage involved the application of the method to selected passages, which demonstrated that the PQRST method was superior to a rehearsal condition and the subject's own pre-intervention strategy in terms of the percentage of main points and details recalled, as well as on a multiple choice recognition task. However, the effects of the strategies were confounded with the time spent using each system, since the PQRST method required more than three times as long as the control condition. Therefore, the efficacy of the study technique *per se* has not been established. Since the self ratings of her memory ability correlated highly with her objective performance, this subjective measure (a 7-point scale) was used to assess the generalization of PQRST training to remembering newspaper articles, following a baseline period of ten days. This demonstrated an improvement in immediate recall

5.9 (5.0) and delayed recall after a day 5.4 (3.6) and a week 5.5 (3.3). The baseline ratings appear in the brackets.

This case study illustrates that the PQRST study technique can be of practical value. Replication with other cases is now required in order to determine the types of subject who may be suitable for this form of training.

E. Self-help techniques

Very little work has been reported on the application of such techniques as self monitoring, self cueing, self reward and punishment, or of self instructions to assist memory functioning.

One of the reasons for the sparse literature on this topic may be the presumed practical problems of relying on subjective criteria for monitoring and training with the memory impaired. However, this is not always a problem with the less severely amnesic person and has been used by Glasgow *et al.* (1977) and Moffat (1982). Furthermore, if awareness is impaired this could be a focus for treatment. A right brain-damaged stroke patient was treated by one of us (N.M.) using self monitoring to help the person realize the existence and extent of his hemi-inattention and then to learn to overcome the problem.

Amnesic patients may of course forget to use self instructions or self cueing techniques. However, as in most applications of self instruction techniques, the covert self statements form the final stage of the treatment once the earlier stages of modelling, prompting and overt and covert practice have been carried out. Thus, prompt cards and other cueing devices such as electronic alarms may be incorporated and maintained during the treatment if necessary.

An example of the use of self instruction with a young, head-injured plumber's mate is given in the sections on external aids and attention training. The treatment of this particular patient incorporated elements of self-instruction techniques to control impulsiveness and also to improve problem-solving ability (Meichenbaum, 1977). These techniques may be used to deal with the self-defeating and negative thoughts faced by some amnesics (see e.g. Glasgow *et al.*, 1977). It is envisaged that self instruction and other cognitive-behavioural techniques will become more widely used with the memory impaired in order to help in the maintenance and generalization of memory enhancement procedures.

F. Attention training

Some investigators have recently advocated attentional training procedures in rehabilitation, particularly following severe head injury (e.g. Trexler, 1982). There are separate issues here which will be examined in turn.

(1) Impairment of attentional processes following brain damage
Subjective reports have often contained complaints of poor concentration and

distractability following head injury (e.g. Moffat, 1978). Recent developments in information processing models of attention (Shiffrin and Schneider 1977) have resulted in more refined measures which distinguish between focussed attention deficts (FAD), that can be assessed using the Stroop Colour Word Test (Stroop, 1935); and Divided Attention Deficits (DAD) which are associated with speed processing as measured by reaction time tasks and the PASAT (Paced Auditory Serial Addition Test, Gronwall and Sampson, 1974).

(a) Focussed attention deficits. On reviewing the literature and on the basis of his own experiments, Van Zomeren (1981) stated that "so far, there is no evidence for a deficit of focussed attention in people who have sustained a head injury".

(b) Divided attention deficits. Slower performance has been noted on reaction time tasks (Miller, 1970), particularly on choice reaction time (Van Zomeren and Deelman, 1978); and also of decreased performance under faster presentation rates on the PASAT (Gronwall and Sampson, 1974).

These reduced rates of the controlled processing of information may be interpreted as a DAD, within the Shiffrin and Schneider model.

(c) Sustained attention. Although there is some suggestion that head-injured subjects show reduced levels of "phasic" alertness in their EEGs (Rizzo et al., 1978), there is little support for reduced tonic alertness (Van Zomeren, 1981); or of impaired vigilance on reaction time (Blackburn, 1958; Dencher and Lofving, 1958) or low event rate tasks (Van Zomeren, 1981).

An exhaustive review of the literature on attention following brain injury is beyond the scope of this chapter, but there is only limited support for the impression of impaired attention following brain damage, particularly when the investigations conform to experimental models of attention.

(2) Treatment of attentional processes
There are a number of centres that have set up attentional training procedures with the brain injured (e.g. Tel Hashomer in Israel, New York and Indianapolis in the US, and Northampton in the UK) generally using reaction time as the training medium. A number of these training programmes have failed to produce evidence of initial impaired performance by the patients on the training tasks. They neither provide adequate documentation of improvements, nor do they establish the generalization of any improvements to other variables. Thus, some of the "training" may represent little more than practice effects on artificial tasks which may have little or no practical benefit. One much neglected study that does address the first two issues (initial impairment followed by improvements during training), was carried out by Blackburn (1958). He found that the brain-damaged group was slower than the control group on a two-choice reaction time task. He then divided these two groups into three instructional conditions: standard ("let us try the experiment again"); urging (providing feedback and reinforcement); and relaxing ("relax and don't concern yourself with what you are doing"). He

then gave each of these selected groups a further 30 trials. The results indicated that the "urging" condition resulted in superior gains to the other instructional conditions for both the control and brain-injured groups.

(3) Generalization of improvements from artificial tasks to real ones
Where attentional training has been carried out at all it has generally been included in a more comprehensive rehabilitation programme or has been limited to case descriptions. Recent developments in attentional training appear to be centred mainly around the use of more sophisticated video games and microprocessor based training procedures (e.g. Lynch, 1981a, 1981b). This is an exciting advance because it usually provides tasks that are interpretable within the framework of theories of attention and information processing. However, it is equally important to ensure that the generalization of training is investigated. Such investigations would not have to be based on the traditional laboratory type of procedure: they could focus on useful daily tasks.

Future investigations might need to distinguish between "external" and "internal" distractors. The former is concerned with the effects of environmental distractors, while the latter presumes that one's own thought processes may wander spontaneously. In helping patients ignore distractors, self instructional techniques may be of value in the regulation of attention.

G. Movement as a mnemonic

There is considerable evidence that motor memory in severe amnesics is less impaired than other memory skills. This was demonstrated by Corkin (1968) with H.M.; Brooks and Baddeley (1976) with two encephalitic and three Korsakoff patients; and by Wilson (1982a) with a stroke patient.

This information may well help therapists, doctors and social workers advise on future employment (e.g. Newcombe and Ratcliffe's (1979) patient mentioned earlier), but can it be utilized in the rehabilitation of memory? Powell (1981) suggested that certain names may be learned by a pattern of motor movements. He gave examples of "Mr Crow", "Mr Hatter" or "Mr Potter". To date no formal studies of this procedure have been demonstrated although one of us (BW) has used it with some success to help one young man with a severe head injury to remember his physiotherapist's name. After several months rehabilitation and memory training he remained with a profound ongoing amnesia. He reliably recalled names of three therapists who regularly worked with him *only* if the initial letter of the name was given to him. A fourth therapist who was called Anita told him he could remember her name as she had "*a neater* way of doing her hair", whereupon she shook her hair. Thereafter, if she simply asked him what her name was he guessed from among the few names available to him, *but* if she shook her hair he always said "Anita". The trouble was that any woman who shook her hair in front of him was also called Anita! Nevertheless, motor coding remains a possible memory aid to be further investigated.

H. Stimulating and exercising memory

Miller (1978) distinguished between restoration of memory function and amelioration of the handicap caused by an impaired memory. The strategies described so far may be considered amelioration procedures: it is not expected that the memory of an amnesic person will improve all round. Rather it is hoped that ways will be found to enable the person to learn some kinds of information more effectively and/or to improve their functioning in some areas of everyday life. As Miller pointed out, it is unlikely that any psychological procedure will restore an impaired memory to its premorbid level. There is little evidence in the literature that intensive practice or training at tasks will improve memory generally (Milner et al., 1968; Brooks and Baddeley, 1976; Wilson, 1982a), and some evidence that it will not (Ericsson et al., 1980). Nor is there firm evidence that training with particular mnemonics or external aids will improve other areas of memory. Wilson's (1981a) patient, for example, was able to learn a certain number of people's names by visual imagery, but his memory for names generally, did not improve. Each one was laboriously and individually learned. On the other hand, most people routinely working with memory-impaired adults (speech therapists, physiotherapists, occupational therapists, nurses and clinical psychologists) frequently employ tasks in which they encourage patients to use their memory. Games such as Pelmanism, Mrs Brown-went-to-town and Kim's game, are sometimes the only procedures therapists use to try to reduce memory impairment. Is there, then a place for memory exercises? At present we do not know but the following points can be made:

(a) in spite of findings that stimulation does not improve the memory of severe global amnesics, it is not known whether this is true for those with less severe impairment. It is possible that mental exercises will have some beneficial effect for this group.

(b) Memory exercises do have face validity i.e. patients and relatives usually believe the exercises are of some value and this, in itself, may be beneficial.

(c) Harris and Sunderland (1981) pointed out that improvement with practice on such games may encourage patients to make an effort with everyday tasks.

(d) The games and exercises can be enjoyable and this, too, could be of indirect therapeutic use by improving the patients' morale.

(e) Harris and Sunderland (1981) also suggest that any neural regeneration may be enhanced by mental exercise.

III. PLANNING AND ADMINISTRATION

A. When to begin memory training

Neurological patients usually receive intensive treatment during the early stages of recovery. The cessation of treatment being determined by adequate recovery or the levelling of performance. However, memory training is generally delayed until a stable baseline has been reached in order for the efficacy of training to be established. Other advantages of delaying the introduction of memory training are

(a) During the early stages of recovery the memory processes may be qualitatively and quantitatively different from the later stable state. So techniques that appear to be appropriate early on may turn out to be inappropriate later.

(b) During recovery from a severe head injury, it has been shown that neuropsychological tests of memory bear little relationship to everyday complaints of forgetting (Sunderland et al., 1981, in press). This may complicate the form of a treatment plan for memory impaired persons.

(c) During this period of recovery motivation to take part in training may be lacking since practical problems of forgetting have not been experienced. Any failures that are noted may be accepted in the belief that memory will return to normal given time.

(d) Delaying the onset of memory training may allow other deficits such as aphasia, concentration or hemi-inattention to reach their optimal level of recovery.

(e) There may be less competition with other rehabilitation therapies; in the early stages, physio-, occupational and speech therapy may all be competing for the patients' most alert periods of the day.

Possible disadvantages of delaying memory training are: (a) patients may have learned maladaptive strategies which are difficult to unlearn, and (b) critical stages may be missed. It is possible that there are critical stages in recovery when cognitive activity may have a special influence on recovery (see Harris and Sunderland, 1981). During such periods memory games and other cognitive tasks may be of special benefit. However, until this is supported by evidence we prefer to follow the more pragmatic approach we have described in this chapter.

B. Matching strategy to patient

The aims of treatment will depend, among other things, on whether or not there is general intellectual impairment or a specific memory deficit. People with general intellectual impairment may be further divided into those with whom the defect is likely to be permanent and those with whom it is likely to be transient (for example, post traumatic amnesia following severe head injury). This distinction will influence the advice given to relatives and other

therapists, but in either case simple strategies of changing certain features of
the environment may be the best one can do, together with Reality
Orientation Therapy (see below).

(1) Strategies for material specific deficits

People without general intellectual impairment may be grouped into those
with a global amnesia, those with a material specific deficit (e.g. verbal or
non-verbal) and those with a modality specific loss (e.g. visual or auditory
memory problems).

Specific verbal deficits will probably be the result of damage to the
dominant hemisphere, perhaps from a stroke, head injury, tumour or
surgery. These can also cause non-verbal deficits if they occur in the non-
dominant hemisphere.

If the damage is permanent and severe the best approach is probably to try
and by-pass the problem by capitalizing on the remaining intact (or relatively
intact) skills. A person with a verbal memory deficit will probably benefit
most from using visual imagery procedures together with external aids. Such a
person will almost certainly find first letter cueing of little or no help.
Conversely, someone with a non-verbal deficit will usually do better with
verbal tasks and should be encouraged to turn non-verbal tasks into verbal
ones as far as possible. If they have topographical memory problems, for
example, it is sometimes possible to use a verbal description to overcome
some difficulties. Patients may do this spontaneously. One man with right
hemisphere damage said "I find my way to the ward by telling myself it's next
to the No-Entry signs". Such spontaneous strategies may indicate the
patient's own preference, which should also be taken into account. It may also
be necessary to encourage use of external aids alongside other strategies.

(2) Strategies for modality specific deficits

Occasionally, a memory problem only manifests itself in one modality.
Patients may, for example, experience difficulty with material they hear but
not with material they read. This is true of some aphasic people and of Shallice
and Warrington's (1970) patient K.F. In other cases the reverse is true, as in
some right hemisphere stroke patients, and may be due to unilateral spatial
neglect (see e.g. Heilman and Valenstein, 1979). Forgetting visual material
can also occur with people who have visual scanning difficulties, perhaps as a
result of brain-stem damage or some other syndrome. If some recovery is still
expected, therapists will probably attempt to reduce the deficit by concentrating on the problem itself. So visual problems may be helped by methods for
improving scanning (Diller, 1980) and verbal problems may be helped by
speech therapy. If the deficit appears to be permanent, however, it may be
possible to use an intact function. People with visual modality problems may,
for example, be encouraged to describe overtly the material they have to
remember. Those with auditory modality problems may be encouraged to
visualize the material. There is considerable overlap between those who have

verbal memory deficits and problems in the auditory modality on the one hand and those with non-verbal deficits and problems in the visual modality on the other. Nevertheless, a distinction can usefully be made. Patients with right parietal damage, for example, sometimes have difficulty with visual material of a verbal and non-verbal nature but have no problems with auditory material. On the other hand, aphasics sometimes have verbal memory problems in both the visual and auditory modalities but little difficulty with non-verbal material whatever the modality.

(3) *Strategies for global deficits*
For those with a global amnesia, external aids will play a vital role. It may also be possible to devise tasks using motor memory to improve performance as described in section II G above. Furthermore, some pockets of ability may remain. Wilson's (1982a) patient was able to use some verbal mnemonics in spite of a severe global amnesia. It is worth investigating whether or not individuals can benefit from one or more of the internal strategies.

Finally, another way of predicting which patients can benefit from one internal strategy, visual imagery, was carried out by Wilson (1982b). She divided brain-damaged patients with mixed aetiologies into three groups on the basis of their ability to remember the Wechsler Logical Memory passage (Wechsler, 1945). Those who were unable to recall anything of the passage an hour later were placed in the severely impaired group. Those who recalled 50% or less of their immediate response were in the moderately impaired group. Those who recalled more than 50% of their immediate response were in the minimally impaired group. Each group was given three lists of paired-associates to learn. The procedure used was similar to that used by Jones (1974). For the first list patients were not given any strategy to aid recall. For the second list, the experimenter drew an image linking the two words (e.g. Nose-Coal was drawn as a large red nose sniffing a lump of coal). For the third list the patients were required to imagine the two words linked together. When tested for delayed recall 2 hours later, all groups benefited from images drawn for them. However, the people in the severely impaired group were unable to benefit from their own mental images. Those in the moderately impaired group were able to benefit from mental images but did better with images drawn for them. The mildly impaired group were able to benefit from both imagery procedures. This suggests that the delayed version of the Logical Memory of the Wechsler Memory Scales can provide information on which amnesic patients can use visual imagery and whether or not they will need someone to draw the images for them.

C. Group treatment

As well as seeing individuals with memory impairment, we both see groups of patients. The memory group at Rivermead Rehabilitation Centre in Oxford is held (by BW) daily, an hour a day, five days a week for 3 to 6 weeks at a time.

There are between 4 and 6 people with varying degrees of deficit in each group. The Birmingham memory group is held (by NM) weekly: an hour a week for 10 to 15 weeks. Again there are four to six people in this group. Working with groups is economically advantageous in that more people can be treated. One treatment technique that is usually tried with groups rather than individuals is Reality Orientation Therapy (ROT) designed for geriatric patients (Brook *et al.*, 1975, Citrin and Dixon, 1977). (This therapy involves teaching, testing and encouraging patients to use essential information about time, place and person.) Because the results from studies such as those with groups of elderly patients have been encouraging, it was decided to start each session of the Oxford Group with the use of ROT techniques.

Evidence for other benefits of group sessions may emerge from an evaluative study of the Oxford memory group currently under way. For example, patients may benefit from interaction with other people having similar problems. It is not uncommon for those with memory difficulties to think they are "going crazy". Also patients can give advice to one another. Furthermore, there are so many tasks, strategies, aids and exercises one can use in a group, that each patient can shine at something. Such success is, no doubt, as important for the brain-damaged as for the rest of us.

D. Evaluation

In order to know whether or not memory rehabilitation programmes are effective, systematic evaluation is essential. Group studies are often unhelpful in such situations as they provide little guidance as to which individuals benefit or fail to benefit from a particular technique. Single case experimental designs would appear to be the most useful tools for evaluation. Hersen and Barlow (1976) and Yule and Hemsley (1977) described these in detail. Widely used in some areas of behaviour modification and behaviour therapy (e.g. Martin, 1981; Yule, 1980) these designs also prove amenable to investigations of cognitive rehabilitation programmes.

The reversal or ABAB design, although simple, is of limited use for three main reasons:
(a) Often it is impossible to revert to baseline conditions. If a patient has been taught to remember a name, for example, it is impossible to "unteach" the name.
(b) There are occasions when a reversal to baseline would be unethical.
(c) It is often impractical to revert to baseline conditions. If someone has been taught not to ask the same question *ad nauseam*, then relatives or staff will not willingly accept a return to the previous level in order to test a hypothesis. Nevertheless, there are occasions when a reversal design is appropriate for demonstrating that changes are due to treatment or an intervention procedure and not to passage of time or spontaneous recovery.

A far more useful single case design is the multiple baseline design which has already been demonstrated earlier in this chapter (see Fig. 1). Wilson

(1982a) used a mutiple baseline across behaviours design with her stroke patient. Other multiple baseline designs include a multiple baseline across settings (see e.g. Carr and Wilson, in preparation) and a multiple baseline across subjects design.

The last of these is usually discussed alongside single case designs because (although it uses several subjects) the problems with very small groups are similar to those encountered when N = 1.

Figure 2 is an example of a multiple baseline across subjects design to investigate the effectiveness of visual imagery. All these patients had predominantly left hemisphere damage.

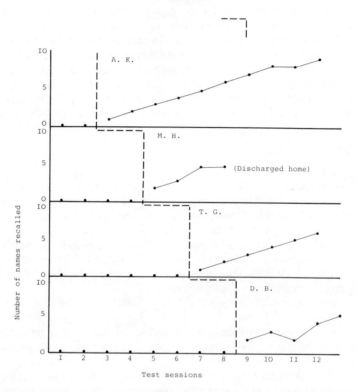

Fig. 2. A multiple baseline across subjects designed to demonstrate the effectiveness of visual imagery for learning names. – – – = visual image introduced.

IV. CONCLUSION

This chapter has described some of the methods employed to help people with memory deficits. We have emphasized amelioration of problems rather than restoration of function. This is because we are pessimistic about attempts to restore function. Furthermore, it is our belief that those of us who attempt to help the memory impaired should concentrate on real, everyday problems rather than on improving recall of experimental material. We should, perhaps, not set our sights too high. Some reduction in the problems faced is usually possible but to seek a total or near-total solution to the memory deficit is almost certain to end in failure. Neither is it always possible to ensure that any techniques learned will generalize to other material or other situations. Instead of asking "How can I improve this patient's memory?" we should perhaps ask "What is the most efficient learning strategy for this particular person?". This may result in a greater reduction of the everyday memory problems. Relatives and others can be taught what to do when the memory-impaired person needs to learn new names, routes or how to accomplish a task. For any individual, different strategies may be necessary for different aspects of the memory problem. Finally, it is important to remember that no strategy, technique or method will suit all patients or all problems. Instead the approach used should be tailored to the individual's needs, problems and personal style.

REFERENCES

Ausubel, D. P. (1960). The use of advance organizers in learning and retention of meaningful verbal material. *Journal of Educational Psychology*, 51, 267–272.

Baddeley, A. D. (1976). "The psychology of memory", Basic Books, New York.

Baddeley, A. D. and Warrington, E. K. (1973). Memory coding and amnesia. *Neuropsychologia*, 11, 159–165.

Barnes, J. (1974). The effects of reality orientation classroom on memory loss, confusion and disorientation in geriatric patients. *Gerontologist*, 14, 138–142.

Blackburn, H. L. (1958). Effects of motivating instructions on reaction time in cerebral disease. *Journal of Abnormal and Social Psychology*, 56, 359–366.

Bransford, J. D. and McCarrell, N. (1975). A sketch of a cognitive approach to comprehension. Some thoughts about understanding what it means to comprehend. *In* "Cognition and the Symbolic Processes" (W. B. Weiner and D. S. Palermo, eds), Erlbaum, Hillsdale, N.J.

Brook, P., Degun, G. and Mather, M. (1975). Reality orientation, a therapy for psychogeriatric patients: a controlled study. *British Journal of Psychiatry*, 127, 42–45.

Brooks, D. N. and Baddeley, A. D. (1976). What can amnesic patients learn? *Neuropsychologia*, 14, 111–122.

Carr, S. and Wilson, B. (In preparation). Promotion of pressure relief exercising in a spinal injury patient. A multiple baseline across settings design.

Carr, S. and Wilson, B. (1982). Teaching a mildly aphasic man to remember names using a face-name association procedure (unpublished case study).

Cermak, L. S. (1975). Imagery as an aid to retrieval for Korsakoff patients. *Quarterly Journal of Studies of Alcoholism*, 34, 1110–1132.

Citrin, R. S. and Dixon, D. N. (1977) Reality orientation: a milieu therapy used in an institution for the aged. *Gerontologist*, **17**, 39–43.

Corkin, S. (1968). Acquisition of motor skills after bilateral medial temporal-lobe excision. *Neuropsychologia*, **6**, 255–265.

Crovitz, H. (1979). Memory retraining in brain damaged patients: the airplane list. *Cortex*, **15**, 131–134.

Crovitz, H., Harvey, M and Horn, R. (1979). Problems in the acquisition of imagery mnemonics: three brain damaged cases. *Cortex*, **15**, 225–234.

Dencher, S. J. and Lofving, B. (1958) A psychometric study of identical twins discordant for closed head injury. *Acta Psychiatrica Neurologica Scandinavia*, **33**, Supplement 122.

Diller, L. (1980). The development of a perceptual-remediation program in hemiplegia. *In* "Behavioral Psychology In Rehabilitation Medicine: Clinical Applications" (L. Ince, ed), Williams and Wilkins, Baltimore.

Diller, L. and Weinberg, J. (1977). Hemi-inattention in rehabilitation: the evolution of a rational remediation program. *In* "Advances in Neurology, Volume 18" (E. A. Weinstein and R. P. Friedland, eds), Raven Press, New York.

Eimas, P. D. (1970). Effects of memory aids on hypothesis behavior and focusing in young children and adults. *Journal of Experimental Child Psychology*, **10**, 319–336.

Ericsson, K. A., Chase, W. G. and Falcon, S. (1980). Acquisition of a memory skill. *Science*, **208**, 1181–1182.

Fowler, R., Hart, J. and Sheehan, M. (1972). A prosthetic memory: an application of the prosthetic environment concept. *Rehabilitation Counselling Bulletin*, **15**, 80–85.

Gianutsos, R. and Gianutsos, J. (1979). Rehabilitating the verbal recall of brain injured patients by mnemonic training: an experimental demonstration using single case methodology. *Journal of Clinical Neuropsychology*, **1**, 117–135.

Glasgow, R., Zeis, R., Barrera, M. and Lewinsohn, P. (1977). Case studies on remediating memory deficits in brain damaged individuals. *Journal of Clinical Psychology*, **33**, 1049–1054.

Greene, J. G., Nicol, R. and Jamieson, H. (1979) Reality orientation with psychogeriatric patients. *Behaviour Research and Therapy*, **17**, 615–618.

Groninger, L. D. (1971). Mnemonic imagery and forgetting. *Psychonomic Science*, **23**, 161–163.

Gronwall, D. M. A. and Sampson, H. (1974). "The Psychological Effects of Concussion", Auckland University Press, Auckland.

Gruneberg, M. M. and Monks, J. (1974). Feeling of knowing and cued recall. *Acta Psychologia*, **38**, 257–265.

Gruneberg, M. M. and Monks, J. (1976). The first letter search strategy. *I.R.C.S. Medical Science. Psychology & Psychiatry*, **4**, 307.

Harris, C. and Ivory, P. (1976). An outcome evaluation of reality orientation therapy with geriatric patients in a state mental hospital. *Gerontologist*, **16**, 496–503.

Harris, J. E. (1978). External Memory Aids. *In* "Practical Aspects of Memory" (M. M. Gruneberg, P. Morris and R. Sykes, eds), Academic Press, London and New York.

Harris, J. E. (1980a). We have ways of helping you remember. *Concord. The Journal of the British Association for Service to the Elderly*. No. 17, 21–27.

Harris, J. E. (1980b). Memory Aids people use: Two interview studies. *Memory and Cognition*, **8**, 31–38.

Harris, J. E. (1984). Remembering to do things; a forgotten topic. *In* "Everyday Memory, Actions and Absent-Mindedness" (J. E. Harris and P. E. Morris, eds),

Academic Press, London, Orlando and New York.

Harris, J. E. and Sunderland, A. (1981). A brief survey of the management of memory disorders in rehabilitation in Britain. *International Rehabilitation Medicine*, **3**, 206–209.

Heilman, K. M. and Valenstein, E. (1979). "Clinical Neuropsychology", Oxford University Press, New York/Oxford.

Hersen, M. and Barlow, D. (1976) "Single Case Experimental Designs: Strategies for Evaluating Behavior Change", Pergamon Press, New York.

Hulicka, I. M. and Grossman, J. L. (1967). Age-group comparisons for the use of mediators in paired associate learning. *Journal of Gerontology*, **22**, 46–51.

Jaffe, P. G. and Katz, A. N. (1975) Attenuating anterograde amnesia in Korsakoff's psychosis. *Journal of Abnormal Psychology*, **84**, 559–562.

Jones, G. and Adam, J. (1979). Towards a prosthetic memory. *Bulletin of The British Psychological Society*, **32**, 165–167.

Jones, M. (1974). Imagery as a mnemonic aid after left temporal lobectomy: contrast between material specific and generalized memory disorders. *Neuropsychologia*, **12**, 21–30.

Kintsch, W. (1974) "The Representation of Meaning in Memory", Erlbaum, Hillsdale, N.J.

Klein, R. M. and Fowler, R. S. (1981). Pressure relief training device: the microcalculator. *Archives of Physical and Medical Rehabilitation*, **62**, 500–501.

Lewinsohn, P. M., Danaher, B. and Kikel, S. (1977). Visual imagery as a mnemonic aid for brain injured persons. *Journal of Consulting and Clinical Psychology*, **45**, 717–723.

Lishman, W. (1978). "Organic Psychiatry", Blackwell Scientific Publications, Oxford.

Lorayne, H. (1975). "Remembering People", W. H. Allen, London.

Lorayne, H. and Lucas, J. (1974). "The Memory Book", Ballantine Books, New York.

Luria, A. R. (1968). "The Mind of a Mnemonist", Basic Books, New York.

Lynch, W. J. (1981a). A guide to Atari videocomputer programs for rehabilitation programs for rehabilitation settings. Paper presented at the Symposium on Models and Techniques of Cognitive Rehabilitation. Indianapolis, January.

Lynch, W. J. (1981b). The use of electronic games in cognitive rehabilitation. Paper presented at the Symposium on Models and Techniques of Cognitive Rehabilitation. Indianapolis, January.

McCarty, D. (1980). Investigation of a visual imagery mnemonic device for acquiring face-name associations. *Journal of Experimental Psychology: Human Learning and Memory*, **6**, 145–155.

Martin, P. (1981). Spasmodic torticollis investigation and treatment using EMG feedback training. *Behavior Therapy*, **12**, 247–262.

Meacham, J. A. and Singer, J. (1977). Incentive effects in perspective remembering. *Journal of Psychology*, **97**, 191–197.

Meichenbaum, D. (1977). "Cognitive-Behavior Modification: An Integrative Approach", Plenum Press, New York.

Miller, E. (1970). Simple and choice reaction time following severe head injury. *Cortex*, **6**, 111–127.

Miller, E. (1978). Is amnesia remediable? *In* "Practical Aspects of Memory" (M. M. Gruneberg, P. Morris and R. Sykes eds), Academic Press, London and New York.

Milner, B., Corkin, S. and Teuber, J. L. (1968). Further analysis of the hippocampal amnesic syndrome: a 14-year follow-up study of H.M. *Neuropsychologia*, **6**, 215–234.

Moffat, N. J. (1978). Reported changes in mood, behaviour and family life associated with a severe head injury. Unpublished master's thesis, University of Exeter.

Moffat, N. J. (1982). Strategies of memory training. Paper presented at the British Psychological Society Division of Clinical Psychology Conference on the Management of Memory and Cognitive Impairment, Nottingham.

Newcombe, F. and Ratcliffe, G. (1979). Long-term psychological consequences of cerebral lesion. *In* "Handbook of Behavioral Neurobiology, Vol. 2" (M. Gazzaniga, ed), Plenum Press, New York.

Patten, B. (1972). The ancient art of memory-usefulness in treatment. *Archives of Neurology*, **26**, 25–31.

Powell, G. E. (1981). *Brain Function Therapy*. Gower Press, Aldershot.

Reason, J. T. (1977). Skill and error in everyday life. *In* "Adult Learning" (M. Howe, ed), Wiley, London.

Rizzo, P. A., Amabile, G., Caporali, M., Spador, M., Zanasi, M. and Morocutti, C. (1978). A CNV study in a group of patients with traumatic head injuries. *Electroencephalography and Clinical Neurophysiology*, **42**, 224–233.

Robertson-Tchabo, E. A., Hausman, C. P. and Arenberg, D. (1976). A classical mnemonic for older learners: A trip that works. *Educational Gerontology*, **1**, 215–226.

Ross, J. and Lawrence, K. A. (1968). Some observations on memory artifice. *Psychonomic Science*, **13**, 107–108.

Rowntree, D. (1970). "Learn How to Study", MacDonald, London.

Shallice, T. and Warrington, E. K. (1970). Independent functioning of verbal memory stores: a neuropsychological study. *Quarterly Journal of Experimental Psychology*, **22**, 261–273.

Shiffrin, R. M. and Schneider, W. (1977). Controlled and automatic human information processing: II Perceptual learning, automatic attending and a general theory. *Psychological Review*, **84**, 127–190.

Stroop, J. R. (1935). Studies in interference in serial verbal reactions. *Journal of Experimental Psychology*, **18**, 643–662.

Sunderland, A., Harris, J. E. and Baddeley, A. D. (1981). Everyday memory and test performance following severe head injury. Paper presented at the British Psychological Society Cognitive Psychology Section Conference on Memory, Plymouth.

Sunderland, A., Harris, J. E. and Baddeley, A. D. (1983a). Do laboratory tests predict everyday memory? A neuropsychological study. *Journal of Verbal Learning and Verbal Behavior*, **22**, 341–594.

Sunderland, A., Harris, J. E. and Baddeley, A. D. (1984b). Assessing everyday memory after severe head injury. *In* "Everyday Memory, Actions and Absent-Mindedness" (J. E. Harris and P. E. Morris, eds), Academic Press, London, Orlando and New York.

Trexler, L. E. (1982). The utilization of microprocessors in the assessment and treatment of subtle attentional disorders. Paper presented at the International Neuropsychological Society meeting, Pittsburgh.

Van Zomeren, A. H. (1981). "Reaction Time and Attention After Closed Head Injury", Swets and Zeitlinger, Lisse.

Van Zomeren, A. H. and Deelman, B. G. (1978). Differential effects of simple and choice reaction time after closed head injury. *Clinical Neurology and Neurosurgery*, **79**, 81–90.

Warrington, E. K. and Weiskrantz, L. (1971). Organizational aspects of memory in amnesic patients. *Neuropsychologia*, **9**, 67–73.

Watts, G. H. and Anderson, R. C. (1971). Effects of three types of inserted questions on learning from prose. *Journal of Educational Psychology*, **62**, 387–394.

Wechsler, D. (1945). A standardized memory scale for clinical use. *Journal of Psychology*, **19**, 87–95.

Williams, M. (1968). The measurement of memory in clinical practice. *British Journal of Social and Clinical Psychology*, **7**, 19–34.

Wilson, B. (1981a). Teaching a patient to remember people's names after removal of a left temporal lobe tumour. *Behavioural Psychotherapy*, **9**, 338–344.

Wilson, B. (1981b). A survey of behavioural treatments carried out at a rehabilitation centre for stroke and head injuries. *In* "Brain Function Therapy" (G. Powell, ed.) Gower Press, Aldershot.

Wilson, B. (1982a). Success and failure in memory training following a cerebral vascular accident. *Cortex*, **18**, 581–594.

Wilson, B. (1982b). Visual imagery as a mnemonic aid for brain damaged adults. Paper presented to the fifth European conference of the International Neuropsychological Society, Deauville, France.

Woods, R. T. (1979). Reality orientation and staff attention: a controlled study. *British Journal of Psychiatry*, **134**, 502–507.

Yates, F. (1966). "The Art of Memory", Routledge, Kegan & Paul, London.

Yule, W. (1980). Identifying problems-functional analysis and observation and recording techniques. *In* "Behaviour Modification for the Mentally Handicapped" (W. Yule and J. Carr, eds), Croom Helm, London.

Yule, W. and Hemsley, D. (1977). Single Case Methodology. *In* "Contributions to Medical Psychology, Vol. 1" (S. Rachman, ed), Pergamon Press, Oxford.

Name Index

* Italic numbers indicate occurrence of names in references.

Subject Index